MW00564111

THE HEBREW PROPHETS

THE HEBREW PROPHETS

An Introduction

JACK R. LUNDBOM

Fortress Press
Minneapolis

THE HEBREW PROPHETS
An Introduction

Copyright © 2010 Fortress Press, an imprint of Augsburg Fortress. All rights reserved. Except for brief quotations in critical articles or reviews, no part of this book may be reproduced in any manner without prior written permission from the publisher. Visit http://www.augsburgfortress.org/copyrights/contact.asp or write to Permissions, Augsburg Fortress, Box 1209, Minneapolis, MN 55440.

Some scripture quotations are based on the New Revised Standard Version Bible, copyright © 1989 by the Division of Christian Education of the National Council of the Churches of Christ in the USA. Used by permission. All rights reserved.

Some scripture quotations are based on the Revised Standard Version of the Bible, copyright © 1946, 1952, 1971 National Council of the Churches of Christ in the USA. Used by permission. All rights reserved.

Cover design: Laurie Ingram
Book design: The HK Scriptorium, Inc.

Library of Congress Cataloging-in-Publication Data

Lundbom, Jack R.
   The Hebrew prophets : an introduction / Jack R. Lundbom.
      p. cm.
   Includes bibliographical references and index.
   ISBN 978-0-8006-9737-2 (alk. paper)
   1. Bible. O.T. Prophets—Criticism, interpretation, etc. I. Title.
   BS1505.52.L86 2010
   224'.061—dc22
                                                      2010012134

The paper used in this publication meets the minimum requirements of American National Standard for Information Sciences—Permanence of Paper for Printed Library Materials, ANSI Z329.48-1984.

Manufactured in the U.S.A.

Dedicated to my students at the
Lutheran Theological Seminary, Hong Kong

CONTENTS

PART 2

POETRY, PROSE, RHETORIC, AND SYMBOLISM IN THE HEBREW PROPHETS

PREFACE

THIS BOOK HAS BEEN A LONG TIME IN PREPARATION. My interest in the Old Testament prophets began when I was very young. I remember sitting at my grandmother's kitchen table listening to her tell me about the mighty Elijah, who made a strong impression on my young mind. Later, I took a course on the Hebrew prophets in college, but only began a serious study of them in seminary and graduate school in the 1960s and early '70s. On a year away from North Park Theological Seminary in Chicago, I took courses on Amos, Hosea, and Jeremiah from William Holladay at the Near East School of Theology in Beirut. Returning home, I sat once again on Sunday mornings and evenings listening to the prophetic preaching of Douglas Cedarleaf, minister of the North Park Covenant Church, my church home. Cedarleaf, when not expounding the parables of Jesus, for which he is also remembered, was preaching powerfully on the dominant themes of the day: the ecumenical movement, civil rights, and issues relating to war and peace. One Sunday evening, he gave a modern rendition of Amos's oracles to the nations (Amos 1–2), which was riveting. His sermon the Sunday morning following the death of President John F. Kennedy, in which he alluded to David's words following the death of Abner, "Do you not know that a prince and a great man has fallen this day in Israel?" (2 Sam 3:38), is one I shall never forget. Someone passed him a note midway in the sermon saying that Kennedy's alleged assassin had now been murdered, and he relayed this to the crowded church. We dispersed after the service in near silence. Linda and I had become engaged the night before, but given the moment, we were unable to tell anyone.

My graduate work began under James Muilenburg, who knew the prophets, taught the prophets, and preached the prophets like no other. In these years, from 1967 to 1974, I divided my time between studying in San Anselmo and in Berkeley, also working in San Francisco, where I drove a mail car for the Bank of America. In Berkeley, graduate seminars and language study were supplemented by daily happenings on the street and the campus of the University of California. One day, I myself entered the fray, taking on a fiery anarchist in front of Sproul Hall during the noontime melee. Driving my bank car to Oakland enabled me to see the drama at the Oakland Induction Center, where the buses of young men I had been following across the Bay Bridge were being delivered to the Center for war duty in Vietnam. I witnessed there the throngs of screaming protesters and a virtual army of police—including California Highway Patrolmen—who kept people at bay so the buses could get to the Center. These were turbulent years, and it was anybody's guess where the disruptions would take us. Similar things were happening elsewhere in the country, but Berkeley is where it all started and where the social unrest was particularly intense. I confess to wondering at times whether this was how a civil war began. Here on the streets of the Bay Area of California, before my very eyes, I was witnessing incidents strangely similar to those I was reading about on the pages of Holy Writ, with some of the more strident individuals claiming to be prophets in their cries against the war, against the university, and against authority of just about any sort. I would have to delve more deeply into my study of the Hebrew prophets, finding out who these individuals really were and assessing more carefully the troubled world in which they lived. This I did, focusing on arguably the greatest of the biblical prophets: Jeremiah ben Hilkiah of Anathoth.

The chapters of this book were first presented to the adult Sunday school class at Trinity Covenant Church in Lexington, Massachusetts. The invitation to teach this class, during January through March of 1976, was extended by my good friend Dr. Donald Wells, pastor of the church. To him, David Bohy, and members of the class I am grateful for a memorable experience. I have given these lectures many times since in churches and in university and seminary classrooms. The lead chapter, "To Be a Prophet . . . ," was delivered in its present form to students at Fudan University in Shanghai, in April 2008, then again in September of that year to students at Ansgar Theological Seminary and Agder University in Kristiansand, and the Lutheran Mission School in Stavanger, Norway.

Interpretations of biblical texts draw upon the Revised Standard Version, the New Revised Standard Version, the Anchor Bible (Jeremiah), or are otherwise my own.

ABBREVIATIONS

AB	Anchor Bible
AJT	*American Journal of Theology*
ANET[3]	James B. Pritchard, ed. *Ancient Near Eastern Texts Relating to the Old Testament.* 3rd ed. With supplement. Princeton: Princeton University Press, 1969.
Ant.	Josephus, *Antiquities*
BA	*Biblical Archaeologist*
BJRL	*Bulletin of the John Rylands Library*
BZAW	Beihefte zur Zeitschrift für die alttestamentliche Wissenschaft
CBQ	*Catholic Biblical Quarterly*
HTR	*Harvard Theological Review*
HUCA	*Hebrew Union College Annual*
ICC	International Critical Commentary
JAOS	*Journal of the American Oriental Society*
JBL	*Journal of Biblical Literature*
JJS	*Journal of Jewish Studies*
JNES	*Journal of Near Eastern Studies*
LCL	Loeb Classical Library
LXX	Septuagint
M[A]	Allepo Codex
M[L]	Leningrad Codex
M[P]	St. Petersburg Codex of the Prophets
MT	Masoretic Text of the Hebrew Bible
OS	*Oudtestamentische Studiën*
SBLDS	Society of Biblical Literature Dissertation Series
SJOT	*Scandinavian Journal of the Old Testament*
VT	*Vetus Testamentum*
VTSup	Supplements to Vetus Testamentum

INTRODUCTION

IN THE MODERN DAY, PARTICULARLY DURING THE
American civil rights movement and the Vietnam War crisis of the 1960s
and 1970s, there was much talk in the church, academy, and public sector
about prophets and messages said to be "prophetic." Certain individuals
were called modern-day prophets, others were said to be delivering prophetic messages, and still others were called upon to be prophetic when
they were not, by those who thought they should be. The times were
unsettled; the post–World War II peace had vanished, and the old had not
yet given way to the new.

At the end of the turbulent 1960s, an article appeared in *Interpretation* by W. Sibley Towner entitled "On Calling People 'Prophets' in
1970."[1] Mentioned here as individuals called prophets by some were William Stringfellow, Martin Luther King Jr., William Sloan Coffin Jr.,
Pope John XXIII, Billy Graham, Jeane Dixon, "the unkempt prophets
of Berkeley," and others. Martin Luther King, leader of the civil rights
movement, was thought by his own father to be a prophet. William Sloan
Coffin, at the historic Riverside Church in New York City, was said to be
carrying on the prophetic preaching of his predecessor, Harry Emerson
Fosdick. Closer to home, my own pastor at the North Park Covenant
Church in Chicago, Douglas Cedarleaf, was not named a prophet per se,
but it was widely agreed both inside and outside the church fellowship
that his preaching in support of the ecumenical movement, civil rights,
issues of war and peace, and opening up the North Park neighborhood
to people of all races was "prophetic." In most of these examples, being a
prophet or speaking prophetically did not consist of divining the future,
although the future was very much in the minds of these individuals; it
meant addressing pressing issues of the day, or "forthtelling," as it was
called.

Towner in his article said that prophetic messages consist of four
great themes:[2]

1

1. an appeal for equity and a call for justice for the politically weak, powerless, and economically outcast (cf. 2 Sam 12:1-7; Amos 8:4-7; Jer 22:13-16);

2. an indictment of corruption in circles of power, wherever it is seen, and at whatever cost might be required (cf. Hos 7:4-7);

3. a call for purification of the religious establishment (cf. Amos 5:21; Hos 4:4-6);

4. a note of hope for redemption, peace, and obedient living (Hos 3:14-15; Jer 31:31-34; Ezek 37:24-28; Isa 35:8-10).

In a telegram sent December 20, 1972, to Billy Graham, Henry W. Andersen, pastor of the First Presbyterian Church in LaGrange, Illinois, and chairman of Chicagoland Key '73, made this appeal to the world-famous preacher:

Dear Dr. Graham:

I have sent telegrams to President Nixon deploring the unlimited bombing the United States is unleashing on Vietnam. My voice before the President is nothing, but you have access to him that no other minister of God has. If you deplore the bombing also, I beg you to raise your voice as a prophet, like Nathan of old, in protest to the President, imploring him to stop the bombing immediately.

Andersen did not receive an answer, so Ernest T. Campbell, minister of the Riverside Church in New York City, read to the assembled throng in this historic church on the Sunday after Christmas an open letter to Billy Graham, asking why Graham had not responded. In it, he said among other things: "The President needs a Micaiah not a Zedekiah, a prophet not a mere house chaplain." Graham answered Campbell and others who had communicated with him, and the telegram, open letter, and Graham's answer were published a couple of months later.[3] In Graham's answer, he said concerning his own ministry:

I am convinced that God has called me to be a New Testament evangelist—not an Old Testament prophet! While some may interpret an evangelist to be primarily a social reformer or political activist, I do not![4]

End of discussion. Billy Graham did not see himself as an Old Testament prophet.

The present book is not about modern prophets or modern prophecy so-called, although I have more than passing interest in both topics. It is about a remarkable number of select individuals in ancient Israel and what made them prophets in their own eyes and in the eyes of others. It lifts up what they said when speaking passionately to kings, the nation's leaders, peoples of foreign nations, and the common folk in ancient Israel. I have held my own analysis of the prophetic messages to a minimum, preferring instead to select from their own words the messages for which they have been remembered. The first portion of the book looks also at various measures given in the Bible for authenticity, that is, tests employed in ancient Israel for determining true prophets from false prophets. The second portion of the book examines how the prophets crafted messages and formed arguments giving their words the power they had, and how the spoken word was supplemented by signs and symbolic action.

For any serious discussion about prophets and prophecy to be carried on in the present day—and there continues to be a need for such at the beginning of the twenty-first century—the Hebrew prophets of the Old Testament must be known and understood. These are the individuals who define both the prophetic office and the prophetic message. I shared this conviction one day with a friend who said he had no interest in the biblical prophets. They lived in a world far removed from ours and had no relevance for today. My friend thought he could form his own views on prophets and prophecy by reading Daniel, Revelation, and modern bestsellers such as Hal Lindsey's *Late Great Planet Earth*.

In the ancient Near Eastern world there were also individuals who boasted of having a vocation similar to Israel's prophets, but they have left no mark and are little more than a curiosity, being studied primarily for purposes of comparing and contrasting to the prophets of Israel. It was the towering figures of Samuel, Elijah, Amos, Hosea, Isaiah, Micah, Jeremiah, Ezekiel, and a select number of others, named and unnamed in the Old Testament, who made a lasting impression, and we need to find out more about who they were, what they were about, and what it was they said. This book seeks to help the reader make these discoveries.

PART 1

Marks, Messages, and Measures of Authenticity in the Hebrew Prophets

1

TO BE A PROPHET . . .

WHAT IS A PROPHET? WE BEGIN BY ASKING A QUESTION people in ancient Israel would probably never have thought to ask. Some might conclude that the Hebrews lacked the reflective power we assume in the modern Western world, or had not the reflective capacity and analytical power of the Greeks, their near contemporaries in the Mediterranean world. The Greeks wrote textbooks on medicine, rhetoric, mathematics, and a number of other subjects, and if prophets had been as defining a group in Greek culture as they were in ancient Hebrew culture—which they were not—we would expect some sort of statement somewhere telling us what it was to be a prophet. But nowhere in the Bible, which is our only real sourcebook for the life and thought of the ancient Hebrews, is there any statement telling us what it was to be a prophet. Fragmented remarks, yes, but nothing more.

There is probably an even better reason for the Bible's lack of a defining statement on the prophetic office. The writers of the Bible would scarcely have analyzed a phenomenon that was common knowledge, and here they were no different than we. Seldom do we ask today, What is a pastor? or What is a priest? Both professions we know well, as they are familiar in the world we inhabit. It is less so with the prophet, although the term has some currency in the modern world. Nevertheless, a great distance in time separates us from the known prophets of antiquity, a great difference between their world and ours, which means we end up having to ask basic questions about what the ancient people knew well and more or less took for granted.

There are six of what I would call "distinguishing marks" of the Hebrew prophet. These set the prophet off from ordinary people, on the one hand, and from other professional types, on the other. The lines are by no means absolute; they give us only a profile, but this is what we need. In one way or another, the Old Testament lifts up each of these marks, indicating that they must have carried weight for the people among whom the prophets lived and moved.

To cite distinguishing marks is not to imply that every prophet possessed all of them, for they did not. One mark, for example, was an ability to perform mighty works, and only a few prophets possessed this gift. But for those who did, it made them prophets in the eyes of others, even though it was doubtless evident that there were other prophets who did not perform mighty works. Not every prophet possessed the whole range of prophetic gifts. Nor were gifts possessed to the same degree, much less manifested in precisely the same way. Prophets never ceased being singular individuals, and it hardly needs saying that no two of them were alike. So while we will be focusing here on what Hebrew prophets had in common, it must not be forgotten that each prophet was unique, he or she a blend of certain defining qualities to which was added a good deal more.

We shall discover that these distinctive marks show up also in prophets and prophetic types whom the Old Testament discredits. Included here would be intermediaries of various description from Babylon, Assyria, Egypt, Moab, and Canaan, also Hebrew prophets who signed on fully or partially with the Canaanite Baals. These marks showed up even in Yahweh prophets who were ultimately discredited. Virtually every mark can be attributed to some prophet whom the Old Testament discredits. Such marks, then, are no guarantee of prophetic authenticity. A connection between these distinctive marks and authenticity does exist, but one does not translate into the other. In chapter 3 we will look at the tests preserved in the Old Testament for distinguishing true prophets from false prophets.

Today it is widely recognized that neither prophecy nor prophetism generally was restricted to ancient Israel. The many extrabiblical texts now in our possession make it clear that Hebrew prophecy has its roots and also came to flower in a larger movement that existed throughout the ancient Near East.[1] Discerning the uniqueness of the Hebrew prophets, which for many is the bottom line issue, is a complex task. Sometimes defining marks will set them off. Other times it will be a perceived authenticity. Still other times it appears to have been behavior judged to be on a higher level than that of their opposite numbers. If any one thing points consistently to the uniqueness and lasting greatness of the Hebrew prophets, it is their *message*. It was a message of words, yes, but even more a total life statement of radical obedience to the living God. What made the Hebrew prophets great is what made Israel—in its best moments—great. Had the Hebrew prophets not borne witness to the living God, they would, like all other prophets and intermediaries who walked the stage of history, have disappeared into the dust and promptly been forgotten. We will take a closer look at their remarkable message, but first let us discover what it is to be a prophet.

THE DIVINE CALL

To be a prophet, in the first place, is to be someone who has received a divine call. Prophets, were they to boast, could boast only of having received a call from Yahweh God. This is the warrant for all the prophet says and does. Hebrew *nābî'* (נָבִיא), which we translate "prophet," most likely means "one who is called."[2] In Akkadian, which predates Hebrew and is a cognate language to Hebrew, *nabû* means "to call," and a *nibîtu* is "one called (by the gods)."

Among Israel's neighbors it was the king who received a call for divine service. Old Babylonian texts from the third millennium B.C.E. report kings being called by the gods.[3] The same was true in Egypt. An Egyptian stele from the reign of Pharaoh Pianche (751–730 B.C.E.) records a call that came to this pharaoh from the god Amun.[4] Amun says:

> It was in the belly of your mother that I said concerning you that you were to be ruler of Egypt; it was as seed and while you were in the egg, that I knew you, that (I knew) you were to be lord.

This call has a similarity to the call of Jeremiah, where Yahweh says to him:

> Before I formed you in the womb I knew you,
>   and before you were born I consecrated you;
>   I appointed you a prophet to the nations.
>
> (Jer 1:5)

Jeremiah's call, however, was not from the womb. It was more remarkable still, being issued *before* he was born, *before* he was conceived. Jeremiah's call took place at a time known only to Yahweh. In typical Hebraic fashion, like the creation of the world itself, the true beginning of things is shrouded in obscurity.

The Assyrian king Esarhaddon (680–669 B.C.E.) also received a divine call. The initiator in this case was the goddess Ishtar.[5] She says:

I am Ishtar of Arbela; I have turned Ashur's favor to you.
When you were small, I chose you. Fear not! Praise me!

Israel's first kings, Saul and David, received calls for divine service, which in both instances were mediated by the prophet Samuel (1 Samuel 9–10; 16). Even earlier, Gideon the judge received a call mediated through a divine messenger to deliver Israel from the Midianites (Judg 6:11-24). Nevertheless, the divine call in Israel appears largely to have been reserved for the prophet. Kings came to power because of success in war, or later, because they stood in a royal line. Priests had a hereditary office and, during the monarchy, were subject to royal appointment.[6] Wise men, who had become a professional class in Jeremiah's time (Jer 8:9; 18:18), and perhaps earlier (Isa 29:14), earned their place in the royal court because of wisdom, discernment, and excellence of speech (Prov 16:21-23). They too received appointment from the king. The prophet seldom if ever had a royal appointment. Most of those who did, like their opposite numbers in neighboring societies, became "rubber stamps" of royal policy and quickly faded into insignificance.

In Israel, the real prophet was typically called to critique kings and governmental policy, which led, as one might expect, to frequent tensions between the prophet and the royal house. Often a prophet became *persona non grata* with the king. Yet even unpopular prophets ate at government expense.[7] Gad, a prophet and a seer, is thought by some to have had an appointment under David. Isaiah, too, may have had a royal appointment under Hezekiah, but if so, he understood himself to be first and foremost in the employ of Yahweh, Israel's true king (Isa 6:1-5). Whatever the prophet's relation to government, it was a call from Yahweh that gave him the office and authority he possessed.

The prophetic movement in Israel began with Samuel,[8] although Samuel also wore the hat of judge and seer. He was the last of the judges. He was also a Nazirite. This was a time of social stress in ancient Israel, when the old was giving way to something new.[9] Yahweh called Samuel while he was still a young boy at the Shiloh sanctuary. Samuel's call came in a night vision, and he needed help in recognizing it (1 Sam 3:2-14). Ironically, the one providing the help, Eli the priest, was singled out in the communication—along with his two sons, Hophni and Phinehas—for judgment. Samuel thus discovered early on what prophets would discover time and again in the future, that receiving a call from Yahweh had its perils. The young Samuel, to his everlasting credit, conveyed the bad news to Eli, and the old man accepted it (1 Sam 3:15-18). Samuel heard again from Yahweh—both by word and by vision—and over time became firmly established as Yahweh's prophet.

Amos reports his call only because he is driven to it. Had he not been pressed for a defense by the hostile priest of Bethel, we may never have heard about his call. Amos says initially that he is *not* a prophet, simply a herdsman and a dresser of vines (Amos 7:14), words that have caused considerable difficulty. Does Amos mean that he is not a prophet at all? Or is he perhaps not a prophet in his own eyes? Possibly he means to say that folks back home in Tekoa do not consider him a prophet. His answer, in any case, is best taken as rhetorical. By emphasizing a lack of professional standing—in his own eyes, in the eyes of others, or both—the opposition is defused. Opposition came in the person of Amaziah, the priest, who addresses Amos as "seer" (7:12). For him "seer" is a term of disparagement, since Amaziah does not view Amos as a prophet. Nevertheless, if Amos began with a disclaimer, he does not end with one, for he goes on to say that he had indeed been called to prophesy:

> Yahweh took me from following the flock, and Yahweh said to me, "Go, prophesy to my people Israel." (Amos 7:15)

No one since has seriously doubted that Amos was called to be one of Yahweh's prophets.

This defense by Amos calls attention to the problem of subjective versus objective testimony. Who knows best who a person really is—that person, or others looking on from a distance? Normally we put greater weight on personal testimony and self-understanding. At the same time, we realize that one's true identity is sometimes known only by others. We see evidence of the latter in the case of John the Baptist, who denied that he was Elijah *redivivus*, simply calling himself "the voice of one crying in the wilderness" (John 1:19-23). But Jesus says that he was "Elijah" (Matt 11:11-14; 17:11-13). Then, too, objective testimony can be divided. Jesus quoted the proverb, "A prophet is not without honor except in his own country" (Mark 6:4; Matt 13:57), which he applied to himself. The proverb could apply also to Amos. Back home, Amos was not a prophet, but at Bethel he was. Despite the hostility of a resident priest, Amos gained a hearing and was reckoned ultimately as a prophet. In the end, all Judaism paid him honor as one of Israel's prophets.

Moses in his own time was not called a prophet, yet by the eighth and seventh centuries B.C.E. he was very much one. Hosea lifts him and

Samuel as the two prophets responsible for Israel's salvation and preservation (Hos 12:13). In the seventh-century book of Deuteronomy, which may be the institutional response to the collected works of Amos, Hosea, and other eighth- to seventh-century prophets,[10] Moses becomes prophet par excellence (Deut 34:10-12). The suggestion has been made that priests played his part when Deuteronomy—or a portion of Deuteronomy—was recited at the yearly festivals (cf. Deut 31:10-13).[11]

Exodus records the call of Moses, which came in the wilderness while Moses was tending the sheep of Jethro, his father-in-law. There he saw a bush aflame, and when he turned aside to look,

> God called to him out of the bush, "Moses, Moses!" And he said, "Here am I." Then he said, "Do not come near; put off your shoes from your feet, for the place on which you are standing is holy ground." And he said, "I am the God of your father, the God of Abraham, the God of Isaac, and the God of Jacob." . . . "Come, I will send you to Pharaoh, that you may bring forth my people, the sons of Israel, out of Egypt." (Exod 3:4-6, 10)

Moses was being called to be the great prophet of deliverance. There were times, of course, when he spoke unmitigated judgment, but his call was to announce and participate in Yahweh's deliverance of an enslaved people (Hos 12:13). He was less than willing, resisting the call when it came to him (Exod 4:10, 13). We see the same later in the case of Jeremiah (Jer 1:6), who was called to be "the prophet like Moses" (Deut 18:15-18; Jer 1:9). But Moses' protestations were to no avail. In the end, Yahweh got his man. It was the same with Jeremiah.

Isaiah received his call on holy ground. The setting was the Jerusalem temple, where the entire interior with its altar and seraphim came alive in a vision. The place was transformed into the throne room of Yahweh. It was a high and holy moment when Yahweh asked for a messenger to run, and Isaiah volunteered. From what some have called the prophet's memoirs, we read:

> And I heard the voice of the Lord saying, "Whom shall I send, and who will go for us?" Then I said, "Here am I! Send me." (Isa 6:8)

The prophet here is modeling himself after the royal messenger. Other prophets employed other models, for example, the "servant" (Isa 20:3), the "watchman" (Isa 21:11-12; Hab 2:1; Ezek 3:17), and the "assayer" (Jer 6:27), but it is the royal messenger that best describes how a prophet is to go about his work. Yahweh wants someone he can "send" and someone who will "go."

In a society lacking modern methods of communication, it was the messenger who delivered the news. In the employ of the king, the royal messenger was privy to the king's business, carrying messages to foreign governments and people of his own country. A staff of messengers waited in readiness in the throne room. When the king had a message he wanted sent, a messenger was called, given the message, and sent on his way to deliver it. Upon arrival, he would preface the message with: "Thus says the king" (2 Kgs 9:18), or "Thus says (King) so-and-so" (1 Kgs 20:3, 5). Isaiah in his vision sees himself as a messenger in the throne room of Yahweh. The call is issued and he steps forward. His message is to go directly to the people (Isa 6:9-13). It is not prefaced by a messenger formula—which Isaiah, for some reason, is not in the habit of using; nevertheless, the word he brings is a direct word from Yahweh the King.

The divine messenger is now known to be a very familiar figure in the ancient Near East. The Mari texts tell us that divine messengers were active in the Upper Euphrates region as early as the eighteenth century B.C.E., some sent by the god Dagan with messages to King Zimri-Lim.[12] Some of the divine messengers in Genesis and Judges may be individuals of a similar type, in which case they should be numbered along with seers as yet other important precursors to the prophets. Hebrew mal'āk (מַלְאָךְ) is translated in our English Bibles as "messenger" or "angel." "Angel" (from Greek angelos) is normally used for the divine messenger, the assumption usually being that reference is to an extraterrestrial being moving between heaven and earth. In some cases, this suits the context, for example, in Jacob's dream at Bethel, where angels are ascending and descending a ladder extending from earth to heaven (Gen 28:12).

Yet other "angels" in Genesis may be earth-bound, professional types attached to a local worship center, comparable to modern-day missionaries or itinerant preachers. There is debate, to be sure, on just how to read these early chapters of Genesis, but if they are legend, as Hermann Gunkel maintained, they would contain a kernel of historical truth and the "messengers of Yahweh" appearing in them could certainly be religious itinerants. Such persons are likely to have appeared to Hagar in the wilderness (Gen 16:7-14), to Abraham and Sarah by the oaks of Mamre (Genesis 18), and again to Abraham as he was preparing to sacrifice Isaac (Gen 22:11). Some years ago the Swedish scholar Alfred Haldar suggested that an individual of this type appeared to the wife of Manoah, telling her

that she would bear a son (Judges 13).[13] As we have said, the messenger
later becomes an important model for the prophet in describing the work
he is called to carry out.

By the mid-ninth century, at the time of Elijah, "messenger of Yahweh" (מַלְאַךְ יהוה, *mal'ak YHWH*) appears to be simply another designation
for the prophet, being used interchangeably with "man of God."[14] The
messenger of Yahweh giving Elijah information and advice in 2 Kgs 1:3,
15 is likely Elisha,[15] who, on another occasion, is the "angel" supplying his
hungry master with food (1 Kgs 19:4-8). Much later, in postexilic times,
Haggai is called a "messenger" (Hag 1:13), and the name Malachi means
literally "my messenger" (Mal 1:1; 3:1).[16]

Jeremiah's call to be Yahweh's prophet was brought home to him in
an orchard near his Anathoth home (Jer 1:1-12). Yahweh, as we have said,
called him before he was born (v. 5), but now he was announcing it to
the young boy, who was probably about the age of Samuel when Yahweh
called him (1 Samuel 3). Jeremiah's call was to be a prophet to the nations,
"to uproot and to break down, to destroy, to build up and to plant" (v. 10).
Jeremiah resisted the call, as Moses had done, but Yahweh overruled him,
saying that he would nevertheless go forth as Yahweh's messenger. The
call was promised a fulfillment in a vision of an "almond blossom," in
which Yahweh said he was "watching over [his] word to do it" (v. 12). One
is reminded of Moses' earlier call coming in a "burning bush" (Exodus 3).
Acceptance came some years later, when Jeremiah "ate" Moses' words in
the temple law book newly found in Josiah's reform (Jer 15:16).[17] Sometime after this, Jeremiah was commissioned by Yahweh to begin his ministry as Yahweh's prophet (Jer 1:13-19).

Ezekiel had the misfortune—or fortune, depending on how you look
at it—of being taken to Babylon in Nebuchadnezzar's deportation of 597
B.C.E., and it was in this strange land, while he sat by the river Chebar, that
Yahweh called him to be a prophet. Yahweh said:

> "Son of man, stand upon your feet, and I will speak with you."
> And when he spoke to me, the spirit entered into me and set me
> upon my feet; and I heard him speaking to me. And he said to
> me, "Son of man, I send you to the people of Israel, to a nation of
> rebels, who have rebelled against me to this very day. The people
> are also impudent and stubborn; I send you to them; and you shall
> say to them, 'Thus said Yahweh God.' And whether they hear or
> refuse to hear (for they are a rebellious house), they will know
> that there has been a prophet among them." (Ezek 2:1-5)

That Ezekiel is also to be Yahweh's messenger can be seen here by the repeated use of the verb "send," also by the messenger formula used to introduce his oracles. The vision here is of the heavenly council, but unlike the vision received by Isaiah, the setting is out-of-doors, which is where Moses, Amos, and Jeremiah received their calls. Ezekiel accepted the call but reports that he left Yahweh's presence in bitterness. For seven days, he says, he could do nothing but sit overwhelmed among his people (Ezek 3:15).

One of the most beautifully articulated calls in all of Scripture comes from someone whose name we do not know. During the last years of Babylonian exile, a prophet in the tradition and spirit of Isaiah arose to whom Yahweh gave a message like the one given to Moses:

A voice cries:

"In the wilderness prepare the way of Yahweh,
    make straight in the desert a highway for our God.
Every valley shall be lifted up,
    and every mountain and hill be made low.
The uneven ground shall become level,
    and the rough places a plain.
And the glory of Yahweh shall be revealed,
    and all flesh shall see it together."

For the mouth of Yahweh has spoken.

(Isa 40:3-5)

The quotes framing this poem show that the crying voice is Yahweh's. This voice continues:

A voice says, "Cry!"
    and I said, "What shall I cry?"
All flesh is grass,
    and all its beauty is like the flower of the field.
The grass withers, the flower fades
    when the breath of Yahweh blows upon it;
        surely the people is grass.
The grass withers, the flower fades,
    but the word of our God will stand forever.

Get you up to a high mountain,
    O herald of good tidings to Zion.
Lift up your voice with strength,
    O herald of good tidings to Jerusalem.
Say to the cities of Judah,
    "Behold your God!"

(Isa 40:6-9)

No two of these calls are alike. Yahweh summons his prophets in a variety of ways. The call may come in a flaming bush or a flowering orchard, on holy ground or in some perfectly ordinary spot on God's earth. But the divine call makes any ground holy ground.

Human responses to the divine call also vary. Some prophets accept the call willingly; others put up resistance, which Yahweh must overcome. How many refused a call from Yahweh we can only guess, but there must have been some, just as there are some individuals in the modern day who resist God's call when it comes to them. These ancient calls were doubtless intensely private affairs, which, only after a period of time, became public knowledge. And we can imagine that prophets made their experiences public in different ways and under different circumstances. Some spoke willingly; others had to allow some time to pass before they could talk about their call openly. And then there was Amos, who related his call only because he was driven to do so. At some point people wanted to know what this man was about and with what authority he spoke. Reporting a call from Yahweh went some way in answering these questions.

We wonder about prophets who left no record of a call. Was there no singular experience for them to report? Or was their call so lacking in drama as to be unworthy of public record? That must have been true for some prophets. We can only speculate here. It would seem, however, that some calling of a general sort must be presupposed in all the prophets.[18] Their language is so personal and direct. Hosea says, "And Yahweh said to me . . ." (Hos 3:1); Micah says, "Hear what Yahweh says . . ." (Mic 6:1); Nahum uses the common messenger formula, "Thus said Yahweh . . ." (Nah 1:12); and Jeremiah says, "The word of Yahweh came to me" (Jer 1:4, 11, 13-14; 2:1; etc.), and "Thus said Yahweh . . ." (Jer 2:1, 5; 6:16; etc.). One can hardly escape the conclusion that all prophets thought of themselves as having been sent by Yahweh. Even false prophets assumed nothing less (1 Kgs 22:24). Yet it remains the case that some prophets left no record of their call.

Other intermediaries—ancient and modern—have claimed an intimate link to the divine. Yet the Hebrew prophet was not satisfied with such a claim. What mattered was that the prophet had heard the divine voice, was conscious of being called, and knew he had a divine message that had to be delivered.

While natural phenomena may have accompanied the divine call, these were of lesser importance—if they had importance at all. Elijah responded not to the wind, the earthquake, or the fire, but only to the *still small voice* (1 Kgs 19:11-12). Hearing was of first importance to the Hebrew prophet. Only after Yahweh's voice had been heard could one venture forth with the divine word, which brings us to the second distinguishing mark of the Hebrew prophet.

THE DIVINE WORD

To be a prophet, in the second place, is to be someone who speaks the divine word. The prophet, in order to be the divine messenger, must have a message. When Yahweh's voice cries to Second Isaiah, the prophet is told that he too must cry (Isa 40:6). He says, "What shall I cry?" and Yahweh tells him.

What we are saying, then, is that hearing must be active hearing. The Hebrew verb "hear" (*šāmaʿ*, שָׁמַע) can also mean "obey" (Josh 1:17; 1 Kgs 12:24; Jer 11:3; etc.). The same is true in English. We say, "Didn't you hear what I said?" or "Why didn't you listen to what I told you?" What we mean in both cases is "Why didn't you *do* what I told you?" or "Why didn't you obey?"

When Yahweh called Amos, he knew he had no option but to obey. Yahweh's voice struck terror into his inner being, even as it had made the whole earth tremble. It was the roar of a lion. Not to respond was unthinkable. Amos says:

> Yahweh roars from Zion
> and utters his voice from Jerusalem;
> the pastures of the shepherds mourn
> and the top of Carmel withers.
> . . . .
> The Lion has roared;
> who will not fear?
> The Lord GOD has spoken;
> who can but prophesy?

(Amos 1:2; 3:8)

Even reluctant prophets knew that in the end they must obey the divine call. Moses knew it, and so did Jeremiah. Jonah, the most reluctant prophet of all, obeyed in the end, and went to speak Yahweh's word to the people of Nineveh.

Because the word of Yahweh was so compelling, we find prophets delivering it in like spirit. One of the great prophetic themes is "obedience," heard in unmistakable clarity at the very beginning of the prophetic movement in the preaching of Samuel. Not once, but twice, Samuel thunders on obedience to King Saul (1 Samuel 13; 15). His second word has become classic:

> Has Yahweh as great delight in burnt offerings and sacrifices
>   as in obeying the voice of Yahweh?
> Behold, to obey is better than sacrifice,
>   and to hearken than the fat of rams.
> For rebellion is as the sin of divination,
>   and stubbornness is as iniquity and idolatry.
> Because you have rejected the word of Yahweh,
>   he has also rejected you from being king.
>
> (1 Sam 15:22-23)

Earlier on, Moses had experienced the disobedience of all Israel, and he anticipated more of the same after his death. Just before he died, as Israel was about to enter the promised land, he taught them a song to carry with them in the years ahead. It is recorded in Deuteronomy 32. It happened much as he said, and the prophets are the ones who rose up to confront the nation with its disobedience to Yahweh and his covenant. Jeremiah struck the note of obedience in his famous Temple Oracles (Jer 7:3-14; cf. 26:4-6).

The spoken word in antiquity was thought to possess great power. Words spoken could not be recalled. The Persian king, for example, was unable to revoke an edict against the Jews even after his sympathies were reversed. All he could do was issue another edict—also irrevocable—that would override the first edict, bringing about the desired result (Esth 8:8). Yahweh's word, although capable of being revoked if he so desired, had the greatest staying power of all. Once it went forth, it did not return empty (Isa 31:2; 55:11). The prophet knew this. He knew that Yahweh would not revoke his call, nor would he likely override one word with another. With this certainty, the prophet went forth as Yahweh's messenger. The word he delivered had the same staying power, meaning that the prophet ended up operating not from a position of weakness but from a position of strength.

Because the prophet was a messenger, more than anyone else in Israelite society he or she became a person of words. Some therefore take *nābî'* (נָבִיא) in an active sense to mean "one who calls." In Exod 7:1, the term comes close to meaning "speaker." Aaron, who was not otherwise a prophet, became a prophet in relation to Moses. (In the same manner, Moses, who was not God, nevertheless became "God" to Pharaoh.) The prophet, in any event, is one who does some "calling" of his own, and this idea is embodied in the Greek word *prophētēs*, from which our word *prophet* comes. A *prophētēs* is "one who speaks for a god and interprets his will to man."[19] The prophet, says Abraham Heschel, is "a person charged with delivering a message and who speaks under the authority of someone else."[20] He possesses what in today's insurance business is called the "power of agency," namely, the authority of the company standing behind the agent. The words of an agent are therefore binding. This same "power behind the power," incidentally, obtains in Jesus' remark to Peter about his being given the keys to the kingdom of heaven (Matt 16:19).

The Hebrew prophet is in true form when, as the divine messenger, he brings forth the divine word. There is Nathan coming to David when David wants to build Yahweh a house, telling him that Yahweh wants rather to build *him* a house (2 Samuel 7). We think, too, of Nathan returning to judge David for taking the wife of Uriah the Hittite, and then seeing to it that Uriah is killed in battle (2 Samuel 12). There is Elijah holding forth on Mount Carmel (1 Kings 18), and the fearless Micaiah, who calls back Yahweh's word to Ahab as they lead him out from the king's presence (1 Kings 22). All the classical prophets—Amos, Hosea, Isaiah, Micah, Jeremiah, Ezekiel, and Second Isaiah—are mighty messengers of the divine word. Prophets in neighboring societies are never so openly critical of the king. When their oracles do contain criticism, there is sufficient ambiguity in them so that the interpretation can be turned around, or the oracle can be made to say something entirely different.[21] Such prophets are inert, much like the 850 prophets of Baal and Asherah who eat at Jezebel's table (1 Kgs 18:19); or the 400 prophets of Yahweh who do the bidding of Ahab on a later occasion (1 Kgs 22:5-12), who may, in fact, be simply the earlier 400 Asherah prophets who have undergone a name change. Jezebel's 400 Asherah prophets appear not to have been killed along with the 450 prophets of Baal (1 Kgs 18:40). All these individuals are rubber stamps of royal policy and know nothing about delivering Yahweh's word.

One can easily see why the Hebrew prophets were feared by kings, priests, other prophets, leading citizens, and the people as a whole. Unlike the articulate wise man, the prophet is no ordinary advisor. When he appears—before the king or anyone–it is to bring a word from Yahweh. And what he says is clear, painfully clear, binding all who hear it. Josiah makes the proper response to the prophetic word of Moses made contemporary by the prophetess Huldah: he tears his robe (2 Kgs 22:11). Jehoiakim, on the other hand, makes an improper response to the prophetic word spoken by Jeremiah, tearing not his garment, but rather the scroll on which the word is written, which he then casts strip by strip into the fire (Jer 36:23-24). A contemptuous act in the eyes of Yahweh.

We must nevertheless recognize that being the divine messenger does not bestow on the prophet unlimited power. Quite the contrary. In fact, it imposes important limitations. Possessing the "power of agency" means that ultimate power and responsibility belong not to the prophet but to Yahweh. Yahweh at all times stands behind the prophetic word; he is the one who will bring it to pass. Messengers today in city corporate life know what this means. They deliver important messages; still, they always remain just messengers. Ambassadors in foreign service know the same limitation. They bring messages to other governments that have far-reaching effects, and their words are binding. Yet they, too, are only messengers. The power they exert always stands behind them; it is never their own. So it is with the prophet. By his word people become ill or are healed, live or die; whole nations rise or fall. Yet behind each momentous word stands Yahweh. The prophet is simply the messenger, nothing more.

Finally, there was the problem in Israel of overzealous messengers delivering Yahweh's word without having been sent. More will be said about them when we come to discuss true and false prophets. Here we repeat only what was said earlier about the signal importance of hearing. A prophet is presumptuous if he speaks a word without having first heard the divine voice. Jeremiah complains about prophets having spoken who had not stood in the divine council to hear what Yahweh had said (Jer 23:18, 21-22). About these Yahweh said:

> I did not send the prophets,
>   yet they ran;
> I did not speak to them,
>   yet they prophesied.
>
> (Jer 23:21)

THE DIVINE VISION

To be a prophet is also to be someone possessed with divine vision. Prophets have vision in the broad sense; that is, they have the capacity to perceive things ordinary people cannot perceive.[22] They see that the times are out of joint, that human life before God is far from what it should be, that judgment is forthcoming, and that after judgment they are the first to anticipate Yahweh's salvation. Prophets also have a visual capacity in the sense that they receive visions and dreams (Num 12:6).

This mark of the Hebrew prophet needs to be nuanced, since the ancient Hebrews have been characterized as being a more auditory people. They are said to discern truth more through the ear than through the eye. The Greeks, by contrast, are characterized as a more visual people.[23] In psychological and theological terms, this means that for the Hebrews the ear plays a more significant role than the eye in receiving divine revelation.

Hebrew prophets hear the divine voice but do not see the divine face. In the oldest traditions of the Old Testament, Moses has the most intimate contact with Yahweh. He alone meets Yahweh "face to face" (Exod 33:11; 34:29), but this is so that Yahweh may *speak* to him. There is no visual dimension to the face-to-face meeting. Yahweh speaks "mouth to mouth" to Moses (Num 12:8). At the time of his call, Moses hears the voice but will not even look for a face (Exod 3:6). Later, when bolder, he requests to see Yahweh's face but is refused (Exod 33:18-23).

Tradition affirms the same regarding Yahweh's revelation to all Israel at Sinai. Deuteronomy 5:4 says that Yahweh spoke there to all the people "face to face," but again, there was hearing only, no seeing:

> Then Yahweh spoke to you out of the midst of the fire; you heard the sound of words, but saw no form; there was only a voice. (Deut 4:12)

Revelation through hearing was extraordinary enough. The Deuteronomic preacher says:

> Did any people ever hear the voice of a god speaking out of the midst of the fire, as you have heard, and still live? (Deut 4:33; cf. 5:26)

Yahweh, then, cannot be looked upon; only his voice can be heard. Hearing always outweighs seeing in the psychology of the Hebrew prophets. When prophetism flowers in the eighth to sixth centuries B.C.E., the resounding call is "Hear the word of Yahweh." Jeremiah criticizes prophets who say, "I have dreamed, I have dreamed," but do not faithfully speak Yahweh's word (Jer 23:23-32).

Having said this, however, we must be careful not to push the point too far. The impression must not be given that vision in the broad sense, or visions in the more restricted sense, is of no importance to the Hebrew prophets. This is not the case. Prophets in every age make some use of the visual sense in mediating divine revelation. Isaiah, Jeremiah, and Ezekiel all have visions accompanying their calls. Ezekiel is also the "watchman" of Israel, and Jeremiah, so outspoken against dreams, has himself visionary experiences on which he lays great importance.

Visions convey to prophets secrets that kings, other prophets, and ordinary people are not privy to. Elisha has the reputation of knowing what the king of Syria talks about in his bedroom (2 Kgs 6:12). Jesus, years later, is confessed to be a prophet by a woman who discovers that he has hidden knowledge about her marital—also nonmarital—life (John 4:16-19).

Visions of the prophets convey coming destruction. Micaiah sees Israel's king dead in battle and all Israel scattered after a Syrian victory (1 Kings 22). Amos has visions of national destruction for northern Israel (Amos 7–9). Jeremiah sees all of Judah destroyed in a vision (Jer 1:13-14). More shocking still is a vision coming to Jeremiah that shows the entire creation returning to primeval chaos (Jer 4:23-26).

Prophets shared this visionary gift with their precursor, the "seer." In 1 Sam 9:9 we read:

> Formerly in Israel, when a man went to inquire of God, he said, "Come let us go to the seer"; for he who is now called a prophet was formerly called a seer.

Samuel was a seer. Saul and his servants seek out Samuel when lost asses cannot be found. It will cost them a fee, but Samuel with his visionary gift can locate them, and he does (1 Sam 9:1—10:16).

Seers, diviners, and other intermediaries of like description were common throughout the ancient world. Visions and oracles were accompanied by fits of ecstasy, a tiny glimpse of which we see in 1 Samuel 10 after Samuel has anointed Saul to be prince over Israel. When Saul gets caught up in ecstasy with a band of prophets, he himself begins to prophesy:

> And when all who knew him before saw how he prophesied with the prophets, the people said one to another, "What has come over the son of Kish? Is Saul also among the prophets?" (1 Sam 10:11)

Outside Israel such individuals were masters of a craft.[24] Harry Orlinsky says of the diviner:

> The novitiate in divination, like the worker in textiles and metals, had to spend many years of hard and closely supervised work in learning his trade. He had to memorize incantations of all sorts. He had to learn to interpret the flight of birds, the formation of livers (hepatoscopy) and entrails (extispicy), the lay assumed by arrows and stones cast out of a container, the relative position of the heavenly bodies (astrology), the smoke and liquid emanating from a special cup or other container (lecanomancy; libanomancy), the significance of dreams and of signs in general; and the like.[25]

Modern counterparts inspect the palms of the hands or read horoscopes to divine the future.

Precisely how different Israelite seers were from diviners and other intermediaries in the neighboring cultures is hard to say, but that there were some differences seems clear, if only because of legislation prohibiting the latter from plying their trade in Israel (Deut 18:9-14). While the Old Testament never outlaws the seer, only a few seers appear after the time of Samuel. Their place was taken by the prophets, with whom they had much in common.[26]

We get a good profile of the seer from Numbers 22–24, where the activities of Balaam are recorded. Balaam, son of Beor, is a non-Israelite hired by Balak, king of Moab, to come and curse Israel. The Old Testament does not call Balaam a seer (nor even a prophet, for that matter);[27] nevertheless, his activity corresponds to that of the typical seer. For one thing, he is hired (Num 22:7). He also performs elaborate sacrifices, which probably indicates that he was attached to some worship center like Samuel, who also presided over sacrifices.[28]

A text discovered at Deir 'Alla in modern Jordan mentions Balaam and contains fragments of an oracle (or oracles) he received and was in the process of reporting. In this text he is called "seer of the gods" (ḥzh 'lhn).[29] In the biblical account, however, Balaam comes off more like a Hebrew prophet; for example, he will speak only what God tells him to speak (Num 22:8, 18, 38; 23:3, 12, 26; 24:13). But he is someone who both sees and hears (Num 24:3-4, 15-16), achieving the former, of course, only after the God of Israel succeeds in opening his eyes (cf. Num 22:21-35).

The Hebrew prophets both see and hear. What disturbs them most are people who can do neither. Isaiah speaks to this with biting irony:

Hear and hear, but do not understand;
  see and see, but do not perceive.
Make the heart of this people fat
  and their ears heavy,
  and shut their eyes,
lest they see with their eyes
  and hear with their ears
and understand with their hearts
  and turn and be healed.
                    (Isa 6:9-10)

Jeremiah, for his part, says this to the people:

Hear this, O foolish and senseless people,
  who have eyes but see not,
  who have ears but hear not.
                    (Jer 5:21)

It is to such people that Yahweh sends his prophets. Little wonder that Yahweh must find someone who can *hear* the divine word, *see* the divine vision, and *speak* both to an insensitive people.

MIGHTY WORKS

To be a prophet is sometimes to be someone able to perform mighty works. Only three Hebrew prophets—four if we include Aaron (cf. Exod 7:1)—were so gifted. Yet an ability to perform mighty works, or miracles as we say, marks one as a prophet of Yahweh.[30] At the conclusion of Deuteronomy, Moses is described as follows:

And there has not arisen a prophet in Israel like Moses, whom Yahweh knew face to face, none like him for all the signs and the wonders which Yahweh sent him to do in the land of Egypt, to Pharaoh and to all his servants and to all his land, and for all the mighty power and all the great and terrible deeds which Moses wrought in the sight of all Israel. (Deut 34:10-12)

In some societies today the prophet is conceived of primarily in terms of being a miracle worker. I discovered this some years ago on a trip to central Africa. Visiting with President Doko of the Communauté

Evangélique a L'Ubangi-Mongala (CEUM), a Christian church in north-west Zaire (Congo), I learned about individuals in the area considered to be prophets. I asked what essentially marked one as a prophet among his people. His response was that the prophet possessed the gift of mir-acle working. Conversations with other African pastors of the CEUM brought forth the same answer. In fact, this was the *only* mark any of them could point to in identifying one as a prophet. Prophet Harris of West Africa (1910–1929) performed exorcisms, healings, and other miracles, and miracles were attributed to Isaiah Shembe (d. 1935), a Bantu prophet in South Africa.[31]

Prior to the exodus, Moses and Aaron performed mighty works before the pharaoh (Exodus 7–10). Aaron turned his rod into a serpent and then proceeded to bring about the first three plagues: turning the Nile into blood, bringing the frogs, and bringing the gnats. Moses per-formed four mighty works: he brought on the plagues of the boils, hail, locusts, and darkness.

The other mighty duo in ancient Israel was Elijah and Elisha, who performed mighty acts of deliverance. They healed the sick and raised the dead. Food and oil were miraculously multiplied, and a city's drink-ing water was made clean. If Aaron could turn a rod into a serpent, Elisha was able to make an ax handle float (1 Kings 17; 2 Kgs 2:19-22; 4:1—6:7).

These prophets did more than see and hear; they were also more than able speakers, if they had that gift at all. What they did was *demon-strate* the power of Yahweh. The magicians of Egypt and Baal prophets of Canaan had limited success at this same sort of thing (Exod 7:11, 22; 8:7; Deut 13:1-2), although their success has been attributed to magic. The great majority of Hebrew prophets, in any case, were not so gifted, and we do not see such power again in Israel until Jesus comes in the spirit of Moses and Elijah (John 6:14; 9:17).

THE DIVINE SPIRIT

To be a prophet is also to be someone filled with the divine spirit. The prophets have *rûaḥ* (רוּחַ), which is translated into English as "spirit" or "wind." Of course, they have their own spirit, but another spirit rushes upon them and controls them in extraordinary ways. This is the spirit of Yahweh, causing them to speak and act with extraordinary passion. Saul, as was pointed out, when meeting a group of spirit-filled prophets was himself brought under the spirit's power. The spirit came also upon David when he was anointed king (1 Sam 16:13), but, unlike Saul, he was conscious of the spirit's presence throughout life (2 Sam 23:2; cf. 1 Sam 16:14).

After David, Israel's kings are not noted for being men of the spirit. The one possessing the gift of the spirit is now the prophet (Neh 9:30), who appears to inherit it from the judges (Judg 3:10; 6:34; 11:29; 13:25; 14:6, 19; 15:14).[32] Only on occasion is Yahweh's spirit said to rest upon priests (2 Chr 20:14; 24:20) and certain other individuals, such as Amasai the military leader (1 Chr 12:18). The day is still a ways off when God's spirit will be poured out upon all people (Joel 2:28-29; John 14; Acts 2). But a foreshadowing of this day appears in Num 11:29, when Moses says to Joshua, "Would that all Yahweh's people were prophets, that Yahweh would put his spirit upon them!"

Here again we must sound a note of caution. The Hebrew understanding of Yahweh's spirit and other spirits is complex. It is also fragmented, at least to us who have but a few biblical texts to inform us. There are, for example, evil spirits such as the one Yahweh sends upon Saul after his own spirit withdraws and is sent to rest upon David (1 Sam 16:14). According to Micaiah, "lying spirits" were sent by Yahweh to the four hundred prophets in the court of Ahab, who, incidentally, believed they were possessed by the spirit of Yahweh (1 Kgs 22:23-24). In addition, there were those empty spirits recognized by the perceptive as being only so much "wind." Here the Hebrew *rûaḥ* means "hot air."

This mark of prophetism is actually played down in the Old Testament. One reason must be the widespread phenomenon of ecstatic prophecy in neighboring cultures.[33] Prophets who showed a tendency to hyperspirituality often ended up being discredited. This was certainly true in the case of the spirit-filled prophets of Baal, who slashed themselves and performed their rain dance on Mount Carmel (1 Kgs 18:27-29), eliciting nothing but wrath and mockery from Elijah.

There were Hebrew prophets, too, who were judged to possess more "wind" than "spirit." Hosea remarked that "the man of the spirit is mad" (Hos 9:7).[34] Micah claimed that insensitive people in his audience would rather sit and listen to "windy" preachers, who push "liquid spirits" on people, than to his cry against social injustice (Mic 2:11). Jeremiah played on the double meaning of "spirit," saying that some prophets he knows will become what they already are: "bags of wind." The word of Yahweh is not in them (Jer 5:13).

At the same time, genuine prophets are inspired people.[35] Micah, despite his comment about "windy preachers," understands himself to be filled with Yahweh's spirit (Mic 3:8). So also Ezekiel (Ezek 2:2; 11:5) and the lesser-known Azariah ben Obed (2 Chr 15:1, 8). The prophet of the exile says this about himself:

> The spirit of Yahweh is upon me,
>   because Yahweh has appointed me
> to bring good tidings to the afflicted;
>   he has sent me to bind up the brokenhearted,
> to proclaim liberty to the captives
>   and the opening of the eyes of those who are bound.
>
> (Isa 61:1)

These words were read in the Nazareth synagogue by Jesus, who then went on to apply them to himself (Luke 4:16-21). We see now why the masses often confessed Jesus to be a prophet.

Because prophets are filled with Yahweh's spirit, they display emotion openly.[36] They speak in a loud voice.[37] When the spirit of Yahweh comes upon them, there is a kind of party atmosphere: music, dancing, loud voices, and the rest. Prophets meeting Saul were playing harps, tambourines, flutes, and lyres. This party atmosphere characterized Pentecost, when the spirit was poured out upon the church. Some thought these spirit-filled people were drunk on wine (Acts 2).

The spirit, however, may work in precisely the opposite way. Instead of causing great excitement, it can have a deep quieting effect, an effect not to be confused with depression, such as Saul experienced when Yahweh's spirit left him and an evil spirit came in its place. Yahweh's spirit had an unmistakable quieting effect upon Ezekiel. At the time of his call, Ezekiel said:

> The spirit lifted me up and took me away, and I went in bitterness
> in the heat of my spirit, the hand of Yahweh being strong upon
> me; and I came to the exiles at Telabib, who dwelt by the river
> Chebar, and I sat there overwhelmed among them seven days.
> (Ezek 3:14-15)

No party this time. Ezekiel sat quietly for seven days! The spirit left him virtually speechless. In both Jeremiah (cf. Jer 15:17) and Ezekiel we see a deep indwelling of Yahweh's spirit—more contemplation, more inner reflection, more prayer, and more confession. More time is spent conversing inwardly with God.

The spirit of Yahweh moves. Like the wind, it comes and it goes (cf. John 3:8). Because of this, the prophets too are moved, sometimes to outward bursts of excitement, other times to deafening silence. One thing is clear. Life for them is not always on an even keel. Sometimes prophets are an octave too high, says Heschel;[38] other times they are an octave too low. But that's how it is to be filled with Yahweh's spirit.

The spirit also moves prophets in the sense that they are people who come and go. Here Elijah provides the classic example. He will appear unexpectedly, then be gone before you know it. One day Elijah met Obadiah, who was the royal steward for King Ahab, and he told Obadiah to announce the prophet's presence to the king (1 Kings 18). Obadiah was surprised to see Elijah, but infinitely more alarmed to accede to the prophet's request, since Elijah was known not to stay around long. Should he leave, Obadiah would be in a perilous position with the king. Obadiah tells Elijah:

> As soon as I have gone from you, the spirit of Yahweh will carry you whither I know not, and so, when I come to tell Ahab and he cannot find you, he will kill me, although I your servant have revered Yahweh from my youth. (1 Kgs 18:12)

Elijah must promise Obadiah that he will not leave, and he honors that promise. Even at the end of Elijah's life, the belief persisted that Yahweh's spirit had taken him to an unknown destination (2 Kgs 2:16).[39]

This mobility that the prophet and others take for granted sets the prophet off sharply from the priest, who is a fixed member of the community. The priest resides at the sanctuary, where he officiates at sacrifices, makes judgments about law, health, and hygiene, and in the early days was on hand to give divine oracles (1 Sam 23:9-12; 30:7-8). He was, for all practical purposes, "a man of God in residence." He does not come to see you; you go to see him, and you know where you can find him. The prophet, on the other hand, is never so tied down. He will appear at the temple to give oracles, lead perhaps in a liturgy, offer prayers, and then be gone.[40] Often he will come to see you, and when he does, it will be at a time you least expect. You may welcome his coming; you may wish he had never come.

As divine messengers, then, prophets were people on the go, and as we have said—their appearances could evoke genuine surprise. Sometimes people dared not ask the divine messenger where he had come from (Judg 13:6); other times people confessed openly that the messenger was sent directly from God. Genesis 21:17 says that when Hagar was about to leave her child to die, a messenger called to her "out of heaven." The expression "out of heaven" tells us not only that the voice was from God but that it came to her as a complete surprise. Today we might say such a voice came "right out of the blue." After all, one is barely able to conceal one's excitement when a messenger of God appears to Hagar at a critical moment, not only showing her the way to water but offering a timely word of hope for the future. Abraham is met in a similar way by a divine messenger when he is about to slay Isaac (Gen 22:11). A voice also comes to him "right out of heaven," which is to say, suddenly and unexpectedly.

To be a prophet, then, is to come and go, the result of being possessed by Yahweh's spirit. The importance of mobility for the prophet persisted even into the late first century C.E., when, in the early church, the false prophet was one who stayed with his host more than two days (*Didache* 11:5).

PRAYER

Finally, to be a prophet is to be someone who prays. In his capacity as divine messenger, the prophet brings messages back to Yahweh, which we call prayers. For the most part these consist of requests. The prophet prays for himself, and he prays on behalf of others, in which capacity he acts as a divine mediator. We learn from Gen 20:7 that intercessory prayer is what marks the prophet.[41] There God speaks to Abimelech about Abraham, saying, "Now then restore the man's wife; for he is a prophet and he will pray for you, and you shall live." Abraham this one time is called a prophet, no doubt because he can pray for the life of another person—in this instance, a foreign king.[42] Jeremiah, too, considers intercession with Yahweh the mark of a bona fide prophet (Jer 27:18).

Thus far, we have said little about the prophet as a mediator, which in neighboring societies was an expected function of the divine intermediary. Indeed, this overshadowed virtually everything else, since ancient religion was bent on influencing the divine will. Prophets and other intermediaries called frantically upon the gods, sometimes even cutting themselves till the blood gushed (1 Kgs 18:28). It was a form of manipulation, like hunger strikes by modern-day prisoners. Such actions were carried out to evoke divine pity, which, it was believed, would lead to divine action. Fasting was another common practice in the ancient world intended to force a divine response.

Ancient sacrificial practice was rooted in the belief that the gods would be beneficent if they were well treated by their human subjects.

The smell of smoke brought pleasure even to Yahweh (Gen 8:21), and it softened him so that he promised never again to send another great flood. When priests offer sacrifices, they act as intermediaries between the people and God.

Prophets are rarely involved in sacrificial worship.[43] With them the accent is a different one entirely. The prophet's commitment is to be in the service of Yahweh. Yahweh calls him, gives him his word, and gives him a measure of vision. When the prophet speaks, it is Yahweh's word that he speaks, and the power he demonstrates is Yahweh's power. Yahweh's spirit controls him. Yet he prays, and people know he prays. So in this one important respect, the Hebrew prophet does stand before God representing the people.[44] He may pray the concerns of his own heart, as Elijah did at Horeb (1 Kings 19), or as Jeremiah did in his many so-called confessions. He may also pray on behalf of the king or on behalf of the nation. When he does, he acts as a divine mediator.

Rarely do we read in the Bible about others praying. Yes, King David prays in his many psalms, Solomon offers a prayer when the temple is dedicated (1 Kings 8), and King Jehoshaphat offers a temple prayer before an important battle (2 Chr 20:5-12). Priests are hardly ever recorded as praying, although they must have done so. The prophet is the important person of prayer.

Certain prophets are remembered for being particularly effective in their intercessory prayers. Moses and Samuel are singled out in Jer 15:1 as the two great mediators in Israel. Countless times they prayed to Yahweh on behalf of the people. Elijah, too, as we mentioned, was a mighty man of prayer. Not only is he the divine mediator when he first emerges as a prophet, but even at the end of his life he is the person through whom Israel's kings are expected to go. Ahaziah is remiss and censured strongly for not coming to him when seeking help for the curing of his illness (2 Kings 1).

The other great mediator and man of prayer is Jeremiah.[45] In his confessions to God, he pours out as no other prophet does his own hurts and the hurts of his people (Jer 8:21). It must have come as a shock to Jeremiah when Yahweh told him to pray no longer (Jer 7:16; 11:14; 14:11). My teacher James Muilenburg used to say that this probably meant he was praying all the time. But when Judah's fate was sealed, mediation was no longer possible. Yahweh said then that he would not even listen to Moses and Samuel were they present to lay the people's case before him (Jer 15:1). But this ban on intercessory prayer was not permanent. After Jerusalem fell, Jeremiah was once again interceding on behalf of the remnant (Jeremiah 42).

Because prophets are divine messengers, they are well placed to make requests of Yahweh. But it may also be because the prophet—assuming that he or she was genuine—was possessed with uncommon integrity. The New Testament says, "The prayer of a righteous person has great power in its effect," with Elijah cited as one such righteous person (Jas 5:16-17). At any rate, not everyone in ancient Israel had equal access to Yahweh. Among those performing acts of mediation, the prophet stood at the forefront. The reason was that he could pray.

THE PROPHETIC MESSAGE— WHAT IS IT?

WE HAVE SEEN WHAT MARKS A PROPHET AS BEING a prophet, and preeminent among these features is that one be enlisted as a messenger to speak on behalf of Yahweh the King. The prophet is a speaker, Yahweh's voice to individuals, to Israel, and to nations of the world. What, then, does the prophet say? What are the messages brought to these individuals and to nations of the world? We must turn now to say something about the prophetic message, which is insufficiently examined in most studies of the Hebrew prophets. After a few general observations, the present chapter will be given over to lifting up the important messages of Old Testament prophets whose messages have been preserved. After a brief introduction to each prophet, we will select those messages that have captured the imagination of people down through the ages. The aim here will be to let each prophet speak for him- or herself. In addition, familiar words we know so well will be left as much as possible in the contexts in which they occur, so as to give them a meaning close to what the prophet originally intended.

FORETELLING AND FORTHTELLING

If people were asked today of what the prophetic message consisted, most would probably say either (1) predictions about the future (foretelling) or (2) censures of current social and political ills (forthtelling). Thus the usual designations of foretelling and forthtelling. Julius Wellhausen and his school deemphasized the foretelling aspect of Hebrew prophecy, in part because with the rise of critical scholarship it was realized that some biblical prophecies, for example, the one naming Josiah as the future destroyer of the Bethel altar (1 Kgs 13:2), were *ex eventu* ("after the event"). In addition, in the view of Wellhausen, prophets were primarily concerned with social and religious ills of the present day. They were forthtellers. But Hermann Gunkel quickly saw the one-sidedness of this view and argued that prophets were from earliest times foretellers of the future.[1] James Muilenburg concurred, saying in support of Gunkel, "The notion held in the past that the prophet did not predict or foretell events is contradicted by every prophet whose words have been preserved."[2]

This having been said, we must also be careful not to distinguish too sharply between foretelling and forthtelling, as prophets rarely did one and not the other. Their messages frequently contained some of both, and excluding one will almost always diminish the importance of the other.

CORRECTIVE SPEECH

Because prophetic speech is largely corrective speech, it is always lop-sided and must not be judged as a balanced presentation on this subject or that. Balance will be found more in the wisdom literature. Abraham Heschel said that prophets were given to much exaggeration and could be enormously unfair in their judgments. He also noted contradictions in prophetic speech without finality. It is, he said, a fragmented word expressed ad hoc.[3]

Prophetic speech, when it is corrective speech, will contain a message people do not want to hear (Mic 2:6; Jer 38:4). People are afraid of prophets preaching doom (cf. Deut 18:22). Of course, prophets also give messages of hope and deliverance, and these will be received not with hostility but with wonder or disbelief. The majority of prophets, however, indict and render judgments, and ancient people—like people today—do not want to hear either.

COVENANT DISOBEDIENCE

Behind all the indictments and judgments of the prophets lay a broken Sinai covenant, which required obedience if it was to stay intact. It has often been pointed out that the word *covenant* appears only infrequently in prophets before Jeremiah, and scholars have wondered why this is so.[4] The answer, it seems to me, is that prophetic preaching is not primarily a call to covenant obedience, nor even a warning of what will happen if Israel disobeys the covenant. We do get some of this preaching in Jeremiah (Jer 7:3-7; 11:3b-5; 21:12), but it is more the message of Deuteronomy than the message of the prophets. In Deuteronomy, Moses is heard admonishing Israel throughout to be careful to do Yahweh's commands, statutes, and ordinances (Deuteronomy 4; 8; et passim), and he describes what will happen if Israel obeys or does not obey. If Israel obeys the covenant, Israel will be blessed and will live long in the land that Yahweh God has given it. But if Israel disobeys, a multitude of curses will fall, the most serious of which will be the loss of the land. There are two ways one can walk. Obedience is the path to life; disobedience is the path to death (Deut 30:15-20). For the blessings and curses fortifying the Sinai covenant, see Deuteronomy 28.

The message of the prophets is different, very different. For them, the covenant is now broken, requiring indictment and judgment if repentance is not forthcoming. Thus in prophetic preaching we encounter what in Greek rhetoric was called the "enthymeme."[5] An enthymeme is a syllogism in which one premise, usually the major premise, is assumed but not present. In order to get the full argument, one must identify the assumed premise, which in our case is the message of Deuteronomy.[6] The argument made by the prophets is the following:

[Deuteronomy: An Israel in violation of the covenant will be punished]
The prophets: Israel has violated the covenant
                 Israel will be punished

When prophets harked back to the Sinai covenant, they were basically conservatives.[7] Jeremiah's big word is not "change," but "return" (šûb, שוב), which translates also as "repent." The "liberals" of Jeremiah's day were those bent on trying new experiments in worship, many of which were imported from religions of neighboring nations. The conservatives were calling people back to their roots.

SOCIAL INJUSTICE

Because the prophets preached about covenant disobedience, they were much concerned about keeping the Law—the Decalogue first and foremost, but also provisions in the Covenant Code and the Code of Deuteronomy. In Deuteronomy, recurring themes were care for the sojourner, orphan, and widow, and justice toward the poor in society. The prophets identified with tragedy in the world, bringing Yahweh's word to bear on adversity and the victims of adversity.

CENSURE OF OTHER NATIONS

Foreign nations had no covenant with Yahweh, yet Yahweh, being God of the whole earth, intended that foreign nations too must be punished for evil they have done. Amos announces the punishment of six nations of the world for gross inhumanity toward one another (Amos 1:3—2:3). Jeremiah says that other nations must be punished because they are wicked (Jer 25:31), proud (Jer 50:31-32), and trusting in their own gods (Jer 50:38; 51:47, 52). The excessive pride (Greek ὕβρις, *hybris*) of nations is a common motif of ancient Near Eastern religion.[8] Foreign nations must also be punished, according to the Old Testament, after they have punished Israel, lest they think that the power to destroy belongs to them. Power belongs rather to Yahweh (Deut 32:26-30).

AUTHENTIC MESSAGES

Prophets make the charge that other prophets are delivering inauthentic messages, which means that true prophets must deliver authentic messages. We will say more about this in the next chapter when we come to discuss measures of authenticity in the Hebrew prophets. Here it will suffice simply to point out in what an authentic message consists and how that message must fit the times in which it is spoken.

Some prophets seem not to understand the conditional element in the Mosaic covenant, which leads them to preach peace when they should be preaching judgment. Their preaching requires no accountability. Other prophets show a basic indifference to evil, which is more insidious than evil itself. Heschel says, "All prophecy is one great exclamation: God is not indifferent to evil."[9] Prophets who are indifferent to evil remain silent about it, talking rather about other things. It was lamented after the fall of Jerusalem that false and misleading oracles failed to expose Judah's iniquity (Lam 2:14). Preaching deliverance and well-being at such a time turned out to be a big lie.

An authentic prophetic message must fit the times. All prophets know well Israel's great messages of the past: that Yahweh is gracious and merciful, that Yahweh is the savior of Israel, and that Yahweh will protect

Israel from enemy attack. But when things have deteriorated to the point where people "call evil good and good evil" (Isa 5:20), when there is no repentance for wrongdoing when such is brought to light, messages of deliverance and well-being should not be preached. Yahweh is not giving those messages at such a time, and prophets who preach them are preaching a false message.

Micah is enraged because immoral prophets, living among immoral leaders, are preaching dependence on Yahweh:

> Yet they lean upon Yahweh and say,
> "Is not Yahweh in the midst of us?
> No evil shall come upon us."
>
> (Mic 3:11)

Is not dependence on Yahweh a commendable message? Yahweh's presence in Israel has been witnessed often enough, his protection proven over and over again. But for Micah, this message is flat because it is being proclaimed as an abstract religious truth, and Yahweh is not in the business of declaring abstract religious truth. Yahweh speaks dynamic words to concrete historical situations, and the historical situation in Micah's day is one in which the leaders of Jerusalem are immoral and the people too are immoral, and preaching dependence on Yahweh at such a time will not wash. Thus an otherwise true message ends up being false. The true message was the one given by Micah, namely, that Jerusalem was deserving of Yahweh's judgment (3:12).

One of Jeremiah's celebrated Temple Oracles was spoken to temple worshipers who were affirming the wondrous salvation of Yahweh while at the same time being engaged in wholesale covenant disobedience. No fewer than six of the Ten Commandments were being broken:

> Behold, you trust in deceptive words to no avail. Will you steal, murder, commit adultery, swear falsely, burn incense to Baal, and go after other gods that you have not known, and then come and stand before me in this house, which is called by my name, and say, "We are delivered!" only to go on doing all these abominations? (Jer 7:8-10)

What are the "deceptive words"? They could be the words Jeremiah has just quoted, "This is the temple of Yahweh, the temple of Yahweh, the temple of Yahweh" (7:4). Or they could be the words "We are delivered!" that follow (7:10). Either way, Jeremiah appears to be quoting words from a temple liturgy, words affirming Yahweh's greatness and the steadfast-ness of the worshiper's faith. But now these words are deceptive, because those speaking them are acting with duplicity before Yahweh, and Yah-weh will have none of it.

The authentic message is one of judgment when judgment is called for. It condemns evil, it announces punishment, and it causes insecurity, as bad as this may seem. Reinhold Niebuhr said that the true prophet in an evil age is one who creates insecurity,[10] and anyone creating insecurity will anger the keepers of institutional religion. But the true prophet is concerned infinitely more with the burning anger of Yahweh.

Inauthentic prophecy is often without originality or independence.[11] Sheldon Blank says that prophets who steal oracles from one another (Jer 23:30) are "dealers in used oracles."[12] Prophets correctly assessing the his-torical situation and Yahweh's response to that situation will come forth with a word fresh and new. Prophets, as we have said, preach a conserva-tive message, but they do not keep alive clichés of the past. John Skinner says that false prophecy

> was fundamentally an unprogressive survival of the ancient prophecy of Israel under conditions to which it was no longer adequate, and under which it was apt to deteriorate into mere flattery of the popular opinion, or even into a means of livelihood (Mic 3:5-8).[13]

MESSAGES OF THE PROPHETS

Early Messengers of Yahweh

Messages delivered by early "messengers of Yahweh" are quite brief, even as their visitations are brief. Their words are timely, however, having to do with urgent matters of the moment while at the same time anticipat-ing momentous events in the near and distant future. In this early period, the prophetic message can be characterized broadly as one of salvation or judgment. Salvation comes as a result of Yahweh's favor; judgment comes because of Yahweh's anger over disobedience, inhumane treatment of people, or some other form of wrongdoing. Yahweh's favor does not require a reason, but judgment always carries with it a reason, and it is a valid reason.

The message Hagar receives from Yahweh's messenger is twofold. She must return to Sarah, from whom she has fled. If this is not a word of judgment, it is at least a rebuke. But she also receives a promise for the future. The child she carries will be a son, and this son will be the father of descendants without number (Gen 16:7-12). The message here, then, is censure and promise, foretelling and forthtelling.

Similarly, when divine messengers visit Abraham and Sarah about the birth of a son (Gen 18:9-15), they accompany their gladsome news with a word of judgment. Sodom, where Abraham's nephew Lot lives together with his family, must be destroyed along with Gomorrah because of the cities' rank wickedness (vv. 16-21). Here the divine messengers appear to be themselves the agents of destruction (19:3), which happens later in the case of Elijah (1 Kgs 18:40), but not with the later prophets, who simply announce the bad news and then let others carry it out. But here we see again a prophecy of both salvation and judgment, one that relates to the present and also to the future: the son promised to Abraham and Sarah is slated for the future; the destruction of Sodom and Gomorrah will take place now. Sodom and Gomorrah's destruction becomes prototypical for the later prophets in announcing the destruction of Israel's wicked cities (Isa 1:9-10; Jer 23:14).

Messengers of Yahweh come later to both of these sons of promise as they are about to die. Hagar has now been sent away by Sarah, and she and the boy are in the wilderness without water. But a message comes confirming the earlier promise. Hagar is then made to see a well from which she can draw water for her dying child (Gen 21:8-19). Something similar happens to Abraham when he is about to sacrifice Isaac on Mount Moriah. A messenger of Yahweh appears to him in timely fashion and tells him not to make the sacrifice. And as he looks up, he sees a ram caught in the thicket that can be sacrificed instead. The messenger then repeats the promise about Abraham being the father of multitudes (Gen 22:9-19).

When Israel is settled in the land and has disobeyed Yahweh by making a covenant with the people who are living there, a messenger of Yahweh comes to speak judgment: the idolatry of the Canaanites will be a continual snare to Israel (Judg 2:1-5). Deborah, a judge taken also to be a prophet, gives Barak and Israel a message promising deliverance over Sisera, a commander of the Canaanite king Jabin (Judges 4). In this age of the judges, Gideon receives a messenger of Yahweh, also called a prophet, who gives him the good news that Yahweh through him will bring Israel victory over the Midianites (Judg 6:7-24). Sometime later, Manoah and his wife receive word from a messenger of Yahweh about the birth of a son, who will become the mighty Samson (Judges 13).

Messages of this early period are almost always about matters of life and death. Children are promised to hopeful parents, and, once born, they are miraculously saved when death appears certain. In the case of Abraham, obedience to Yahweh is critical for the salvation of his son. Whole peoples are also promised deliverance in battle, and entire cities receive messages of doom. These early divine messengers almost always address individuals, not entire nations. But the messages they give are much the same as messages delivered by the classical prophets to Israel and nations of the world.

Samuel: Prophet of Obedience

The most remembered message of Samuel is the one he addressed to Saul about obeying the voice of Yahweh. Yahweh had said that Saul must utterly destroy the Amalekites, sparing neither persons nor animals (1 Samuel 15). Yet Saul spared Agag, the king, and the best of the animals. The latter, he claimed, were to be sacrificed to Yahweh. As a reault, Samuel delivers this word to Saul:

> Has Yahweh as great delight in burnt offerings and sacrifices
>   as in obeying the voice of Yahweh?
> Behold, to obey is better than sacrifice
>   and to hearken than the fat of rams.
> For rebellion is as the sin of divination,
>   and stubbornness is as iniquity and idolatry.
> Because you have rejected the word of Yahweh,
>   he has also rejected you from being king.
>   (1 Sam 15:22-23)

This was not the first time. Saul disobeyed an earlier prophetic word, commencing the sacrifice at Gilgal before Samuel had arrived. As a result, he was told then that his kingdom would not continue (1 Sam 13:8-15). Obedience, again, was the defining test: Abraham passed, Saul failed.

Nathan: Prophet of the Covenants

The prophet Nathan delivered three important messages to King David. The first was a good news message that David, instead of being given the go-ahead to build a house for Yahweh, would have a house built for him. Yahweh was promising him a perpetual line of descendants (2 Samuel 7). But after David's adultery with the wife of Uriah the Hittite, and the murder of Uriah, Nathan's message to David was riveting judgment (2 Samuel 11). After hearing the prophet's story of a rich man who snatched a poor man's ewe lamb, upon which the king was asked to render a judgment, David gave a correct verdict on the rich man. But Nathan then turned to the king and said, "You are the man!" David was judged for violating the sixth and seventh commandments, yet because he repented, he did not lose the kingship, as Saul did. His punishment was that the sword would not depart from his house, that evil would arise against him within his house, and that the child born to him and Bathsheba would die (2 Sam 12:1-15). Finally, when David's son Solomon was born, Nathan returned to pronounce the son beloved by Yahweh (vv. 24-25).

Gad: Prophet to David about the Census

David's other prophet (and seer) was a fellow named Gad, who came to the king with a word of judgment after David had taken a census (2 Sam 24:10-14). David's infraction is unclear, but there seems to have been disapproval of his military motives. A prophet speaking to David against war was unusual, but it would be a common message from later prophets, notably Isaiah and Jeremiah, to the kings of Judah. Gad's message was also unusual in that David was given his choice of punishment. He could have (1) three years of famine, (2) three months of pursuit by the enemy, or (3) three days of pestilence. David chose three days of pestilence, and it came. Jeremiah later gave Judahites a choice of punishment, although none the people would likely have chosen (Jer 15:1-2).

Elijah: Prophet of Yahweh Alone

Elijah's message to an Israel living in violation of the first commandment was that Yahweh alone was God (1 Kings 18). Elijah's very name meant "Yahweh is God," the confession people made after Yahweh bested the prophets of Baal on Mount Carmel (1 Kgs 18:39). This mighty defender of Yahweh returned to pass judgment on Ahab and his wife Jezebel for a miscarriage of justice, the latter having arranged the seizure of a vineyard belonging to Naboth the Jezreelite (1 Kings 21). The Israelite king and his wife had violated the ninth commandment on not bearing false witness (vv. 8-13). Then, at the end of his life, Elijah judged King Ahaziah for seeking out Baalzebub (= Baalzebul) of Ekron regarding a illness to which he had fallen victim (2 Kings 1)—judgment once again for a violation of the first commandment.

Elijah also had a message for private citizens, accompanying it with mighty works. His prophetic word saved the widow of Zarephath and her son from famine, and then in another message, coupled with a miracle, the son was spared a second time (1 Kgs 17:8-24).

From Elijah we also hear personal confessions, similar to those that come later in great number and are articulated more elaborately by Jeremiah. Elijah, like Moses and Samuel before him, bared his soul to Yahweh, and his confessions along with the divine answers he received are an important part of his prophetic message (1 Kgs 19:4-18). While in the wilderness fleeing from Jezebel, Elijah was visited by another messenger of Yahweh who provided him with food (vv. 5-7).

Elisha: Prophet against Moab and Syria

Elisha, after giving Jehoshaphat and Jehoram a prediction of victory over Moab (2 Kgs 3:11-20), prophesied also victories over Syria. The last of these was on his deathbed (2 Kgs 6:11—7:20; 13:14-19). Elisha was an international figure, bringing Yahweh's message to none other than the king of Syria. When Benhadad was sick, Elisha journeyed to Damascus to tell Hazael that he, albeit by devious means, would become the next Syrian king (2 Kgs 8:7-15; cf. 1 Kgs 19:15). Jeremiah later would do much the same, sending messages to neighboring kings who had come to Jerusalem to discuss rebellion against Nebuchadnezzar (Jer 27:1-11).

Elisha delivered a life-giving message, accompanied by a miracle, to the wife of one of the sons of the prophets (2 Kgs 4:1-7) and repeated the feat of his master Elijah by delivering a life-giving message, accompanied by another mighty work, to the Shunammite woman and her son (2 Kgs 4:8-37). This incident and the one earlier by Elijah recall visitations to Hagar and Abraham at which time both of their sons were spared. Elisha later told the Shunammite woman to leave the country because Yahweh had decreed a famine (2 Kgs 8:1-2). On another occasion Elisha judged his servant Gehazi for being unprincipled in taking money from Naaman the Syrian. Gehazi as a result took on the leprosy from which Naaman had just been cleansed (2 Kgs 5:19-27).

Amos: Prophet of Justice and Righteousness

Amos was a shepherd and a dresser of vines in Tekoa, a Judahite city just south of Jerusalem. Called by Yahweh to prophesy against northern Israel (Amos 7:15), Amos preached during the reigns of Uzziah in Judah (783–742 B.C.E.) and Jeroboam II in Israel (786–746 B.C.E.), two years before "the earthquake" (1:1). The latter no doubt gave credibility to his prophecy (8:8; 9:1-4). This earthquake must have been a major one, for it was mentioned also by Zechariah (Zech 14:5) and later by Josephus (*Ant.* 9.222-27). Its date has been put at c. 760 B.C.E., there being possible archaeological evidence for it in Hazor Stratum VI.[14] The prophecies of Amos are usually dated between 765 and 755 B.C.E., shortly before those delivered by Hosea. The Old Testament gives us little background information on Amos. He is known only to have preached once at Bethel, a northern sanctuary, where he was sent home straightaway by Amaziah, the resident priest (7:10-17). It is possible, however, that he preached elsewhere and over an extended period of time.

The mid-eighth century brought prosperity to Israel and Judah. Jeroboam II and Uzziah were both strong kings, having restored the combined national borders to nearly what they were at the time of Solomon. The Assyrians had the Syrians in check by 802 B.C.E.,[15] but by the mid-eighth century Assyria also was weak. Currently there was no problem with Egypt. During the early eighth century B.C.E., both Israel and Judah appear to have been at peace, but things changed radically for both kingdoms, especially Israel, when Tiglath-pileser ascended the Assyrian throne in 745 B.C.E.

The book of Amos opens with a sweeping indictment and judgment on eight nations. Yahweh is a roaring lion in Zion, and Amos has no choice but to speak his terrible words (1:2—3:8). Israel's six near neighbors are judged for gross inhumanity. Yahweh has no covenant with any of them; nevertheless, as God of heaven and earth, Yahweh is fully justified in punishing them. Damascus (= Syria) threshed people of Gilead with threshing sleds of iron (1:3); Gaza (= Philistines) and Tyre (= Phoenicians) delivered whole populations to Edom as slaves (1:6, 9); Edom (= Esau) cast off all pity in pursuing his brother with the sword (1:11); Ammon ripped open pregnant women in Gilead (1:13); and Moab burned the bones of the king of Edom to lime (2:1).

When Judah came up for review, it was judged for rejecting Yahweh's law and walking in lies (2:4). Covenant violation is clear. Against Israel, charges of covenant violation are made specific. Amos thunders against Israel for injustices to the righteous and poor, and says that Yahweh will not revoke the nation's punishment:

Because they sell the righteous for silver
  and the needy for a pair of sandals—
they who tamp the earth with the head of the poor
  and push aside the way of the afflicted.
A man and his father go into the same maiden
  so that my holy name is profaned.
They lay themselves down beside every altar
  on garments taken in pledge.
And in the house of their God they drink
  the wine of those who have been fined.

(Amos 2:6b-8)

Israel is indicted also for making Nazirites violate their vows and for telling prophets not to prophesy. Yahweh here reminds the people that he is the one who raised up prophets and Nazirites (2:11-12). But in the most damning word in this opening discourse, the weightiest prophecy in the entire book, Amos tells Israel that because of her special status as a chosen people, Yahweh will punish her. Yahweh says:

You only have I known of all the families of the earth;
  therefore I will punish you for all your iniquities.

(Amos 3:2)

The preaching of Amos has a universalism not found in the preaching of his contemporary, Hosea. Salvation history is here universalized: Yahweh says that he moved the Ethiopians, the Philistines, and the Arameans (Syrians) just as he brought up Israel from Egypt (9:7). Israel is no better than Hamath the great, or Gath of the Philistines (6:2). In three doxologies in the book, Yahweh is praised as not only God of Israel but God of heaven and earth and God of creation and destruction (4:13; 5:8-9; 9:5-6).

Throughout the book of Amos, we encounter two important themes: social justice and righteousness. There is a strong ethical concern in this prophet. He is concerned with injustice in the city gate (= the court), accumulated wealth, and worship rendered hollow when no justice obtains in the land. Samaria is rife with oppression, violence, and robbery, which Amos says is a result of people not knowing how to do right (3:9-10). Injustice occurs in the marketplace (8:4-6). People are afflicting the righteous, taking bribes, and pushing aside the needy in the gate. Amos says that things have become so bad that the prudent are forced to become silent (5:12-13).

Amos has particularly strong words for the rich. Rich women in Samaria oppress the poor while living in opulence. Amos says to them:

> Hear this word, you cows of Bashan
>   who are on Mount Samaria,
> who oppress the poor, who crush the needy,
>   who say to their husbands, "Bring something to drink!"
>
> (Amos 4:1)

Rich men of Samaria are also living the easy life. Amos says to them:

> Woe to those who are at ease in Zion
>   and to those who feel secure on Mount Samaria,
> the notable men of the first of the nations
>   to whom the house of Israel comes.
>
> (Amos 6:1)

Things have become desperate for the poor:

> They hate the one who reproves in the gate,
>   and they abhor the one who speaks the truth.
> Therefore because you trample on the poor
>   and take from them levies of grain,
> you have built houses of hewn stone
>   but you shall not live in them;
> you have planted pleasant vineyards
>   but you shall not drink their wine.
>
> (Amos 5:10-11)

Again the prophet speaks to Samaria's opulence:

> Woe to those who lie upon beds of ivory
>   and lounge on their couches,
> and eat lambs from the flock
>   and calves from the stall,
> who sing idle songs to the sound of the harp
>   and like David improvise on instruments of music,
> who drink wine in bowls
>   and anoint themselves with the finest oils,
>   but are not grieved over the ruin of Joseph.
>
> (Amos 6:4-6)

The "cows of Bashan" will meet a terrible end, being taken away with hooks from their places of ease (4:2). The rich men of Samaria, who give no thought to a day of judgment, are helping to bring it about (6:3). The rich who live in opulence and care not for the ruin of the nation will be the first to go into exile (6:7). Pride comes in for strong censure, the result of turning justice into poison and the fruit of righteousness into wormwood (6:8, 12-13). Destruction will come to the luxurious houses, falling even upon Yahweh's sanctuary at Bethel (3:14-15; 6:11). There will be much lamenting on this new "passover" (5:16-17). The whole land will mourn (8:8).

Amos delivers a strident attack on Israel's sanctuaries and the activities occurring there. An elaborate worship apparatus was not needed in the wilderness (5:25). Amos seems not to be as concerned as Hosea about worship of Baal, saying only that young men and women who swear by false gods in the sanctuaries will one day faint for thirst, fall, and never rise again (8:13-14). Israel in all this was busy in the service of Yahweh (5:22). Amos calls the unrighteous and unjust to seek Yahweh and to stay away from these sanctuaries slated for destruction, including the southernmost worship center at Beersheba (5:4-6). The prophet is also ironic in railing against Israel's holy places, telling people on one occasion: Keep on with your bloody worship! (4:4-5). On another occasion Yahweh says in one of Amos's prophetic words:

I hate, I despise your festivals,
    and I take no delight in your solemn assemblies.
Even though you offer me your burnt offerings and grain
        offerings,
    I will not accept them;
and the offerings of well-being of your fatted animals
    I will not look upon.
Take away from me the noise of your songs;
    I will not listen to the melody of your harps.
But let justice roll down like waters,
    and righteousness like an everflowing stream.
                                        (Amos 5:21-24)

Prior punishments by Yahweh were meant to be redemptive; however, they had no effect. Natural disasters and wars descended upon Israel, but still the nation did not return (4:6-11). Amos therefore says, "Prepare to meet your God, Israel!" (4:12). Amos has interceded on the people's behalf, and twice Yahweh has held back the punishment. But now Yahweh will no longer hold back: the high places, sanctuaries, and royal house of Jeroboam will be destroyed (7:1-9). This is the preaching that kindles the anger of the priest at Bethel.

As a result of this breakdown in Israel's community life, an adversary will surround her and bring down her strongholds (3:11; 6:8). It will be the nation's end (8:1-2). A Day of Yahweh is coming, but not like those in the past, when Yahweh fought on behalf of Israel. This will be a day of darkness and not light (5:18-20). The earth will be darkened in broad daylight; it will be a day of great mourning (8:9-10). One will hear painful sounds and a painful silence (8:3). It will be

> as if someone fled from a lion
>   and was met by a bear,
> or went into the house and rested his hand against the wall
>   and was bitten by a snake.
>
> (Amos 5:19)

The adversary is never identified, even though in a few years everyone knew it was Assyria. In 3:9 LXX, Assyria is summoned to witness the evil in Samaria, but the MT of this verse reads "Ashdod."

Amos speaks about a surviving remnant (5:15; 9:8), but it will not amount to much:

> As the shepherd rescues from the mouth of the lion two legs, or a piece of an ear, so shall the people of Israel who live in Samaria be rescued, with the corner of a couch and part of a bed. (Amos 3:12)

In one house all ten men will die, and a kinsman will come by to cremate (6:9-10). When Yahweh inflicts his blow upon the sanctuary, no one will escape, no matter where they flee (9:1-4). In another oracle, however, Amos says that the destruction of Israel's cities will leave a remnant of 10 percent (5:3). To the resident priest of Bethel, who told Amos not to prophesy, Amos has a harsh word from Yahweh: his wife will become a city prostitute, his children will die by the sword, his land will be parceled out, and he along with others will be carted off into exile (7:16-17). Amos says ironically that the Israelites will accompany their idols into exile (5:26-27). In aimless wanderings some will meet up with a famine not of food and water but of hearing the words of Yahweh (8:11-12).

There is divine compassion and a call to repentance in Amos, but neither is prominent in his preaching. Amos calls people to seek good and hate evil, and to establish justice in the gate. If they do so, he says that Yahweh "may be gracious to the remnant of Joseph" (5:14-15).

At the end of the book of Amos is hope for the future, but the hope seems targeted for Judah rather than Israel, which could be explained by Amos having hailed from Judah. Some take this as a later add-on. These closing words state that Yahweh will restore the Davidic city, fertility to the land, and Israel's fortunes, and that Israel will once again inhabit its land in security (9:11-15).

Second Moses: Prophet of the Song

One of the most strident prophetic messages of the Old Testament comes in a poem composed by someone we do not know. It is the Song of Moses in Deuteronomy 32, in which the author is assuming the prophetic voice of Moses. Most scholars date the song between the tenth and the eighth century B.C.E., but I think it may well precede the preaching of Amos and Hosea, since it focuses not on the settlement in Canaan, as is widely assumed, but on the Transjordanian settlement after Israel defeated the Amorite kings Sihon and Og. I take its composition to predate Tiglath-pileser III's destruction of Transjordan and Galilee in 734 B.C.E.

After a word of introduction calling upon heaven and earth to give ear (Deut 32:1-3), the song begins by celebrating the greatness of Yahweh, which it contrasts with the foolishness of Israel (vv. 4-9). Yahweh's defining salvation of Israel is then recounted (vv. 10-14), after which Israel is indicted for being unfaithful in going after other gods (vv. 15-18). A sentence is thus meted out to unfaithful Israel (vv. 19-22). This indictment and sentence are summarized by Huldah in her oracle of 622 B.C.E., after a law book was found during repairs to the temple (2 Kgs 22:16-17).[16] The message here, which makes this song genuine prophecy, is that Israel stands indicted because it has forgotten Yahweh and made him angry by sacrificing to other gods. Therefore Yahweh's wrath is promised to burn in judgment like an unquenchable fire. The song continues by describing the extent of Israel's punishment (vv. 23-27), and it looks at this punishment in retrospect (vv. 28-33). The tone then changes dramatically as the future salvation of Israel is promised (vv. 34-38), and the song draws to a close by returning to reiterate the greatness of Yahweh, this time contrasting it with the impotence of Yahweh's adversaries (vv. 39-42). A conclusion calls heaven and earth to praise Yahweh for avenging his adversaries and purifying his land (v. 43).

Hosea: Prophet of Divine Compassion

Hosea was a home-grown prophet of northern Israel, a contemporary of Amos, active in the years just prior to Samaria's fall. The superscription to his book has him prophesying during the reigns of Jeroboam II and Joash in Israel, and Uzziah, Jotham, Ahaz, and Hezekiah in Judah. This is the same prosperous period in north and south to which Amos speaks. Most scholars doubt that Hosea was around in Hezekiah's reign (715–687 B.C.E.), which, if he was, would mean that he survived the fall of Samaria (722 B.C.E.). But he may have been active for thirty years or so, between 755 and 725 B.C.E. The more traditional reckoning assumes a considerable overlap with Isaiah, but even with a shorter ministry for Hosea, there would have been some overlap. Isaiah received his call in 742 B.C.E. In a number of Hosea's oracles, both Israel and Judah are addressed (5:9-14; 10:11; 11:12; 12:2), although Judah's faithfulness contrasted with Israel's lies and deceit in 11:12 may be the work of a later Judaic editor.

Hosea's burden was that Israel—referred to often as Ephraim—was unfaithful to Yahweh; the covenant was viewed by him as a marital relationship between Yahweh and Israel. Unfaithfulness consisted of going after other gods, a violation of the first commandment. Hosea drove the point home by marrying a whore and having children of whoredom (Hosea 1–3). Names given to his children correlated with three themes of his preaching: (1) "Jezreel," which meant that Israel would experience military defeat in the Valley of Jezreel; (2) "Not Pitied," which meant that Yahweh would no longer have pity on Israel and would not forgive her; and (3) "Not My People," which meant that the Sinai covenant was now defunct (1:4-9).

In the book's opening discourse (Hosea 2), Yahweh indicts Israel for having chased after the Baals, not realizing that it was Yahweh who gave her the grain, wine, oil, and other good things after settlement in the land. Because of this, Hosea said Yahweh would strip her bare in the sight of her lovers and terminate her feasts, new moons, Sabbaths, and appointed feasts, which had been carried on for Baal, not Yahweh (2:1-13). Because Israel had dealt faithlessly with Yahweh, the children she bore were alien children (5:7).

Besides unfaithfulness, Israel lacked a knowledge of God, which became a prominent theme in Hosea's preaching (4:1, 6; 5:4; 6:6). Because there was no knowledge of God,

> swearing and lying and murder and stealing and
> adultery break out; bloodshed follows bloodshed.

(Hos 4:2)

Yahweh must therefore indict Israel because no one else in the society had the warrant to do so. Kings, priests, and prophets were all incapable of judgment, so bad had they become (4:4-9). Baal worship, drunkenness, and sexual misconduct consumed not only the young brides but the men as well, who trafficked with whores (4:11-14).

Israel was living in gross violation of the Sinai covenant, at the center of which lay the Ten Commandments. Hosea mentions the Sinai covenant, while Amos does not. In 8:1 Hosea says that Israel has broken Yahweh's covenant and transgressed Yahweh's law. The prophet cites even Adam's disobedience as Israel's transgression of an early covenant (6:7). Evildoing, he says, exists on both sides of the Jordan:

> Gilead is a city of evildoers,
>   tracked with blood.
> As robbers lie in wait for someone,
>   so the priests are banded together;
> they murder on the road to Shechem,
>   they commit a monstrous crime.
> In the house of Israel I have seen a horrible thing;
>   Ephraim's whoredom is there,
>   Israel is defiled.
>
> (Hos 6:8-10)

The law in Deut 25:13-16 may be in the back of Hosea's mind when he says that Israel is like a trader with false scales; he loves to oppress (12:7).

Israel's violation of the second commandment prohibiting images is behind Hosea's censure of the worship going on in the northern sanctuaries (4:15). Israel has become an inebriated people joined to idols, which will only bring shame (4:17-19). Idolatrous calves stand at Samaria (8:5-6) and Beth-aven, the disparaging name given to Bethel (10:5-6). By casting images and idols of silver, the sinning continues. People kiss calves (13:2)! Israel itself has become like a stubborn heifer (4:16). But the day will come when people will mourn the Bethel calf. The idolatrous priests will wail for its departed glory when the thing itself is carted off to Assyria as tribute to the great king. Israel will be ashamed of its idol. The calf of Samaria will be broken in pieces. The high places of "Aven" will be destroyed, with thorns and thistles growing up on their altars. People will then call for the mountains to cover them, the hills to fall upon them (10:8). Hosea says that evil began at Gilgal, which is where Yahweh came to hate Israel (9:15). But false worship flourishes on both sides of the Jordan—in Gilead and in Gilgal—so

Yahweh will destroy altars in both places (12:11). Gilead was overrun by King Tiglath-pileser in 734 B.C.E. Bethel, because of its great wickedness, has horrible indignities to look forward to (10:15).

Because Israel has played the whore and departed from her God, she will go to a foreign land where drink offerings and sacrifices will not please Yahweh (9:1-4). Hosea asks what people will do then on the days of the appointed festivals (9:5). Using an agricultural metaphor, Hosea says that Israel is a luxuriant vine; the more fruit it yielded the more altars it built. Its sacred pillars were improved. But because Israel's heart is false, Yahweh will break down both altars and pillars (10:1-2). Israel will become like the morning mist, like the dew that goes early away (13:3). Yahweh asks once again at the end of the book, "What more has Ephraim to do with idols? It is I who answer and look after you" (14:8).

Because of sin, Yahweh will leave his people so they cannot find him (5:6, 15). What they must do is acknowledge their guilt and seek his face. They can use these words:

> Come, let us return to Yahweh,
>> for it is he who has torn, and he will heal us;
>>> he has struck down, and he will bind us up.
> After two days he will revive us;
>> on the third day he will raise us up,
>>> that we may live before him.
> Let us know, let us press on to know Yahweh;
>> his appearing is as sure as the dawn.
> He will come to us like the showers,
>> like the spring rains that water the earth.
>
> (Hos 6:1-3)

There is great pathos in Hosea's preaching. The prophet probes the very heart of Yahweh, discovering Yahweh's deep frustration over Israel's (and Judah's) sin and wondering what he should do about it. Yahweh decrees punishment, but only reluctantly. Yahweh says:

> What shall I do with you, O Ephraim?
>> What shall I do with you, O Judah?
> Your love is like a morning cloud,
>> like the dew that goes away early.
> Therefore I have hewn them by the prophets,
>> I have killed them by the words of my mouth,

and your judgment goes forth as the light.
For I desire steadfast love and not sacrifice,
  the knowledge of God rather than burnt offerings.

(Hos 6:4-6)

Sacrifice and burnt offerings have become subordinate to steadfast love and the knowledge of God. Hosea says a good deal about steadfast love, which is covenant love. Hosea also has much to say about God's love for Israel (9:15; 11:1, 4; 14:4) and Israel's love of God (6:4), although the latter, he says, was fleeting. Love of God and love for God were major themes in Deuteronomy, raising the question of who influenced whom. Yahweh would have redeemed his wayward and rebellious people, but they were speaking lies against him. They did not cry to Yahweh from their hearts, but wailed on their beds and gashed themselves for grain and wine—presumably in Canaanite cultic rites (7:13-15). Israel sows the wind and reaps the whirlwind. Standing grain will yield no meal, and if it did, foreigners would devour it (8:7-8).

Hosea is well acquainted with the exodus and wilderness tradition (2:15; 12:9). Yahweh says through him:

Yet I have been Yahweh your God
  ever since the land of Egypt.
You know no God but me,
  and besides me there is no savior.
It was I who fed you in the wilderness,
  in the land of drought.
When I fed them, they were satisfied;
  they were satisfied, and their heart was proud;
    therefore they forgot me.

(Hos 13:4-6)

Here are echoes of the Song of Moses (Deut 32:10-18), which will be heard again in oracles from the prophet Jeremiah (Jer 2:2-8).

Hosea sees the folly of Israel's foreign policy. It will bring only judgment:

Ephraim has become like a dove,
  silly and without sense;
    they call upon Egypt, they go to Assyria.
As they go, I will cast my net over them.
  I will bring them down like birds of the air.

I will discipline them according to the report
  made to their assembly.

(Hos 7:11-12)

Bankrupt foreign policy goes hand in hand with alien worship:

For they have gone up to Assyria,
  a wild ass wandering alone.
    Ephraim has bargained for lovers.
. . . .
When Ephraim multiplied altars to expiate sin,
  they became to him altars for sinning.
Though I write for him the multitude of my instructions,
  they are regarded as a strange thing.
. . . .
Now he will remember their iniquity
  and punish their sins.
They shall return to Egypt.

(Hos 8:9-13)

Again on misguided foreign policy in the precincts of Samaria:

Ephraim herds the wind
  and pursues the east wind all day long.
They multiply falsehood and violence;
    they make a treaty with Assyria,
      and oil is carried to Egypt.

(Hos 12:1)

Recalling perhaps Elijah's word to Ahaziah (2 Kings 1), Hosea sees Ephraim and Judah going to Assyria for their sickness. Assyria cannot cure them. Yahweh will thus become like a lion to both Ephraim and Judah (5:13-14). Yahweh would like to heal Israel, but no one calls upon him (7:1-7). Ephraim mixes herself with peoples; she "is a cake not turned." As a result, foreigners have devoured her strength, and she does not even know it (7:8-9).

Israel's failure to return to Yahweh and seek him results from pride (7:10), that father of all vices that receives censure in other preaching from this prophet (5:5; 13:6). Israel is proud to have become rich, believing that she has not sinned (12:8). But her pride is self-damning; people neither return to Yahweh nor seek him (7:10). There was a time when

Ephraim spoke and other people trembled, but then she incurred guilt through Baal and died (13:1). Hosea on one occasion calls for people to sow righteousness and reap steadfast love; it is time, he says, to seek Yahweh (10:12). Jeremiah is anticipated in Hosea's preaching about "returning / repenting." Because Israel has not returned to Yahweh, she will return to "Egypt," that is, Assyria (11:5).

In delivering Yahweh's indictment, Hosea harks back to patriarchal traditions, noting that Jacob (Israel) did become reconciled to his brother Esau (12:2-6). He says:

> In the womb he took his brother by the heel,
>   and in his manhood he strove with God;
>   he strove with the angel and prevailed.
> He wept and sought his favor.
>
> (Hos 12:3-4a)

Jacob's vow at Bethel is recalled (12:4b), after which comes a doxology (v. 5) and a call for Israel to return (v. 6). At the end of the book, Hosea calls again for people to return, giving them words they can say (14:1-3).

Kingship comes in for strong censure with this prophet, with Yahweh recalling the battle over choosing a king in the first place. Now Yahweh asks:

> Where now is your king, that he may save you?
>   Where in all your cities are your rulers,
> of whom you said,
>   "Give me a king and rulers"?
> I gave you a king in my anger,
>   and I took him away in my wrath.
>
> (Hos 13:10-11)

Israel set up kings, but not through Yahweh. The nation's "revolving-door kingship" (8:4-6) probably refers to the short reigns of Zechariah (746–745), Shallum (745), and Menahem (745–737). Israel will lament not having a king, but when people do not fear Yahweh, what good will a king do (10:3)? Samaria's king will perish "like a chip on the face of the water" (10:7, 15). Assyria, says the prophet, shall be their king (11:5).

Israel's princes are also judged, compared by the prophet to people removing the landmark (5:10). Officials have become rebels, for which reason Yahweh loves Israel no more (9:15). Strong words are also spoken against priests and prophets. Priests are destroyed for a lack of knowledge, and for having forgotten the law of their God (4:6). The prophet is a fool, says Hosea; the man of the spirit is mad. A fowler's snare is on all his ways (9:7-8). Yet Hosea knows that Yahweh's word has come through the prophets (12:10). By a prophet Yahweh brought up Israel from Egypt, and by a prophet Israel was preserved (12:13).

There is an unmistakable romanticism in Hosea, which will turn up again in Jeremiah. An opulent, well-fortified Israel is rejected, with the prophet longing for the earlier days of Yahweh's care and Israel's faithfulness in the wilderness (2:14). Hosea says that Israel has forgotten its Maker in building its palaces and fortifying its cities (8:14). The nation trusts in its power and large army, but war will come and the nation will be destroyed (10:13-14). Yahweh speaks tenderly about finding Israel in the wilderness:

> Like grapes in the wilderness I found Israel,
> > like the first fruit on the fig tree, in its first season,
> > > I saw your ancestors.
> But they came to Baal-peor
> > and consecrated themselves to a thing of shame
> > > and became detestable like the thing they loved.
> Ephraim's glory shall fly away like a bird—
> > no birth, no pregnancy, no conception.
> Even if they bring up children,
> > I will bereave them until no one is left.
> Woe to them indeed
> > when I depart from them.
>
> (Hos 9:10-12)

The problem came with the settlement, where Hosea echoes the Song of Moses in saying that it all began in Transjordan after Moses defeated the Amorite kings and Israelite tribes were settled in their land. The preeminent act of apostasy was at Baal-peor (Num 25:1-5).

More pathos comes in another of Hosea's prophecies:

> Once I saw Ephraim as a young palm planted in a lovely meadow,
> > but now Ephraim must lead out his children for slaughter.
> Give them, O Yahweh—
> > what will you give?
> Give them a miscarrying womb
> > and dry breasts.
>
> (Hos 9:13-14)

Recalling Israel's salvation history, Yahweh says:

> When Israel was a child, I loved him,
>   and out of Egypt I called my son.
> The more I called them,
>   the more they went from me.
> They kept sacrificing to the Baals
>   and offering incense to idols.
> Yet it was I who taught Ephraim to walk,
>   taking him up by his arms,
>   but they did not know that I healed them.
> I led them with cords of human kindness,
>   with bands of love.
> I was to them like those who lift infants to their cheeks;
>   I bent down to them and fed them.
>
>   (Hos 11:1-4)

Hosea reveals a God set on punishing Israel, but one who nevertheless is ambivalent about doing so, so filled is he with compassion for his people:

> How can I give you up, Ephraim?
>   How can I hand you over, O Israel?
> How can I make you like Admah?
>   How can I treat you like Zeboiim?
> My heart recoils within me;
>   my compassion grows warm and tender.
> I will not execute my fierce anger;
>   I will not again destroy Ephraim.
> For I am God and no mortal,
>   the Holy One in your midst,
>   and I will not come in wrath.
>
>   (Hos 11:8-9)

Hosea here uses a favorite expression of Isaiah, referring to Yahweh as the "Holy One of Israel." In another oracle Yahweh asks:

> Shall I ransom them from the power of Sheol?
>   Shall I redeem them from Death?
> O Death, where are your plagues?
>   O Sheol, where is your destruction?
>   Compassion is hid from my eyes.
>
>   (Hos 13:14)

In addition to his message of judgment, Hosea delivers a clear word of hope for the future. It is introduced at the very beginning of the book. Whereas Yahweh had said to Israel, "You are not my people," now he will say, "Sons of the living God!" The people of Israel and Judah shall be united under one head, with Hosea now saying, "Great shall be the day of Jezreel" (1:10-11). After Yahweh renews the bliss of the wilderness period, Israel will once again call Yahweh "my husband," indicating that a divorce has not taken place (2:14-17). This new day will see a future covenant in which Yahweh says:

> I will make for them a covenant on that day with the beasts of the field and with the birds of the air and the creeping things of the ground. And the bow and sword and weapon of war I will abolish from the land. And I will make them lie down in safety. (Hos 2:18)

Yahweh appears here to be brokering a covenant between Israel and the created order, whereby Israel will be betrothed to Yahweh forever, heaven and earth together will bring fertility to the land, and the names of Hosea's children will be reversed (2:19-23). In taking back Gomer, Hosea shows that Yahweh still loves Israel, even though it turned to other gods and ate their cakes of raisins. It is anticipated that after Israel has been without a king, without sacrificial worship, and without priestly mediation, it will seek Yahweh under a new Davidic king (3:1-5).

There is other hopeful preaching in the book. The day will come when people will go after Yahweh, the Roaring Lion, and trembling souls will be returned to their homes (11:10-11). Yahweh says about this future time:

> I will heal their disloyalty;
> I will love them freely,
> for my anger has turned from them.
> I will be like the dew to Israel;
> he shall blossom like the lily,
> he shall strike root like the forests of Lebanon.
> His shoots shall spread out;
> his beauty shall be like the olive tree,
> and his fragrance like that of Lebanon.
> They shall again live beneath my shadow;
> they shall flourish like a garden.

They shall blossom like the vine;
　　their fragrance shall be like the wine of Lebanon.

(Hos 14:4-7)

Micah: Prophet against Urban Oppression

Micah was a late-eighth-century Judahite prophet, a contemporary of
Isaiah, who lived through the final destruction of the northern kingdom
in 722 B.C.E. The superscription to his book has him active during the
reigns of Jotham (742–735 B.C.E.), Ahaz (735–715 B.C.E.), and Hezekiah
(715–687 B.C.E.), although there is some doubt whether he was preaching
as early as Jotham's reign. A ministry during Ahaz and Hezekiah's reigns
is clear. Micah announces a judgment against Samaria when the city is
still standing (Mic 1:6). His judgment on Jerusalem (Mic 3:12) and the
impact it had on Hezekiah are reported in Jer 26:18-19.

Micah was from Moresheth, a town near Gath in Israel's Shephelah,
which is the foothill district between the Judean hills and the coastal plain.
The Shephelah separates Judah from Philistine territory. Moresheth was
about six miles north of Lachish and twenty-three miles southwest of
Jerusalem. Since Micah is named in the superscription without patronym, some believe he came from a family of little or no importance.

With idolatrous worship flourishing in Samaria and Jerusalem, Yahweh says he will descend from his holy temple and lay waste both capitals
(1:2-9). Micah can only lament and wail.

What is the transgression of Jacob?
　　Is it not Samaria?
And what is the high place of Judah?
　　Is it not Jerusalem?
Therefore I will make Samaria a heap in the open country,
　　a place for planting vineyards.
I will pour down her stones into the valley
　　and uncover her foundations.
All her images shall be beaten to pieces,
　　and her wages shall be burned with fire,
　　　　and all her idols I will lay waste.
For as the wages of a prostitute
　　they shall again be used.
For this I will lament and wail;
　　I will go barefoot and naked.

I will make lamentation like the jackals,
  and mourning like the ostriches.
For her wound is incurable;
  it has come to Judah.
It has reached to the gate of my people,
  to Jerusalem.

(Mic 1:5b-9)

Like his predecessor Amos, Micah was outraged at social injustice, which lay at the heart of an oracle delivered against Jerusalem. The climactic lines were later cited by elders attending the trial of Jeremiah (Jer 26:18). Micah said that all of Israel's leaders were caught up in wrongdoing:

Hear this, you rulers of the house of Jacob
  and chiefs of the house of Israel,
who abhor justice
  and pervert all equity,
who build Zion with blood
  and Jerusalem with wrong!
Its rulers give judgment for a bribe,
  its priests teach for a price,
    its prophets give oracles for money.
Yet they lean upon Yahweh and say:
  "Surely Yahweh is with us!
    No harm shall come upon us."
Therefore because of you
  Zion shall be plowed as a field.
Jerusalem shall become a heap of ruins,
  and the mountain of the house a wooded height.

(Mic 3:9-12)

People lie in bed thinking up evil, and then do it when morning comes. They covet fields and seize them; they oppress both a man and his house. Therefore Yahweh will rain evil on such a people, who will weep bitter tears when captors are seen parceling out their fields (2:1-5).

Micah finds that people do not want to hear judgment preaching. They say disgrace will not overtake them. How can Yahweh's patience be exhausted (2:6-7)? In frustration, Micah says:

If someone were to go about
  uttering hot air and lies,

saying, "I will preach to you of wine and strong drink,"
    such a one would be the preacher for this people!

(Mic 2:11)

When injustice is rife, when leaders hate good and love evil, treating people like so much flesh being readied for consumption, and then cry to Yahweh, Micah warns that Yahweh will not answer (3:1-4). Problems exist with other prophets. Micah says:

Thus says Yahweh concerning the prophets
    who lead my people astray,
who cry "Peace" when they have something to eat
    but declare war against those who put nothing into their
        mouths.

(Mic 3:5)

But these prophets, also seers and diviners who are plying their trade, shall be put to shame, for God will give no answer through them. As for Micah himself, he is filled with power and the spirit of Yahweh, with justice and might, to declare to Jacob his transgression and to Israel his sin (3:6-8).

Threats and predictions of doom resume in chapters 6–7, although here Micah's preaching takes on a softer tone. Yahweh has a controversy with Israel, asking what he has done to deserve the treatment he is receiving. Yahweh has performed great and mighty acts, beginning with Israel's deliverance from Egypt (6:1-5). Then in a truly great passage Micah says that justice, steadfast love, and walking humbly with God count for more than worship and are what Yahweh requires:

"With what shall I come before Yahweh
    and bow myself before God on high?
Shall I come before him with burnt offerings,
    with calves a year old?
Will Yahweh be pleased with thousands of rams,
    with tens of thousands of rivers of oil?
Shall I give the firstborn for my transgression,
    the fruit of my body for the sin of my soul?"
He has told you, O mortal, what is good,
    and what does Yahweh require of you
but to do justice, and to love steadfastness,
    and to walk humbly with your God?

(Mic 6:6-8)

Micah cites injustice and dishonesty in the marketplace, where rich cheat poor with bad scales and bags of false weights. Yahweh, he says, has already begun to strike Israel down, and the sated wicked can now look forward to gnawing hunger. They will sow and not reap, tread olives and not rub their bodies with oil, tread grapes but not drink the wine. Samaria and its inhabitants will become a desolation. Why? Because people have kept the statutes of Omri and Ahab, not the statutes of Yahweh (6:9-17).

Micah says, "Woe is me," comparing himself to one who has nothing to eat after the summer fruit harvest. He says:

The faithful have disappeared from the land,
    and there is no one left who is upright.
They all lie in wait for blood,
    and they hunt each other with nets.
Their hands are good at doing evil;
    the official and the judge ask for a bribe.
And the powerful speaks the desire of his soul,
    and they weave it together.
The best of them is like a brier,
    the most upright of them a thorn hedge.
The day of your watchmen, your punishment, has come;
    now their confusion is at hand.

(Mic 7:2-4)

It is a time to put no trust in a friend, a confidant, or even the one who lies in one's embrace. Enemies are members of one's own household. As for Micah himself, he will look to Yahweh and wait for the God of his salvation, trusting that Yahweh will hear him (7:5-7).

There is hopeful preaching at the center of Micah's book (chapters 4–5), and opinions differ as to whether it emanates from the prophet or was added later. Two things need to be factored in. One is a reform said to have been carried out by King Hezekiah (2 Kgs 18:4, 22 = Isa 36:7), in which the king removed high places, altars, and other cult symbols in a move to purify and centralize worship of Yahweh in Jerusalem. Second Chronicles 29–31 gives this reform extended coverage. Some doubts have been expressed whether such a reform actually took place, but a window of opportunity did exist between 712 and 701 B.C.E. This reform could have impacted Micah's preaching. Jeremiah 26:19 says that Hezekiah humbled himself upon hearing Micah's judgment on Jerusalem, which could explain Micah's softer tone from this point on.

The second thing to be factored in is Sennacherib's attack on Jerusalem in 701 B.C.E., at which time the city was nearly taken. It was spared, and according to the biblical report, Yahweh brought about its deliverance (2 Kgs 19:32-36 = Isa 37:33-37). There are problems here in the reconstruction of historical events, but at some point Yahweh did deliver the city. In light of this deliverance, Micah, like Isaiah, may have turned to preaching a future hope.

Already in chapter 2 is a hopeful word for Israel:

> I will surely gather all of you, O Jacob,
> I will gather the survivors of Israel.
> I will set them together
> like sheep in a fold,
> like a flock in its pasture;
> it will resound with people.
> The one who breaks out will go up before them;
> they will break through and pass the gate.
> Their King will pass on before them,
> Yahweh at their head.

(Mic 2:12-13)

In 4:1-4, a passage repeated with slight variation in Isa 2:2-3, Micah says that in future days the temple on Mount Zion will be reestablished; to it people will again stream to receive instruction from Yahweh. Regarding Yahweh, he says:

> He shall judge between many peoples
> and shall arbitrate between strong nations far away.
> They shall beat their swords into plowshares,
> and their spears into pruning hooks.
> Nation shall not lift up sword against nation,
> neither shall they learn war any more.
> But they shall sit each person under his own vine
> and under his fig tree, and none shall make him afraid,
> for the mouth of Yahweh of hosts has spoken.

(Mic 4:3-4)

In this future day, a remnant of the lame and the afflicted will be transformed into a strong nation, and Yahweh will reign in Zion, a city given back its former dominion and sovereignty (4:6-8). The oracle in 4:9-10 calls upon daughter Zion to writhe and groan at having to leave for Babylonian exile; however, it goes on to say that Yahweh will redeem his people from there. One wonders here if Babylon is not a substitute for Assyria, since it is from Assyria that exiles will be rescued in 5:6. Assyria was the world power at the time, not Babylon, and it is unlikely that Micah is anticipating the exiles of 597 B.C.E., 586 B.C.E., and later, which were to Babylon. Another passage describes Zion's degradation among the nations as being left like so many sheaves on the threshing floor, but a day will come when Zion will rise up and do some threshing of its own (4:11-13).

Micah sees beyond a present siege to the day when Israel will have a new king. Bethlehem is addressed in a passage later given messianic interpretation (5:1-4):

> But you, O Bethlehem of Ephrathah,
> who are one of the little clans of Judah,
> from you shall come forth for me
> one who is to rule in Israel,
> whose origin is from old,
> from ancient days.
> (Mic 5:2)

This king will feed the people in the strength of Yahweh, and they will rest secure (v. 4).

Peace will come when the Assyrians enter the land and Israel's rulers will rescue her (5:5-6). Jacob's remnant will depend on no one; her hand shall be raised against her adversaries, and they shall be cut off (5:7-9). Micah also envisions a day when Yahweh will strip the nation of its military might, but will at the same time cut off its soothsayers and idolatrous images. Disobedient nations will then be subjected to the divine wrath (5:10-15).

The book of Micah concludes with what appears to be a liturgy (7:8-20). It builds on the prior word of v. 7, where the prophet says he must wait for Yahweh. The enemy will not have the final word, for in the end Yahweh will vindicate his people (vv. 9-10). Israel's cities will be rebuilt, and exiles will come home from Assyria and Egypt. Finally, Yahweh is acclaimed as a God who pardons iniquity, remaining faithful to the covenant made with Abraham and the fathers (vv. 18-20).

Isaiah: Prophet of Holiness and the Holy One

The superscription of Isaiah's book says that Isaiah, son of Amoz, had a vision concerning Judah and Jerusalem in the reigns of Uzziah (783–742

B.C.E.), Jotham (742–735 B.C.E.), Ahaz (735–715 B.C.E.), and Hezekiah (715–687 B.C.E.), kings of Judah (Isa 1:1). This puts him roughly a couple of decades after Amos and Hosea, prophets to the northern kingdom, and makes him a contemporary of Micah, who prophesied against Judah and Jerusalem. Supplementary prose gives information on the prophet and the background for prophecies spoken during the reigns of Ahaz (chapters 7–8) and Hezekiah (chapters 36–39). Still, the problems of trying to reconstruct a career for this brilliant prophet are formidable, some would say impossible. The biblical account of Sennacherib's entry into Judah is unclear (2 Kgs 18:13—19:37 = Isaiah 36–37) as to whether there was one campaign or two. To correlate Isaiah's prophecies with known events of the late eighth century is also difficult, as all commentators know. Because Isaiah appears throughout life to have had ready access to the king, he is thought by some to have come from a good family, to have had a good education, and to have been well acquainted with affairs of the royal court.

Isaiah's prophecies are contained in chapters 1–39 of the book bearing his name, with chapters 36–39 being a historical appendix largely repeated in 2 Kings 18–20. Prophecies in chapters 40–66 emanate from one or two unknown prophets in the exilic and postexilic periods and are not assigned by modern critical scholars to Isaiah of Jerusalem (see below, p. 106, "Second Isaiah: Prophet of the Incomparability of Yahweh").

Isaiah received his call to be a prophet in the year King Uzziah died, that is, 742 B.C.E. (6:1). In an extraordinary temple vision, he was struck by Yahweh's holiness, and also by the depths to which sin had taken root in the nation. These two convictions, Yahweh being the Holy One of Israel (1:4 et passim) and Judah being a sinful nation in violation of the Sinai covenant, control all his preaching. In his call, Isaiah sees Yahweh enthroned as King and hears heavenly voices calling to one another:

"Holy, holy, holy is Yahweh of hosts;
    the whole earth is full of his glory."

The pivots on the threshold shook at the voices of those who called, and the house filled with smoke. And I said: "Woe is me! I am lost, for I am a man of unclean lips, and I live among a people of unclean lips; yet my eyes have seen the King, Yahweh of hosts!"

(Isa 6:3-5)

After one of the seraphs cleansed Isaiah's mouth with a live coal from the altar, and his sin and guilt were removed, Yahweh put out the call for a divine messenger and Isaiah stepped forward, saying, "Here I am; send me" (6:8). But he was told that the people to whom he would go were hardened disbelievers incapable of taking correction. Yahweh's words to both people and prophet bristle with bitter irony:

> Keep listening, but do not comprehend;
>> keep looking, but do not understand.
> Make the mind of this people dull
>> and stop their ears
>> and shut their eyes,
> so that they may not look with their eyes
>> and listen with their ears
> and comprehend with their minds
>> and turn and be healed.
>> (Isa 6:9-10)

The prophet asks how long this must go on. Yahweh says until the cities are a wasteland without inhabitant, and the land is utterly desolate. Even if a tenth remains, it will be burned like a terebinth or an oak, with only the stump remaining. But a ray of hope comes at the end. Yahweh says, "The holy seed is its stump" (6:11-13). An indestructible remnant will survive, repent, and become a purified people (1:24-27). This idea of a "remnant" is a hallmark of Isaiah's preaching. He names one of his sons "A Remnant Shall Return" (7:3).

The book opens with a prophecy echoing Isaiah's predecessor Hosea:

> Hear, O heavens, and give ear, O earth,
>> for Yahweh has spoken.
> Sons I have reared and brought up,
>> but they have rebelled against me.
> The ox knows its owner
>> and the ass its master's crib;
> but Israel does not know,
>> my people do not understand.
>> (Isa 1:2-3)

In his early preaching, Isaiah faced a situation similar to what Amos and Hosea faced in the north. Israel had become corrupt during the long reign of Jeroboam II (786–746 B.C.E.), and an array of social and political evils had to be attacked head-on. In Judah it was the prosperity that came during the long reign of Uzziah (783–742 B.C.E.): land and wealth had been concentrated in the hands of a few; the rich were exploiting the poor (3:14-15; 5:8); injustice was rife; princes and judges were corrupt (1:23; 5:23;

10:1-2; 29:21); and innocent blood was on many hands (1:10-23). Debauchery and drunkenness characterized the upper classes (3:16-23; 5:11-12, 22; 28:1-8; 32:9-20), but they would be dealt with when Yahweh's wrath could be contained no longer. Isaiah says about once-faithful Jerusalem:

> How the faithful city has become a harlot,
>   she that was full of justice.
> Righteousness lodged in her,
>   but now murderers.
> Your silver has become dross,
>   your wine mixed with water.
> Your princes are rebels
>   and companions of thieves.
> Everyone loves a bribe
>   and runs after gifts.
> They do not defend the orphan,
>   and the widow's cause does not come to them.
>   (Isa 1:21-23)

Isaiah had a strong word for worship carried on when terms of the covenant were being compromised or were forgotten entirely. Yahweh did not want burnt offerings and sacrifices, Isaiah said, and could endure appointed festivals no longer. Even though people spread their hands giving long prayers, Yahweh would not listen. They must instead "cease to do evil, learn to do good, seek justice, correct oppression, defend the orphan, plead for the widow" (1:16-17).

Yahweh's call for covenant obedience puts the question of repentance squarely in the lap of the people. He speaks as a judge in a court of law:

> Come now, let us reason together,
>   says Yahweh.
> Though your sins are like scarlet,
>   they shall be white as snow.
> Though they are red like crimson,
>   they shall become like wool.
> If you are willing and obedient,
>   you shall eat the good of the land.
> But if you refuse and rebel,
>   you shall be devoured by the sword,
>   for the mouth of Yahweh has spoken.
>   (Isa 1:18-20)

Then follows a promise that Yahweh will vent his wrath on his foes, where the foes are the people in Judah. Judges like those in former days will be restored, and Jerusalem will once again be the faithful city, redeemed by justice and those practicing righteousness (1:24-31; cf. 4:2-6).

Isaiah has a harsh word for foreign religious practitioners and also for the idolatry imported during the reigns of Uzziah and Jotham. Uzziah (Azariah) rebuilt Elath to control Red Sea traffic (2 Kgs 14:21-22), and trade was being carried on with Tarshish in faraway Spain. In the first of two oracles, Isaiah asks Yahweh not to forgive this idolatry (2:6-11); and in a second, he tells people to turn away from human beings, who are of no account (2:12-22). In a future Day of Yahweh, holy terror will be unleashed against human pride and everything high and lifted up. People will then be humbled, will cast away their idols to bats and moles, will flee into caves; and Yahweh alone will be exalted. Isaiah has a particularly harsh word for Jerusalem and Judahite leaders who oppress the poor, which brings anarchy. Yahweh will enter into judgment with these leaders (3:1-15).

In a classic passage, Isaiah likens the nation to a well-tended vineyard that ought to have yielded good grapes, but brought forth something quite different (5:1-7; cf. 3:14):

> Let me sing for my beloved
>   my love-song concerning his vineyard.
> My beloved had a vineyard
>   on a very fertile hill.
> He dug it and cleared it of stones
>   and planted it with choice vines.
> He built a watchtower in the midst of it
>   and hewed out a wine vat in it.
> He expected it to yield grapes,
>   but it yielded wild grapes.
> And now, inhabitants of Jerusalem
>   and people of Judah,
> judge between me
>   and my vineyard.
> What more was there to do for my vineyard
>   that I have not done for it?
> When I expected it to yield grapes,
>   why did it yield wild grapes?
> And now I will tell you
>   what I will do with my vineyard.

I will remove its hedge,
    and it shall be devoured.
I will break down its wall,
    and it shall be trampled down.
I will make it a waste;
    it shall not be pruned or hoed,
        and it shall be overgrown with briers and thorns.
I will also command the clouds
    that they rain no rain upon it.
For the vineyard of Yahweh of hosts
    is the house of Israel,
and the people of Judah
    are his pleasant planting.
He expected justice
    but saw bloodshed;
righteousness
    but heard a cry!
            (Isa 5:1-7)

The sorry state into which Jerusalem had fallen is addressed in Isaiah's six "woes" of 5:8-25. "Woe" is declared upon the rich, greedy landowners; upon drunks, liars, and the conceited; and upon the unjust among Jerusalem's elite. People call good evil and evil good (5:20). Such godless behavior cannot be tolerated by the Holy One of Israel (5:19, 24; cf. 6:3), whose anger is kindled because of it. He will whistle for a punishing nation to come speedily from the ends of the earth, and the day of its arrival will be darkness and distress (5:24-30). Isaiah had a warrant for this "woe" preaching: in his call, he had recognized his own uncleanness and said, "Woe is me" (6:5). The two passages have been deliberately juxtaposed in the biblical text.

With the accession of Ahaz, Isaiah came into direct conflict with national policy. In 735-733 B.C.E., a crisis had developed: Rezin, king of Syria, and Pekah, king of northern Israel, had attacked Jerusalem in order to compel Ahaz to join an anti-Assyrian coalition, leaving the much-frightened Judahite king to appeal for Assyrian aid. Isaiah, taking with him his son, "A Remnant Shall Return," went to meet the king. He told him not to worry about the current threat, for it would be of short duration. These two "smoldering stumps of firebrands" would not be around for long (7:1-9). An oracle against Damascus contained the same message (17:1-11). If the king would not believe, he would not be established (7:9). Later Isaiah went to see Ahaz again, telling him this time to ask for a sign from Yahweh. The king refused, so Isaiah gave him a sign, the famous "Immanuel" prophecy, signifying that Yahweh's promises to David were sure and that the two kings would be gone before the young child reached majority. As a result of wrongheaded policy and unbelief, great calamity would descend upon the nation (7:10-25).

The name of Isaiah's second son, "The Spoil Speeds, the Plunder Hastens," aims to give king and people the same message (8:1-15). Isaiah tells them, "Let [Yahweh] be your fear, and let him be your dread" (8:13). Assyria is only a temporary peril. But neither king nor people would listen, showing the hardness of heart Isaiah had been warned about in his call. Ahaz went on to send tribute money to Tiglath-pileser III, and thus surrendered his independence (2 Kgs 16:7-8). Isaiah, his word rejected, bound up his prophecy as a future witness, gave it to his disciples, and withdrew from public life. He would wait for Yahweh and place his hope in him. A day of distress, gloom, and deep darkness lay ahead for Judah (8:16—9:1). Events proved Isaiah right. Jerusalem was not taken by Rezin and Pekah (7:1). The Assyrians overthrew Damascus in 732 B.C.E. and took Samaria a decade later. In the year Ahaz died, Isaiah gave an oracle against Philistia (14:29-32).

From perhaps this time, or later at the time of Hezekiah's accession in 715 B.C.E., come Isaiah's messianic prophecies in 9:2-7 and 11:1-9. At that time, however, they simply looked forward to an ideal Davidic king who would inaugurate a new order. These prophecies loomed large in later Judaism and became even more important for the church in anchoring the life and ministry of Jesus in earlier prophecy. The first passage:

> The people who walked in darkness
>> have seen a great light.
> Those who lived in a land of deep darkness,
>> on them light has shined.
> You have multiplied the nation;
>> you have increased its joy.
> They rejoice before you
>> as with joy at the harvest,
>>> as people exult when dividing plunder.
> For the yoke of their burden
>> and the bar across their shoulders,
> The rod of their oppressors
>> you have broken as on the day of Midian.
> For all the boots of the tramping warriors

and all the garments rolled in blood
    shall be burned as fuel for the fire.
For a child has been born for us,
    a son given to us.
Authority rests upon his shoulders,
    and he is named
Wonderful Counselor, Mighty God,
    Everlasting Father, Prince of Peace.
His authority shall grow continually,
    and there shall be endless peace
for the throne of David and his kingdom.
    He will establish and uphold it,
with justice and with righteousness
    from this time onward and forevermore.
The zeal of Yahweh of hosts will do this.

                                  (Isa 9:2-7)

The second passage:

A shoot shall come out from the stump of Jesse,
    and a branch shall grow out of his roots.
The spirit of Yahweh shall rest upon him,
    the spirit of wisdom and understanding,
the spirit of counsel and might,
    the spirit of knowledge and the fear of Yahweh.
        His delight shall be in the fear of Yahweh.

He shall not judge by what his eyes see
    or decide by what his ears hear.
But with righteousness he shall judge the poor
    and decide with equity for the meek of the earth.
He shall strike the earth with the rod of his mouth,
    and with the breath of his lips he shall kill the wicked.
Righteousness shall be the belt around his waist
    and faithfulness the belt around his loins.

The wolf shall live with the lamb;
    the leopard shall lie down with the kid,
the calf and the lion and the fatling together,
    and a little child shall lead them.

The cow and the bear shall graze;
  their young shall lie down together,
    and the lion shall eat straw like the ox.
The nursing child shall play over the hole of the asp,
  and the weaned child shall put its hand on the adder's den.
They will not hurt or destroy
  on all my holy mountain.
For the earth will be full of the knowledge of Yahweh
  as the waters cover the sea.

(Isa 11:1-9)

Another prophecy in 2:2-4 describes the peace that will reign in the messianic age, but since it is repeated with slight variation in Mic 4:1-3, its authorship remains unknown. People will go to Yahweh's holy mountain to be taught Yahweh's ways, and when Yahweh rises to judge the nations, they shall learn war no more.

Northern Israel is censured in the four prophecies of 9:12, 17, 21; and 10:4, each of which concludes with a refrain that occurs also in 5:25. The background suggests a date about 737 to 732 B.C.E., when Tiglath-pileser III was laying waste the Israelite populations in Transjordan and Galilee, and Israel was being attacked by Syria and the Philistines (9:12). The northern kingdom was brought down by Shalmaneser IV, and surrendered finally to Sargon II in 722 B.C.E. Its population was exiled to Assyria. In oracles spoken during this time, Israel is cited for pride and arrogance (9:8-12); said to be suffering because of godless leaders great and small (9:13-17); and rife with anarchy and internal strife (9:18-21). A climactic "woe" is addressed to leaders and judges who no longer practice justice to the poor and needy. They exploit orphans and widows, which, according to Deuteronomy, is a clear violation of the Sinai covenant (10:1-4). As a result, Yahweh's anger will not be turned back from Judah's northern neighbor. Punishment is sure.

Isaiah in these oracles focuses on Assyria, a godless nation that Yahweh is using to punish his people. Assyria is the "rod of his anger" (10:5) that will punish both Samaria and Jerusalem (10:5-11). Isaiah knows, however, that Assyria is but a tool in Yahweh's hand, and that in the end Yahweh will take care of the haughty pride of this plundering nation (10:12-14). In a classic passage, Assyria is seen as being no match for the Holy One of Israel. Isaiah says:

Shall the ax vaunt itself over the one who wields it,
  or the saw magnify itself against the one who handles it?
As if a rod should raise the one who lifts it up,

or as if a staff should lift the one who is not wood!
Therefore the Lord, Yahweh of hosts,
 will send wasting sickness among his stout warriors.
And under his glory will be kindled
 a flame like a burning fire
The light of Israel will become a fire,
 and his Holy One a flame.
And it will burn and devour
 his thorns and briers in one day.
The glory of his forest and his fruitful land
 Yahweh will destroy, both soul and body,
  and it will be as when an invalid wastes away.
The remnant of the trees of his forest will be so few
 that a child can write them down.

(Isa 10:15-19)

This prophecy is followed by others announcing a future hope for Israel, when a remnant will return and will lean upon the Holy One of Israel (10:20-34). This was the thrust of Isaiah's later preaching. Not only will Yahweh bring down the mighty Assyria, but he will exercise judgment on nations that have harassed Judah and will gather dispersed exiles from these nations (11:10-16; 12:1-6).

In the middle of the book is a collection of oracles against foreign nations, some of which may be of anonymous origin, and some of which have been combined with hope for Israel, or with a restoration of sorts for the nation in question: Babylon (13:1—14:23; 21:1-10); Assyria (14:24-27; 17:12-14); Philistia (14:28-32); Moab (15–16); Syria (17:1-3); northern Israel (17:4-11); Egypt (chapter 19); Egypt and Ethiopia (chapter 20); Edom (21:11-12); the Arabian tribes (21:13-17); and Tyre (chapter 23). Babylon is wicked, arrogant, and proud and will know the terrible force of Yahweh's wrath on the day of his coming (13:11-13), when also its idols will be shattered (21:9). Babylon's fall will bring with it Yahweh's compassion for Israel, which will turn to taunt its former oppressor (14:1-23). Assyria and Philistia have oppressed other nations, but now they themselves will experience the heavy hand of oppression. Moab is censured for its arrogant pride (16:6). When calamity strikes, it will get no help from its gods (16:12). Egypt, too, in confusion brought on by Yahweh, will get no help from its idols, mediums, or wise men (19:1-15). Yahweh will terrorize that nation (19:16-17). But afterward Egypt will be converted to Yahweh, will know prosperity, and will have peaceful relations with Israel and Assyria. The latter, too, will be converted to Yahweh (19:18-25). Yahweh will bring down the pride of Tyre (23:9-12), but after seventy years sweet melodies will again be heard from this harlot nation, whose merchandise will be dedicated to Yahweh (23:15-18).

Included in this cluster of oracles against the nations are others of a related nature. In 18:1-7 is an oracle against ambassadors from Ethiopia who have come to Jerusalem advocating revolt against Assyria. Isaiah opposed this. Assyria will be crushed without help from other nations. A possible date for this oracle would be the beginning of Hezekiah's reign, when Judah was asked to join a revolt against Assyria promoted by the Philistines and Egypt (714–712 B.C.E.).

In 22:1-14 is Isaiah's oracle concerning the Valley of Vision, directed toward a city engaged in revelry on the eve of disaster. An invasion—presumably by the Assyrians, aided by mercenaries from Elam and Kir (v. 6)—will occur on the fateful Day of Yahweh. The city is not named. Some think it is Jerusalem at the time of Sennacherib's invasion of 701 B.C.E. ("daughter of my people" in v. 4 sounds like Judah; Judah is explicitly mentioned in v. 8; and "city of David" and "Jerusalem" are mentioned in vv. 9-10), but since the oracle occurs amid oracles against foreign nations, another city (in Judah) could be the referent.

In 22:15-25 is an oracle against a certain Shebna, a steward of foreign extraction in Jerusalem's royal house who was a person of influence in the city (cf. 36:3). He had a grand tomb built for himself. Shebna appears to have been promoting an alliance with Egypt against Assyria, a policy that Isaiah opposed, and for this reason he comes in for harsh censure from the prophet. Shebna will be violently hurled into exile, and Eliakim will replace him.

Chapters 24–27 contain a cluster of oracles on the Day of Yahweh that will bring judgment on the nations (chapter 24) and salvation for Israel (chapters 25–27). The prophecy is eschatological, almost but not quite apocalyptic in nature, although some claim that chapter 24 announces the last judgment. The prophecy appears not to derive from Isaiah of Jerusalem, dated as it is by most scholars to the postexilic period. Isaiah 25:8 states that Yahweh in this future day "will swallow up death forever" and "will wipe away tears from all faces"; and in 26:19 is one of the rare mentions of resurrection from the dead in the Old Testament.

In chapter 24 Yahweh promises ruin of the entire land, its effect being felt by everyone in society, high and low. Mirth will cease in country and city. The heavens, too, will languish because people have broken the covenant, here said to be an everlasting covenant (v. 5). What covenant this is cannot be said. Some say it is the covenant God made with Noah (Gen 9:8-17), but that covenant contains no statutes capable of being violated.

Nevertheless, in the midst of this dismal forecast, the poet hears distant voices singing for joy (vv. 14-16). The day will dawn, after punishment is complete, when Yahweh will reign on Mount Zion and show his glory there (v. 23).

Chapter 25 contains songs and prophecies of redemption. The opening song celebrates the ruin of some alien city (vv. 1-5); a feast for all peoples to be celebrated on Mount Zion (vv. 6-9); and Yahweh's judgment on proud Moab (vv. 10-12). In chapter 26 a thanksgiving song and supplication are heard in Judah. The song of procession into Jerusalem begins:

> We have a strong city;
>> he sets up salvation
>>> as walls and bulwarks.
> Open the gates
>> that the righteous nation may enter,
>>> who keeps faith.
> You keep him in perfect peace
>> whose mind is stayed on you
>>> because he trusts in you.
> Trust in Yahweh forever,
>> for Yahweh God is an everlasting rock.
>
> (Isa 26:1-4)

After a confident belief that some proud city—perhaps Moabite (cf. 25:11) but maybe Edomite, since it is said to be lofty (cf. Jer 49:16; Obad 3)—will be overthrown (26:5-6), a psalm continues with supplication and affirmations (26:7-19), much like what we find in the Psalter. An appeal is made for the overthrow of an enemy, and peace for Israel. Next is the astonishing statement that those fallen in battle will be resurrected from the dead, something that will not happen to the fallen of the enemy (26:19; cf. v. 14). The poet knows, however, that despite these yearnings he must wait for Yahweh (26:7-9). People are told to hide themselves until Yahweh's wrath is over (26:20-21).

Yahweh's judgment on nations of the world at the beginning of chapter 27 uses mythical imagery: his sword will crush Leviathan, the fleeing serpent of the sea, and will slay it (27:1). Yahweh then sings a song of his vineyard (vv. 2-6), reversing the thrust of the earlier song in 5:1-7. In days to come Israel will take root and blossom and will fill the whole world with its fruit (27:6). What follows is an explanation of Israel's suffering, which, it is hoped, will lead to the removal of sin when Israel's idols are crushed. But Yahweh's people still lack discernment, for which reason they are unable to see Yahweh's favor (vv. 7-11). But in a future day exiles banished to Assyria and Egypt will hear a great trumpet blast and will come to worship Yahweh on his holy mountain in Jerusalem (27:12-13).

Isaiah had better relations with King Hezekiah, who, according to a lower chronology, took the throne in 715 B.C.E. According to this chronology, Isaiah had been out of public life for perhaps eighteen years. During Hezekiah's reign, Isaiah had a more positive impact on national policy. Hezekiah carried out a major reform (2 Kgs 18:4, 22 [= Isa 36:7]; 2 Chronicles 29–31), which no doubt was in response to the preaching of Isaiah and Micah, and though it was short-lived, it did away with the Assyrian religion imported into Judah by Ahaz. This reform most likely began sometime after Hezekiah took the throne in 715 B.C.E. and continued perhaps until the arrival of Sennacherib in Palestine in 701 B.C.E. Assyrian records tell us that Sargon II carried out no campaigns into Palestine between 712 and 706; and after he died in 705, Judah would have been free to renounce openly the Assyrian gods and consolidate prior gains before Sennacherib regained control of the empire and invaded Judah in 701. Hezekiah is said to have humbled himself also at the preaching of Micah (Jer 26:19), and to have humbled himself when the Assyrians invaded Judah in 701 B.C.E. (Isa 37:1-4). This brought forth from the prophet a divine oracle against Assyria (37:22-29 = 2 Kgs 19:21-28). When the king was sick and was told by Isaiah that he would die, he prayed with tears to Yahweh for recovery, and it was granted to him (38:1-8; 2 Kgs 20:1-11). The historical appendix (38:9-20) includes a psalm composed by the king after he recovered.

Things did not go well for Hezekiah a decade or so after he became king. Once Sennacherib had taken the Assyrian throne (704 B.C.E.), Hezekiah joined a rebellion against him, led by Ashdod (14:28-32; 18; 2 Kgs 18:7), and sent envoys to negotiate a treaty with Egypt. Isaiah was against the scheme, calling an alliance with Egypt a "covenant with death" (28:14-22; 30:1-17; 31:1-3) and also a rebellion against Yahweh. While the rebellion was being planned, Isaiah walked barefoot clad only in a loincloth like a war prisoner (chapter 20), protesting Judah's reliance on Egypt and predicting disaster. But Judah's leaders were a godless lot, mocking the prophet and telling him rather to speak "smooth things" (30:10). A second time Isaiah wrote up his prophecy as a witness for the future (30:8).

But Isaiah was convinced that Jerusalem would be delivered from the Assyrian threat if it put its trust in Yahweh. Assyria had been the instrument of Yahweh's judgment, but now Yahweh would act against the hubris of this nation and rescue Jerusalem (chapters 36–37). Even though Hezekiah had to pay tribute money to Sennacherib in one of his attacks on Jerusalem (2 Kgs 18:13-16), in the end the city was spared. After this dramatic eleventh-hour deliverance (in 701 B.C.E., or 688 B.C.E. according to the lower chronology), Isaiah disappears from public view and is heard from no more.

The oracle in 1:4-9 is spoken against the background of Sennacherib's campaign in 701, where Isaiah's words "the daughter of Zion is left like a booth in a vineyard" corroborate the report of the Assyrian text stating that Sennacherib destroyed forty-six Judahite cities and countless small villages, leaving Hezekiah in Jerusalem "like a bird in a cage."[17] The Valley of Vision oracle in 22:1-14 may also come from this time.

Chapter 28 opens with a woe oracle against the proud drunkards of northern Israel (28:1-4), spoken before Samaria's fall in 722 B.C.E. It is supplemented by a promise that Yahweh in that day will be a crown of glory to the remnant of his people (28:5-6). The chapter continues with oracles on the same theme directed against Judah, perhaps uttered during Hezekiah's early reign when a revolt was being planned against Assyria, otherwise just prior to the invasion of Sennacherib in 701 (28:7-29). Judah's leaders, like the leaders in Samaria, were also drunk on wine and reeling, erring in vision and stumbling in their judgment (28:7). Isaiah mocks their scoffing. Because Jerusalem's rulers remain intransigent, Yahweh says:

> Behold, I am laying in Zion for a foundation
>   a stone, a tested stone,
> a precious cornerstone, of a sure foundation.
>   He who believes will not be in haste.
> And I will make justice the line
>   and righteousness the plummet.
> And hail will sweep away the refuge of lies,
>   and waters will overwhelm the shelter.
> Then your covenant with death will be annulled,
>   and your agreement with Sheol will not stand.
> When the overwhelming scourge passes through,
>   you will be beaten down by it.
> (Isa 28:16-18)

Isaiah's words end by citing the farmer's methods of plowing, sowing, and threshing various crops. God, says the prophet, shows a similar wisdom in acting out his plan in history (28:23-29).

What follows in chapters 29–32 are more woes on those who advo-
cate a national policy relying on Egypt. Isaiah has now come to believe
that Yahweh will deliver Jerusalem from its formidable enemy, doubtless
Sennacherib, who was besieging the city. Chapter 29 begins with a "woe"
on Ariel (Jerusalem) for the distress about to come, but then speaks of a
sudden visitation by Yahweh that will turn disaster into triumph (29:1-8).
Jerusalem's people are rebuked with bitter irony for their blindness and
unbelief (29:9-12), a reminder of what Isaiah had been warned about in
his call (6:9-10). Yahweh promises that he will do "marvelous things" for
people carrying on "religion by rote" (29:13-14). Another "woe" follows
on those hiding from Yahweh—perhaps also from the prophet—and the
planned alliance with Egypt. Isaiah says:

> Woe to those who hide deep from Yahweh their counsel,
>   whose deeds are in the dark,
> and who say, "Who sees us?
>   Who knows us?"
> You turn things upside down!
>   Shall the potter be regarded as the clay,
> that the thing made should say of its maker,
>   "He did not make me,"
> or the thing formed say of him who formed it,
>   "He has no understanding"?
>   (Isa 29:15-16)

Reliance on Egypt will come to nothing (29:17-21). But once the crisis is
past, people will sanctify the "Holy One of Jacob," and those in error will
come to understanding (29:22-24).

Isaiah has more stern words for those who rely on Egypt (30:1-7). He
says:

> Woe to the rebellious children, says Yahweh,
>   who carry out a plan, but not mine;
> who make an alliance, but against my will,
>   adding sin to sin;
> who set out to go down to Egypt
>   without asking for my counsel,
> to take refuge in the protection of Pharaoh
>   and to seek shelter in the shadow of Egypt.
> Therefore the protection of Pharaoh shall become your shame,
>   and the shelter in the shadow of Egypt your humiliation.

For though his officials are at Zoan
  and his envoys reach Hanes,
Everyone comes to shame
  through a people that cannot profit them,
that brings neither help nor profit,
  but shame and disgrace.

(Isa 30:1-5)

And again:

An oracle concerning the animals of the Negeb:
Through a land of trouble and distress,
  of lioness and roaring lion,
    of viper and flying serpent,
they carry their riches on the backs of donkeys,
  and their treasures on the humps of camels,
    to a people that cannot profit them.
For Egypt's help is worthless and empty;
  therefore I have called her
    "Rahab who sits still."

(Isa 30:6-7)

Isaiah's answer is to trust Yahweh and wait patiently for him. Yahweh God, the Holy One of Israel, says:

In returning and rest you shall be saved;
  in quietness and in trust shall be your strength.
And you would not, but you said,
  "No! We will speed upon horses";
    therefore you shall speed away.
And "We will ride upon swift steeds";
  therefore your pursuers shall be swift.
A thousand shall flee at the threat of one,
  at the threat of five you shall flee,
till you are left
  like a flagstaff on the top of a mountain,
    like a signal on a hill.
Therefore Yahweh waits to be gracious to you;
  therefore he exalts himself to show mercy to you.
For Yahweh is a God of justice;
  blessed are all those who wait for him.

(Isa 30:15-18)

The supplementary prose of 30:19-26 promises grace for the faithful remnant. People will hear the words of their Teacher (vv. 20-21); they will rid themselves of their idols (v. 22); and Zion's populace will once again see the earth yield in abundance and cattle grazing in lush green pastures (vv. 23-24). The sun and the moon will shine with greater splendor (v. 26). In 30:27-33 Yahweh promises that the Assyrians will be terror-stricken at his voice, with a burning place having long ago been prepared for them.

The polemic against an Egyptian alliance continues in chapter 31. Isaiah speaks a woe against those who trust in horses and chariots but do not look to the Holy One of Israel (31:1-3). Yahweh will protect Jerusalem, and the nation should therefore turn to him (31:4-9). Chapter 32 speaks of a messianic king in a future idealistic age. At this time the blindness and deafness of people will be reversed; the eyes of those who see will not be closed, the ears of those who hear will hearken, and rash minds will have good judgment. Moreover, the fool will no longer be called noble (32:1-8). However, the women of present-day Jerusalem—young and old—are promised future anxiety because the land will not yield and the city will be deserted. Jerusalem will become the habitation of wild animals until Yahweh's spirit is poured out from on high. At that time righteousness and justice will prevail, the fruit of which will be peace, quietness, and renewed trust (32:9-20).

The last of six woes is against a destroyer who has not himself been destroyed, but a treacherous day awaits him (33:1). A petition is then made for Yahweh to be gracious to those who wait for the Exalted One, who will come to fill Zion with justice and righteousness (33:2-6). Judah at present lies in ruins, with covenants broken and witnesses despised, but Yahweh will rise against the invaders, sinners in Zion will tremble, and the righteous will dwell in a secure place with bread to eat and water to drink (33:7-16). In coming days, people will see "the king in his beauty," and Zion will be both a city of joyous feasts and a quiet habitation. No one will say, "I am sick," and people will be forgiven their iniquity (33:17-24).

Chapters 34-35 are taken by many to emanate from a later prophet, perhaps Second (or Third) Isaiah, whose oracles appear in chapters 40–66. Chapter 34 predicts Yahweh's wrath against nations of the world, with Edom singled out for special mention (34:5-17). Chapter 35 promises Zion a happy future, a day when Yahweh will prepare a highway for a singing host to return, when joy and gladness will fill the air, and sorrow and sighing will flee away (35:10).

Zephaniah: Prophet of the Day of Yahweh

Zephaniah, in the superscription of his book, is said to have been a descendant of Hezekiah, one of Judah's better kings (1:1). He was thus of royal blood and would, in all likelihood, have been acquainted with the goings-on in royal circles. The superscription also says that Yahweh's word came to him during the reign of Josiah (640–609 B.C.E.), which would make him an older contemporary of Jeremiah. The early years of Josiah saw Judah attempting to undo the apostasy of Manasseh, who reigned fifty-five long years. During this time, Hezekiah's reform was dismantled, old Canaanite and current Assyrian worship were brought into the temple, and much innocent blood was shed, including that of Manasseh's own son (2 Kgs 21:1-18).

In Zephaniah's opening oracle, Yahweh says that he will sweep away everything, including Judah and Jerusalem. Syncretistic worship has caused people to turn from Yahweh and no longer seek him (1:2-6). A coming Day of Yahweh is announced when those responsible for this sorry state of affairs will be punished. Israel knew an earlier Day of Yahweh, when Yahweh led his people to defeat of their enemies. But now holy war has been declared on Judah. People are told to be silent, for Yahweh has prepared a sacrifice and readied guests for the punishment of Judah's officials, the king's sons, and all who dress in foreign attire. They stand guilty of violence and fraud (1:7-9). Merchants, too, who think that Yahweh will do nothing will be punished. All their labor will be for nought, for others will come to plunder their goods and lay waste their houses (1:10-13). This future day echoes Amos's day of wrath and gloom (Amos 5:18-20). Zephaniah says:

> The great day of Yahweh is near,
>   near and hastening fast.
> The sound of the Day of Yahweh is bitter;
>   the warrior cries aloud there.
> That day will be a day of wrath,
>   a day of distress and anguish,
> a day of ruin and devastation,
>   a day of darkness and gloom,
> a day of clouds and thick darkness,
>   a day of trumpet blast and battle cry
> against the fortified cities
>   and against lofty battlements.
>   (Zeph 1:14-16)

The ominous day will come because people have sinned against Yahweh, and nothing can save them. Terrible it will be, consuming the whole earth (1:17-18).

Zephaniah's Day of Yahweh will impact other nations. It will also descend upon the shameless Philistines, although anyone of that nation who seeks Yahweh may escape the divine wrath (2:1-4). A hopeful word for Judah follows. Judah's remnant—for there will be one—will possess the seacoast meadows when Yahweh remembers it and restores its fortunes (2:5-7).

Judgment will come against Moab and Ammon, both of whom have taunted Yahweh's people. They shall become like Sodom and Gomorrah. A remnant of Yahweh's people will plunder them. Moab and Ammon are censured for their pride, also for their boasting and scoffing against Yahweh's people. Their gods will shrivel up, and bowing down now before Yahweh will be the coastlands and islands (2:8-11). A fragmented judgment is spoken against Ethiopia (2:12). Then, climactically, the heavy hand of Yahweh will come upon proud Assyria. Nineveh will be transformed into a wasteland for wild animals (2:13-15).

Zephaniah returns in chapter 3 to address Judah, beginning with a searing "woe" oracle against rebellious, defiled, oppressing Jerusalem, who listens to no one, refuses correction, and does not trust in Yahweh. Her officials, judges, prophets, and priests are all guilty of wrongdoing. Prophets are faithless and priests violate the law. Yahweh, by contrast, is righteous and without wrong, unlike the unjust, who know no shame (3:1-5). Yahweh has cut off the nations in hopes of making Jerusalem accept correction, but is saddened to learn that his people have returned the favor by becoming even more corrupt (3:6-7).

Yahweh says, "Wait for me, for the day when I arise as a witness." Reference here is to the day when Yahweh will pour out his indignation on all the earth. At that time, the speech of peoples will be changed so that they will call upon Yahweh's name. Dispersed ones will return home bearing offerings (3:9-10). On that day, Jerusalem will not be shamed, because the proud and haughty will all be removed from Yahweh's holy mountain (3:11). Yahweh says:

> For I will leave in the midst of you
> a people humble and lowly.
> They shall seek refuge in the name of Yahweh,
> the remnant of Israel.
> They shall do no wrong
> and utter no lies.

Nor shall a deceitful tongue
   be found in their mouths.
Then they will pasture and lie down,
   and no one shall make them afraid.

(Zeph 3:12-13)

Once this transformation has occurred, Zion will rejoice because Yahweh will have taken away all judgments against her and turned away her enemies. Yahweh will reign victoriously in her midst; exiles will come home; Zion's glory will return, and her fortunes will be restored (3:14-20).

Habakkuk: Prophet at the Watchtower

About the prophet Habakkuk we again know nothing, having only the prophecies attributed to him. Because of talk in 1:6 about Yahweh arousing the Chaldeans—that is, the Babylonians—the prophecies in this book are dated by some c. 598 B.C.E., a year before Nebuchadnezzar entered Judah and forced Jerusalem's surrender. Others date some oracles in the book before the Battle of Carchemish (605 B.C.E.), when the Babylonians defeated the Egyptians.

In his first oracle, Habakkuk asks how long he must cry to Yahweh to end the violence and trouble he sees and have Yahweh not answer him. The prophet is weary of seeing wrongdoing—the law slackened, justice being perverted, and the wicked surrounding the righteous (1:1-4). Yahweh answers by saying that he is doing something Habakkuk will scarcely believe. He is rousing the Chaldeans, a fierce and impetuous nation, who will take care of the problem. They too will come to do violence and will incur guilt for their transgressions, since might is their god. But Yahweh is calling on them all the same to traverse the land (1:5-11). Habakkuk then responds to the "Holy One," asking how it can be that Yahweh will allow such a ruthless enemy to destroy without mercy. Yahweh keeps creating new human lives, but the Chaldeans keep catching and consuming them like so many fish out of the sea. The prophet wants to know how long this can go on (1:12-17).

Habakkuk decides to take up his place in the watchtower. Here he will wait for Yahweh's answer to his complaint (2:1). Yahweh says to him:

Write the vision
   and make it plain on tablets,

so that a runner may read it.
For there is still a vision for the appointed time;
    it speaks of the end, and does not lie.
If it seems to tarry, wait for it;
    indeed it will surely come, it will not delay.
Look at the proud!
    their spirit is not right in them,
        but the righteous shall live by their faith.

(Hab 2:2-4)

What is the content of this vision? We are not sure. It could be the five woes that follow, or else the psalm of chapter 3, in which God's mighty power is recited. Habakkuk, in any case, says that he is prepared to wait patiently for the day of calamity (3:16b). For now, Yahweh simply tells the prophet that the spirit of the proud is not right and that the righteous shall live by their faith (cf. Gal 3:11; Rom 1:17; Heb 10:38). Yahweh gives him assurances that the arrogant will not endure (2:5).

Habakkuk's five "woes" are prophetic invectives. The first woe is against the one who is greedy and arrogant, namely, Nebuchadnezzar. He heaps up plunder but will himself be plundered. Judgment will come because of bloodshed and violence (2:6b-8). The second woe is against the one who pillages and amasses wealth by wrongdoing. Nebuchadnezzar is building a house that will not stand. He will be shamed and will forfeit his own life (2:9-11). The third woe is against the one who builds cities by iniquity, referring again to the Babylonian king. Habakkuk asks a question and then answers it:

Is it not from Yahweh of hosts
    that peoples labor only to feed the flames,
        and nations weary themselves for nothing?
But the earth will be filled
    with the knowledge of the glory of Yahweh,
        as the waters cover the sea.

(Hab 2:13-14)

Verse 14 is an almost verbatim quotation of Isa 11:9b.

The fourth woe is spoken against the one who makes neighboring nations drink the cup of his wrath only so that he can gaze upon their shame. Habakkuk says the same will happen to him when Yahweh passes to him the cup of wrath. Cruel Babylon is again judged for bloodshed and violence, perpetrated even against the animals (2:15-17). The fifth woe is against the one who expects life and teaching from idols (2:18-20). Babylon's idols are mocked as worthless, dumb, and inert. The woes conclude with a confession that has become another signature of this prophet:

> But Yahweh is in his holy temple;
> let all the earth keep silence before him.
>
> (Hab 2:20)

The psalm in chapter 3 is thought by many to be an ancient hymn later added to the book. A Habakkuk scroll from Qumran does not contain the chapter. But others point out that this psalm is well integrated into the book, saying that it could be Habakkuk's answer to the earlier question (3:1-19). Its mythological and historical imagery celebrate the mighty acts of Yahweh—from hoary antiquity to the salvation of his people. When Habakkuk hears this, he trembles and says:

> I wait quietly for the day of calamity
> to come upon the people who attack us.
>
> (Hab 3:16b)

The prophet's final words rejoice in Yahweh, the God of his salvation, even though fields now yield no food and flocks are cut off from the fold. Yahweh has become Habakkuk's strength and has given him new vigor in life.

Huldah: Prophetess of the Temple Scroll

Huldah the prophet is the woman who delivered an important prophetic message after the temple law book was found during Josiah's reform (622 B.C.E.). The high priest Hilkiah, Shaphan the scribe, and others went to Huldah to obtain an oracle from her. Judah received a riveting judgment for abandoning Yahweh,[18] but King Josiah, because he was penitent, would be spared from seeing the evil that would come upon the place (2 Kgs 22:14-20).

Joel: Prophet of the Outpouring Spirit

About the prophet Joel we also know next to nothing; the superscription of his book tells us simply that he was the son of Pethuel (Joel 1:1). On the basis of internal evidence, the book is dated by scholars anywhere from the late preexilic period to the postexilic period, with dates in the latter ranging from early (sixth century B.C.E.) to late (fourth century B.C.E.). The walls of Jerusalem are standing (2:7, 9), which means that if the book is postexilic, it would have to postdate Nehemiah's rebuilding in the sixth century. The author is familiar with the temple, the priesthood, and cultic practices generally (1:9, 13-14; 2:15-17), which means that if the book is postexilic, it has to be later than 515 B.C.E., when the Second Temple was dedicated.

In 3:1-3 the Babylonian exile and dispersion seem to be in the past, but one does not know whether these verses of prose belong to the original book or were added later. If the locust parade and what follows in 1:4-7 refer to the coming of the Babylonian army, then the prophecy must predate the fall of Jerusalem in 586 B.C.E. Joel 3:6 states that the people of Judah and Jerusalem were sold to Greeks, but this could have occurred anytime between the seventh and the fifth centuries B.C.E. Some poetic lines and phrases have close or exact parallels to other prophetic utterances, for example, "pastures of the wilderness" in 1:19-20 (cf. Jer 9:10; 23:10); "the great and terrible Day of Yahweh" in 2:11, 31 (cf. Mal 4:5); "in Mount Zion . . . there shall be those who escape" in 2:32 (cf. Obad 17a); "Yahweh roars from Zion, and utters his voice from Jerusalem" in 3:16 (cf. Amos 1:2); "my holy mountain" in 2:1 and 3:17 (cf. Isa 11:9; 56:7; 57:13; 65:11, 25; 66:20; Obad 16; Zeph 3:11); and "the mountains shall drip sweet wine" in 3:18 (cf. Amos 9:13). But these parallels are inconclusive for determining a date for the book. We do not know when Joel prophesied. The prophet is placed here simply because a preexilic date for his message is possible. But, again, we do not know.

The prophet begins by asking if anyone can remember an enemy invading Yahweh's land that wrought such devastation. It is a story to tell one's children and grandchildren (1:2-3). The prophet portrays this devouring enemy in his famous "locust parade":

> What the cutting locust left
>   the swarming locust has eaten.
> What the swarming locust left
>   the hopping locust has eaten.
> And what the hopping locust left
>   the destroying locust has eaten.
>
> (Joel 1:4)

This verse may be a reference to an actual locust plague, as many scholars assume, or it may be a portrayal of the enemy nation coming to wreak havoc on Judah (cf. Amos 7:1-2; Jer 5:17).

People are called to lament the destruction, priests in particular, for offerings will be cut off from the sanctuary. Priests are to assemble the elders and proclaim a fast (1:5-14). Joel sees this as a frightful Day of Yahweh, when not only food will be cut off, but also joy and gladness. Even groans from the animals will be heard (1:15-18). Joel cries to Yahweh because pastureland and trees have been devoured by fire. Brooks have no water for the wild animals (1:19-20).

Like Amos and other prophets of doom, Joel sees the Day of Yahweh as a day of darkness, not light (2:1-2; Amos 5:18-20). The enemy will enter a land lush like the garden of Eden, but will leave it a desolate wilderness. It is a mighty war machine; its arrival on horses and in chariots will leave people paralyzed. Soldiers will descend upon the city and be running upon its walls (2:3-9). All of heaven and earth will tremble at the enveloping darkness, which will be Yahweh uttering his mighty voice. The Day of Yahweh is great and very terrible—"who can endure it?" (2:10-11).

But Joel says there is still time for people to return to Yahweh:

Yet even now, says Yahweh,
  return to me with all your heart,
with fasting, with weeping, and with mourning;
  rend your hearts and not your garments.
Return to Yahweh your God,
  for he is gracious and merciful,
slow to anger, and abounding in steadfast love,
  who relents from punishment.

(Joel 2:12-13)

Yahweh may relent and leave a blessing behind (2:14). People are therefore urged once again to proclaim a fast and make sure everyone is there. At this time, the priests are to plead with tears for Yahweh's mercy (2:15-17).

The turning point of the book is at 2:18, where Yahweh is now said to become jealous for his land and to have pity on his people. He therefore answers the prayer of the priests, promising to send grain, wine, and oil, enough so that people will be fully satisfied. Yahweh says further that he will remove the nation's northern enemy, driving it into a parched land (2:18-20). The land will be glad and rejoice. Beasts, too, need fear no more, for pastures will again be green. Fertility will return. Yahweh will now carry out a reverse of the earlier "locust parade" (2:21-27). Yahweh says:

The threshing floors shall be full of grain;
    the vats shall overflow with wine and oil.
I will repay you for the years
    that the swarming locust has eaten,
the hopper, the destroyer, and the cutter,
    my great army, which I sent against you.

(Joel 2:24-25)

Then comes Joel's great prophecy about the outpouring of Yahweh's spirit, which is quoted by Peter at Pentecost (2:28-32; Acts 2:17-21). Joel says:

Then afterward I will pour out my spirit on all flesh;
    your sons and your daughters shall prophesy;
        your old men shall dream dreams,
        and your young men shall see visions.
Even on the male and female slaves,
in those days, I will pour out my spirit.

(Joel 2:28-29)

This outpouring will be accompanied by portents in heaven and on earth, and those who call upon the name of Yahweh shall be saved (2:30-32; cf. Rom 10:13).

Yahweh will restore the fortunes of Judah and Jerusalem, at which time the nations will be judged (3:1-3). Foreign nations will be judged because they scattered Israel, dividing up its land and giving its children to immoral practices or selling them into slavery (3:2-3). The Phoenicians will be requited for robbing Jerusalem and selling Judahites to the Greeks (3:4-8). Yahweh will sell their sons and daughters to the Sabeans, a punishment befitting the crime.

A Day of Yahweh awaits the nations, and people are told to beat their plowshares into swords. Judgment of the nations will take place in the Valley of Jehoshaphat, also called the Valley of Decision (3:9-15). Yahweh will roar from Zion (cf. Amos 1:2), only this time he will be a refuge to his people. This cosmic warfare will occur so that people will know that he is Yahweh, the God who dwells on his holy mountain in Zion (3:16-17). This new day will see the earth yield in great abundance, and a fountain will stream forth from the temple (3:18; cf. Ezek 47:1-12; Rev 22:1). Egypt and Edom get a final word of judgment for violence done to Judah and for shedding innocent blood (3:19). Judah will henceforth be inhabited because "Yahweh dwells in Zion" (3:20-21).

Nahum: Prophet against Assyria

About Nahum we again know virtually nothing, except that he gave an oracle against Nineveh and came from an unknown place called Elkosh (1:1). This prophet has a one-theme message against Assyria, which ceased being a world power when the Babylonians and Medes destroyed Nineveh in 612 B.C.E. Nahum prophesied before or at the time of this event.

Nahum's first vision is an abbreviated acrostic in 1:2-8, which announces Yahweh as a God who takes vengeance on his adversaries. Yahweh is slow to anger, but he will not clear the guilty (1:3; cf. Exod 34:6-7). Assyria is then addressed, being asked if she did not in fact plot against Yahweh (1:9-11). An oracle to Judah and Assyria follows, first assuring Judah that Assyria will afflict her no more (1:12-13), then telling Assyria that Yahweh will cut off images from its house of gods (1:14). Judah is then comforted by a messenger coming with good tidings, proclaiming peace (1:15; cf. Isa 52:7). Judah is told to keep her feasts, since the wicked shall never again come against her. Some suggest that because of this positive attitude toward feasts, Nahum may have been a cultic prophet. This is a different message, in any case, from the one we get in Jeremiah, who was silent about Nineveh's fall. Moreover, Jeremiah would not have agreed with Nahum that the wicked would never again come against Judah. It is remarkable that Nahum speaks no condemnation of Judah, nor does he call for repentance or reform of the Judahite nation.

Judgment on Nineveh continues. With an enemy about to destroy her, Nahum imagines that Yahweh is restoring the majesty of Israel (2:1-2). The attack on Nineveh is vividly portrayed: the palace trembles, women are captured and led away, and the place is plundered (2:3-9). A mocking lament follows (2:10-12). Yahweh is against this city; the voice of its messengers shall be heard no more (2:13).

Nineveh, that city of bloodshed and accumulated booty, is now seen filled with dead bodies (3:1-3). Nahum heaps scorn on her. Yahweh has said:

> Because of the countless debaucheries of the prostitute,
>   gracefully alluring, mistress of sorcery,
> who enslaves nations through her debaucheries
>   and peoples through her sorcery,
> I am against you, says Yahweh of hosts,
>   and I will lift up your skirts over your face.
> And I will let nations look on your nakedness
>   and kingdoms on your shame.

I will throw filth at you
   and treat you with contempt
     and will make you a spectacle.
Then all who see you will shrink from you and say:
   "Nineveh is devastated; who will bemoan her?"
    Where shall I seek comforters for you?
(Nah 3:4-7)

Nineveh is compared to Thebes, Egypt's capital, which fell in 663 B.C.E., and Nineveh will share the fate of Thebes (3:8-17). A closing word addresses the king of Assyria, whose nobles sleep. All who hear the news of Nineveh's fall will clap their hands, for what nation has ever escaped her cruelty (3:18-19)?

Jeremiah: Prophet of the New Covenant

About Jeremiah we know a good deal, considerably more than about any other Hebrew prophet. The superscription of his book tells us that he was the son of Hilkiah, one of the priests living in the village of Anathoth, just three miles or so north of Jerusalem. Yahweh's word came to him first in the thirteenth year of Josiah (640–609 B.C.E.), which was 627 B.C.E., also during the reign of Jehoiakim (609–598 B.C.E.), and to the end of the eleventh year of Zedekiah (597–586 B.C.E.), when Jerusalem fell to Nebuchadnezzar, Israelite nationhood came to an end, and the remaining Judahites were taken into Babylonian captivity (1:1-3). According to later material in the book, Jeremiah survived the demise of the Israelite nation and continued to prophesy after Jerusalem's destruction. After his release by Nebuzaradan (39:11-14; 40:1-6), he joined the reconstituted community at Mizpah (586–582 B.C.E.) and was then taken forcibly to Egypt after the Babylonian-appointed governor, Gedaliah, was murdered and the Mizpah community disbanded. In Egypt, Jeremiah lived long enough to preach to Judahite exiles there, before disappearing from view. Later tradition has it that he died in Egypt.

Jeremiah learned of his call to be a prophet when he was a young boy, and he reports the divine revelation in 1:5-12. In this report, he says that Yahweh called him before he was conceived in his mother's womb, which means that the call lies veiled in mystery. Only Yahweh knows when it was issued. Jeremiah did not accept the call at the time he learned about it, and Yahweh too said his word would be watched over until it was fulfilled (1:12). Acceptance came when the law book was found in the temple in

622 B.C.E., and Jeremiah consumed the words written on the scroll (15:16). These words, in all likelihood, were a portion of the Song of Moses (Deut 32:15-22). Jeremiah understood himself to be the "prophet like Moses" of Deut 18:18. Soon afterward, in a second revelation, Yahweh commissioned Jeremiah to begin his public ministry (1:13-19). In this divine word, Yahweh promised to break the nation, but Jeremiah was promised rescue from those trying to break him. This promise was reiterated later during a time of personal crisis (15:19-21).

The core of Jeremiah's prophecies given during his early career (622–605 B.C.E.) is found in chapters 1–20, which constitute the First Edition of the Jeremiah book. In this collection are oracles on apostasy and repentance (2:1—4:4); oracles and laments addressing the mayhem brought on by a "foe from the north" (4:5—10:25), and personal laments by the prophet (chapters 11–20). Preaching on other themes is interspersed among these three basic collections.

Jeremiah's prophecies on apostasy begin with the romantic notion that Israel was loyal to Yahweh in the wilderness (2:2-3), but after settlement in the land the people abandoned Yahweh. Yahweh asks what wrong the people found in him, and the answer, of course, is none at all (2:5, 31). Yahweh is the fountain of living water, yet people reject him for idols that are nothing more than broken cisterns (2:13; cf. 17:7-8, 13). In a despondent mood, Jeremiah questions whether this can be true, at least for him personally (15:18), but in better moments he knows that idols are the false resource; they cannot bring rain (14:22), nor have they power to save (2:27b-28; 11:12). Yahweh fills the creation (23:24), sends rain (5:24; 14:22), and controls the sea (5:22).

Jeremiah probes deeply into the nature of Yahweh. Yahweh is a God who "knows" (12:3; 15:15; 18:23; 29:23). He knows people and events, not only events that are current but also those planned for the future (1:5; 29:11; 33:3). Yahweh "remembers," too, both the good and the bad (2:2; 14:10), though in forgiveness he ceases to remember (31:34). Yahweh has the capacity to "see" (12:3; 16:17; 32:24), even in the temple darkness or other secret places where evildoers imagine God cannot see (7:11; 23:24). More important, Yahweh is a God who acts. Many do not believe this (5:12), perhaps because Jeremiah has announced him as the people's enemy. But to faithful individuals, such as Jeremiah, Baruch, and Ebed-melech the Ethiopian, protection and salvation are both promised and delivered (1:17-19; 45:5; 39:15-18). Yahweh is a righteous judge (11:20), although Jeremiah cannot understand why he allows the wicked to prosper (12:1-2). Yahweh will vindicate himself eventually (5:9, 29; 9:9), and the humble can expect to receive divine mercy (3:12-13). Jeremiah discovers more than once that Yahweh can be overpowering, particularly when the prophet is suffering (1:6-8; 20:7; 32:25-26), but he is filled with rejoicing when deliverance comes (20:13).

Jeremiah has extraordinary insight into the human condition. He says much about the people "forsaking Yahweh" (2:13; 16:11; 17:13; 19:4), which can be seen in the nation's misguided foreign policy, that is, reliance on Egypt and Assyria (2:14-19). People are said also to have "forgotten Yahweh" (2:32; 3:21; 13:25; 18:15; cf. Deut 32:18), which, in concrete terms, means that they do not know the true source of their abundant crops. Baal worship, sexual adventurism, and indulgence in fertility rites associated with the "no gods" are flagrant violations of the Sinai covenant (2:20-37; 5:7; 22:20-21; cf. Deut 32:13-15; Hos 2:8). Moreover, people were sacrificing their children on altars in the Ben Hinnom Valley (7:31-32; 19:5-6). All this can bring only shame to the nation (2:36-37; 3:25). Jeremiah says that there is one answer to Judah's apostasy: a return/repentance (chapter 3). Yahweh says, "If you return, O Israel, . . . to me return" (4:1).

The "foe from the north" (4:6; 6:22; cf. 1:14-15) was at first ravaging bands (2 Kgs 24:2), but basically it was Babylon, which sent the marauders on their errands and later came with its own army to bring the nation down. Babylon is the "lion come up from his thicket" (4:7), "watcher from a distant land" (4:16), the "nation from antiquity . . . whose language you do not know" (5:15). Jeremiah says of this foe:

> Its quiver is like an open tomb;
>   all of them are mighty men.
> It shall consume your harvest and your food;
>   it shall consume your sons and your daughters;
>   it shall consume your flocks and your herds.
> It shall consume your vines and your fig trees.
> It will beat down your fortified cities—
>   in which you trust.
>
> (Jer 5:16-17)

In a stunning vision, Jeremiah views the coming catastrophe as a return to primeval chaos (4:23-26; cf. 9:10-11). Yahweh would consider pardoning Jerusalem, but a righteous person could not be found in the city (5:1-8). Jeremiah is sufficiently grounded in wisdom thought to realize that next to godlessness is foolishness, and the latter malady has contributed not a little to the nation's precarious condition. Foolish leaders are singled out for special mention (10:21; 14:18). People are fools; they do not "know" Yahweh (4:22; 5:21). Judah's lack of knowledge picks up from the Song of Moses, Hosea, and Isaiah (Deut 32:6; Hos 4:1, 6; 5:4; 6:6; Isa 1:3). Knowing Yahweh, for Jeremiah, means "knowing his way" (5:4-5), "knowing his ordinances" (8:7), and doing justice to the poor and needy (22:16). People, however, are wicked, unjust to orphans, widows, and the needy, and they murder the innocent poor (2:34; 5:26-28; 7:9; 22:3). Jeremiah says:

> For from the least of them to the greatest of them,
>   everyone is shaving off profit.
> And from prophet all the way to priest,
>   everyone commits falsehood.
> They have healed the brokenness of my people
>   ever so lightly, saying,
> "Peace, peace,"
>   when there is no peace.
> They should have been very ashamed when they committed
>   abomination;
>   indeed they are not at all ashamed;
>   indeed to show deep humiliation, they do not know.
> Therefore they shall fall among those falling;
>   at the time I reckon with them, they will stumble.
>   (Jer 6:13-15 = 8:10b-12)

With the covenant being grievously violated, worship is rendered hollow, and Yahweh will have none of it (6:16-21; 7:1-15, 21-26). Yahweh says:

> Why is it frankincense comes to me from Sheba
>   and the good cane from a distant land?
> Your burnt offerings are not acceptable;
>   your sacrifices are not pleasing to me.
>   (Jer 6:20)

Jeremiah is therefore left to lament over the destruction of people and land (8:22—9:2; 9:10-11), and he calls for professional wailing women to do the same (9:17-22). Concluding the "foe-lament" cycle are liturgical pieces affirming Yahweh as the incomparable God of Creation and the Portion of Jacob (10:1-16). The crafted idols are admittedly beautiful, but inert:

> Like a field scarecrow are they, since they don't speak;
>   they must be carried, since they don't take a step;

do not fear them, for they don't do evil.
And also to do good is not in them.

(Jer 10:5)

Beginning in chapter 11, we learn that Jeremiah early on preached in support of the Josianic reform, but when the reform came to a full stop under Jehoiakim, and Judah returned to the wickedness of earlier generations, words of harsh judgment were forthcoming from the prophet. The Sinai covenant, as set forth in Deuteronomy, contained curses for non-compliance (11:1-5). The covenant was also something you do, and Judah was not doing it (11:6-8). Finally, the covenant was declared broken, which meant that Yahweh would rain curses upon his people (11:9-13). Other passages in chapters 1–20 seem to indicate that Jeremiah supported the reform during the reign of Josiah (4:1-4, 14; 6:16; 7:3-7; 17:19-23, 24-27; 18:1-10, 11-12).

Jeremiah experienced particularly hard times during Jehoiakim's reign. He angered the king at the outset by preaching in 609 B.C.E. that the temple would be destroyed like Israel's first sanctuary at Shiloh, and for this message Jeremiah was put on trial for his life (7:12-15; 26:1-19). From this period probably come many of the prophet's personal confessions (chapters 11–20), although some may date from an earlier time (11:18-23). In these confessions, Jeremiah goes public about his suffering, either proclaiming his own innocence (12:1-3; 15:10; 18:19-23) or simply probing for a divine answer (15:15-18; 10:23-24; 17:13-18). Yahweh sometimes tells the good prophet that he will vindicate him or attend to his enemies (11:21-23; 15:11-12), or that the prophet himself stands in need of correction (15:19-21), or that Jeremiah must simply accept his suffering, for things will likely get worse (12:5-6; cf. 10:19). In one case, Jeremiah answers his own complaint about being called to prophetic office with a confident word that he will not be overcome by the opposition (20:7-10, 11-13). In another case, Jeremiah's complaint is answered with a prior word given to him, affirming the hidden wisdom of Yahweh (20:14-18; 1:5).

Because Judah is so set in her evil ways, Yahweh tells Jeremiah not to pray on her behalf (11:14-17; cf. 7:16-20). Yahweh will abandon his house, his heritage, and his beloved people to the enemy (12:7-13). Jeremiah warns the people that pride will lead to their fall, for which reason they must humble themselves (13:15-17). The young king Jehoiachin and the queen mother receive this message in 597 B.C.E. just before Jerusalem surrenders to Nebuchadnezzar and the first group of Judahites are carted off to Babylonian exile (13:18-20). Following oracles focus on Jerusalem's sin and uncleanness, with Jeremiah asking how long such must go on? (13:21-23, 24-27; 15:13-14; 16:10-13, 16-18; 17:1-4, 9-10, 11).

Jeremiah is particularly reflective about the nature of sin and how it works in individuals and in the nation as a whole. The depth to which sin goes, also its scope, taxes the prophet's understanding to the limits. Israel's abandonment of her God is something other nations would not think of (2:11), her rebellion greater than that of chaotic sea waters (5:22-23). People behave like instinct-driven animals (2:23-25; 5:7-8). Sin, however, is old, extending back to Israel's earliest generations (2:20; 7:22-26; 22:21; 32:30). Yet if past generations were bad—and they were (2:5; 16:19)—the buildup of sin over the years makes the present generation worse (16:12).

In his early preaching, Jeremiah affirms the long-standing belief that punishment for the father's sins will be meted out upon the children and grandchildren (2:5-9). But later he states, along with his younger contemporary Ezekiel, that each person must die for his own sin (31:29-30; cf. Ezekiel 18). A return to health and well-being has now become impossible (8:15, 22; 14:19; 30:12-15). It seems as if everyone is evil (5:4-5; 6:13 [= 8:10]; 9:4-5). Sin goes deep (2:22; 17:1). "The heart," says Jeremiah, "is deceitful above all things; . . . who can know it?" (17:9). Sinful people become hardened, intractable people; punishment has no effect upon them; they are without shame, and calls for them to repent go unheeded (2:30; 3:3; 5:3; 6:15 [= 8:12]). Refining or winnowing the Judahite people proves to be impossible (6:27-30; 15:5-9). Jeremiah says that they are unable to change their evil behavior (8:4-7; 13:23), which is to say that sin has an irreversible quality. Lustful urges cannot be given up (2:25), and people sink deeper into their sorry state of affairs. Those caught up in wrongdoing tend to be superficial and unknowing, both with respect to the intentions of others—also Yahweh—and about what they themselves are doing. They can be shortsighted, not knowing what their end will be (5:31). Jeremiah notes how cavalier the wicked are, how they vacillate and wander about aimlessly (2:36; 4:1; 31:22; cf. Hos 7:11). They do not lay things to heart—not even their land, which has been ravaged by war (12:11). Women are extravagant in their dress, not realizing that the "lovers" they attract care nothing for them and would willingly kill them (4:30; 30:14). Even confessions of sin now have no efficacy, since real change does not occur (14:7-9, 20-22). On one occasion, Jeremiah says that people know the ordinances of Yahweh but continue to break them (5:5); they talk of Yahweh even though he is distant from their hearts (12:2). And in one of his confessions, Jeremiah says that people cannot direct themselves in the right way; correction, therefore, must come from Yahweh (10:23-24).

Behind all the prophet's talk about sin and judgment lies a broken covenant. Jeremiah prayed that Yahweh, for his part, would not break the covenant (14:21); nevertheless, it was broken, and Israel bore the responsibility (2:20; 5:5; 11:10). In one of his celebrated Temple Oracles, five of the Ten Commandments forming the core of the Mosaic covenant are said to have been broken: those prohibiting stealing, murder, adultery, false oaths, and going after Baal or other gods, the most serious infraction of all (7:9; cf. 2:8; 5:2; 9:2-6; 16:11; 18:15). Other broken commands are those pertaining to idols (8:19; cf. 10:14 [= 51:17]), the Sabbath (17:19-27), and coveting the wife of one's neighbor (5:8).

Fortunately, evil cannot go on forever. Yahweh's anger is finally kindled to the point where he must defend his good name. Judgment is the result. People have brought it upon themselves (2:17, 19; 4:18); it is "the fruit of their doings" (17:10). Yahweh's judgment always carries with it a reason, and that reason is sin (1:16; 4:17; 5:6; 8:14; 13:22; 30:14-15).

The exile, however, will offer a door of hope for the covenant people. Once it is over, people will confess Yahweh not as the one who delivered Israel from Egypt but as the one who delivered Israel from the north country and other places to which they were dispersed (16:14-15; 23:7-8). Jeremiah thus looks ahead to a new day and a new knowledge of Yahweh (16:19-21).

In the midst of Jeremiah's personal laments are two communal laments (14:2-6, 17-19b), two communal confessions and petitions (14:7-9, 19c-22), and two rejections of mediation by the prophet (14:10-16; 15:1-4). They were spoken in connection with a severe drought that Judah was experiencing. With the land in shambles after foreign invasions, who will stop to inquire after Jerusalem's welfare? Yahweh says:

> For who will have pity upon you, Jerusalem,
>   and who will condole with you?
> And who will turn aside to ask
>   after your well-being?
> You, you abandoned me . . .
>   backward you went away.
> So I stretched out my hand against you and destroyed you.
>   I was weary of relenting.
> I winnowed them with a fork
>   in the gates of the land.
> I made childless, I killed my people;
>   from their ways they did not turn back.
> Their widows became more numerous to me

than the sand of the sea.
I brought to them—upon the mother of the young man—
a devastator at noonday.
I let fall upon her suddenly
agitation and terrors.
The one who bore seven languished,
her throat choked.
Her sun went down while it was yet day;
she was shamed and disgraced.
And the rest of them to the sword I will give
before their enemies.

(Jer 15:5-9)

On a more personal level is a psalm cursing the man who trusts in others but turns away from Yahweh. He will become like a juniper in the wilderness, and will not live to see the later good that will come. The one trusting in Yahweh is like a tree transplanted by water; he will not fear when the heat comes, for his leaves will remain green and he will continue to bear fruit (17:5-8).

Jeremiah is told that he himself may not marry and have children (16:1-4). Because of the perilous times, he must also absent himself from mourning feasts and feasts more joyful in nature (16:5-7, 8-9). Jeremiah calls for a more rigorous Sabbath observance, saying that keeping the Sabbath is life (17:19-27). From a visit to the potter's shop, Jeremiah learns that Yahweh can reshape nations in the same way a potter reshapes vessels of clay. In the case of Judah and Jerusalem, Yahweh is shaping evil against them. But things could go the other way if people turned from their evil (18:1-12). In another oracle, Yahweh says he will scatter the people like the east wind, showing them his back, not his face (18:13-17). Resorting once again to imagery from the potter's shop, Jeremiah likens Judah to a broken decanter because of its idolatrous ways, the most heinous of which was the sacrificing of children in the Ben Hinnom Valley (19:1-13). A summary of this message, given subsequently in the temple courtyard, so angered Pashhur the priest that he put Jeremiah in stocks for the night. When released the next morning, Jeremiah had harsh words of judgment for Pashhur, extending also to include his family and friends (19:14—20:6).

Jeremiah had particularly sharp words for Judah's kings and prophets, some of which were collected in an appendix to the First Edition (chapters 21-23). Kings are judged here because they do not practice justice and righteousness, do not give aid to the poor, and do not rescue the weak from oppressors (21:12; 22:3-5, 15-17). Jehoiakim spends lavishly on buildings for himself, but neglects the weightier matters of justice and righteousness—a complete misunderstanding of his office and what it requires of him (22:13-17). "Lebanon South" will therefore be destroyed by the enemy (22:6-9, 20-23). Jeremiah echoes Deuteronomy's concern for justice and for giving aid to the poor (2:34; 5:28; 7:5-7). Jeremiah utters a lament for Jehoahaz (22:10-12), but Jehoiakim gets a "non-lament" (22:18-19). Jehoiachin is lamented when taken off to Babylon in 597 B.C.E. (22:24-30). The message to Zedekiah is that he and Jerusalem will be given into the hands of Nebuchadnezzar, king of Babylon (21:1-7). The people, for their part, are presented with the way of life and the way of death. The way of life is leaving the city and surrendering to the enemy; the way of death is remaining in the city, and dying by sword, famine, or pestilence (21:8-10). Zedekiah receives the same dreadful message on later occasions (34:1-7; 37:3-11, 17-21; 38:14-28), although in 38:14-28 he is told that he too could save his life by surrendering to the enemy. The king-prophet collection closes with a woe oracle against the shepherds (kings) who have scattered the sheep of Yahweh's pasture. But Yahweh says that after these shepherds are attended to, he will raise up shepherds who will do the job right (23:1-4). Following is a messianic oracle promising a righteous branch for David who will do justice and righteousness in the land (23:5-6; cf. 33:14-16). His name will be "Yahweh Is Our Righteousness," a deliberate play on and reversal of the name "Zedekiah," which means "My Righteousness Is Yahweh." The future king will be a complete turnaround from Zedekiah, embodying the precious commodity of righteousness, which the present king does not.

Prophets are judged because of adultery, lying, and prophesying by Baal (5:31; 14:14; 20:6; 23:9-12, 13-15; 29:23, 24-32), also for preaching "peace, peace, when there is no peace" (6:14; 8:11). From Jeremiah's point of view, prophets delivering a peaceful message have not stood in the divine council; they are messengers who run without being sent (23:18, 21-22; 29:31). The word of Yahweh is not in them (5:13); their dreams are nothing but figments of their own imagination (23:16-17, 25-32). Lies building on lies become self-reinforcing, as these prophets must resort to "stealing" oracles from one another (23:30). "Burdens" (that is, oracles) are contrived, and Yahweh says the prophets themselves are "burdens" that he will cast off (23:33-40).

After the capture of Jerusalem in 597 B.C.E. and the departure of leading citizens to Babylon, Jeremiah preached that the future lay with the exiles, not with the people remaining in Judah. In his vision of the two baskets of figs in chapter 24, he said that the good figs were Judahites who had gone to Babylon; the rotten figs were Judahites left behind in the land. In letters sent to the exiles in Babylon (29:1-28), Yahweh's message to the exiles was this:

> Build houses and live in them; and plant gardens and eat their fruit. Take wives and beget sons and daughters, and take for your sons wives, and your daughters give to husbands, and let them bear sons and daughters. Yes, multiply there, and do not decrease. And seek the welfare of the city where I have exiled you, and pray on its behalf to Yahweh, for in its welfare will be welfare for you. (Jer 29:5-7; cf. v. 28)

Nebuchadnezzar of Babylon had been appointed Yahweh's servant for a time, and nations of the world would have to serve him. Judah would be brought to ruin, but then after seventy years of Babylonian rule, Yahweh would reckon with Babylon for its iniquity (25:1-14; 27:1-22; 28:1-17). Miscellaneous oracles against Judah and the nations follow (25:30-31, 32-33, 34-38), which are to be dated sometime after 605 B.C.E.

Jeremiah was called to be a prophet to the nations (1:5, 10), and in this capacity he was appointed Yahweh's cupbearer to serve up the wine of wrath to nations of the world (25:15-29). Judah would be judged first, then the other nations (25:28-29). Specific oracles were spoken against nine nations: Egypt (46:2-28); the Philistines (47:1-7); Moab (48:1-47); Ammon (49:1-6); Edom (49:7-22); Damascus (49:23-27); Kedar and the desert tribes (49:28-33); Elam (49:34-39); and Babylon (50:1—51:58). With all of these nations Yahweh had no covenant, but they merited punishment because of their wickedness, hubris, and idol worship (25:31; 50:31-32, 38; 51:47, 52). Some prophecies, or add-on prophecies not from Jeremiah, state that Babylon "sinned" against Yahweh (50:14), that its land was "filled with guilt" (51:5), and that Yahweh would repay this nation for destruction done to his temple (50:28; 51:11). Later, when their punishment is over, Yahweh will have compassion on all these nations except Babylon, at which time they will be reinhabited (46:26; cf. 12:14-17) and their fortunes restored (48:47; 49:6, 39). Jeremiah also looks to the day when enemy nations will learn the ways of Yahweh and swear by his name (12:16).

In the Book of Restoration, a separate collection in the larger book of Jeremiah, a number of largely hopeful oracles and other prophetic utterances look ahead to Judah's restoration after the exile is over (chapters 30–33). Jeremiah in his call was designated not only "to uproot and break down" but also "to build up and to plant" (1:10). The poetic core of this collection contains judgment oracles combined with oracles of hope, and in the latter portion laments combined with words of comfort and promise (30:5—31:22). Some oracles of hope may have been directed to northern Israelites exiled to Assyria, in which case they would have been uttered early in Jeremiah's career. These exiles are now called to return to Zion (31:4-6, 7-9; cf. 3:12-14).

An oracle on Jacob's time of distress (30:5-7) is joined to an oracle telling Jacob not to be afraid (30:10-11); Judah's incurable blow (30:12-15) is joined to an oracle saying that Yahweh will heal Judah's wounds (30:16-17). At the center of this well-crafted structure is an oracle about the rebuilding of Jerusalem (30:18-22); a formula restating the covenant (30:22); Yahweh's desert storm (30:23-24; cf. 23:19-20); another formula restating the covenant (31:1); and three hope oracles about Israel finding grace in the wilderness, Yahweh returning a remnant of Israel, and the One who scattered Israel now acting to gather her (31:2-14). Then a lament about Rachel weeping over her sons (31:15) is joined to an oracle telling Rachel to weep no more (31:16-17); and a lament of Ephraim rocking in grief (31:18-19) is joined to an oracle stating that Yahweh still remembers Ephraim and yearns for him (31:20). The core concludes with a word telling exiles departing for Babylon to return to their cities (31:21-22).

A supplement to this core with the refrain "Look, days are coming" affirms that Israel's future will have both continuity and discontinuity with the past (31:23-40). In the first oracle, Yahweh promises that once again people will bless the holy mountain, that is, Jerusalem (31:23-26). Then follows a cluster of three oracles: (1) a promise of future sowing of the seed of humans and the seed of beasts in a united Israel-Judah; (2) a promise of population growth and restoration of the land, complete with new plantings and new buildings; and (3) a divine oracle stating that people will no longer speak the old proverb about the fathers eating sour grapes and the children's teeth being set on edge, for each person will die for his own sin (31:27-30).

Then comes the most important message of all from Jeremiah: Yahweh promises to make a new covenant with the house of Israel and the house of Judah. It will not be like the old covenant, which the people broke. This new covenant will mark a new beginning in the divine-human relationship, because (1) it is given without conditions; (2) it will be written on the hearts of people, in a way that the Sinai covenant was not; and (3) it will be grounded in a wholly new act of divine grace, that is, the forgiveness of sins (31:31-34). Then come three poetic oracles affirming Yahweh's ongoing covenants with all creation and with Israel (31:35, 36, 37), the latter appearing to reaffirm the covenant made with Abraham. A final "Look, days are coming" oracle in the supplement says that the measuring line will once again go out in Jerusalem, and the city will be rebuilt (31:38-40).

Jeremiah makes a forcible statement about the nation's return by buying a field in his home village of Anathoth. The transaction took place when Jerusalem was under siege and would soon fall to the Babylonians (chapter 32). The word here was that fields would one day be bought and sold again in the land (32:15, 42-44). Included in the chapter are two oracles of judgment against Jerusalem (32:26-29, 30-35) and an oracle promising an "eternal covenant" for the future (32:36-41), which is simply the "new covenant" going by another name. It underlines the unconditional and eternal nature of the covenant that will replace the broken Sinai covenant.

Chapter 33 contains more preaching on restoration and ongoing covenants. Yahweh says in the opening oracle:

Thus said Yahweh who made it,
   Yahweh who formed it to establish it.
     Yahweh is his name.
Call to me and I will answer you,
   and let me tell you great things and hidden things
     you have not known.

                         (Jer 33:2-3)

A second oracle promises a healed city of Jerusalem and a healed people. Replacing the stench of rotting corpses will be the sweet smell of peace and security (33:4-9). Two following oracles promise the return of joyful sounds to Jerusalem and Judah's cities (33:10-11), and the return of pastureland in which shepherds will be seen resting their flocks (33:12-13). The oracle about a righteous Davidic king in a righteous city recasts slightly the messianic oracle of 23:5-6 (33:14-16). Remaining oracles reaffirm existing covenants. The Davidic and Levitical lines will continue (33:17-18, 19-22), and a final oracle states that the seed of Jacob (Israel) and the seed of David (Judah) can be counted on to continue (33:23-26).

Prose chapters following the Book of Restoration carry forth the covenant theme. Zedekiah and the people are severely censured for making a covenant providing liberty to male and female slaves, but then reneging on the covenant, taking the slaves back. Jeremiah thus proclaims to them a "liberty" to the sword, pestilence, and famine (34:8-22). Chapter 35 reports a commendation given earlier during the Jehoiakim years to the seminomadic Rechabites for remaining obedient to Jonadab son of Rechab, their father, who commanded them not to drink wine. The people of Judah and Jerusalem, by contrast, have been disobedient to commands given them by Yahweh.

During the final days leading up to the capture of Jerusalem and Israel's loss of nationhood, Jeremiah was unswerving in his prophecy that Jerusalem would be taken and the nation would fall (38:2-3). For this message, he endured much suffering. After the city was taken and exiles were lined up for the long trek to Babylon, Jeremiah was released and given the choice to go to Babylon or remain in the land. He hesitated briefly, but then decided to remain in the land (40:4-6). From this point on, Jeremiah's message was that the remnant should stay in the land, not go to Egypt, as many wanted to do (41:17-18; 42:1-22; 43:1-4).

But the remnant went to Egypt anyway, and after they arrived there, Jeremiah's message to the exiles was to abandon worship of the Queen of Heaven, also that Nebuchadnezzar would come to that land and their fate would be the same as those who held out in Jerusalem: sword, famine, disease, and captivity (43:8-13; 44:1-30).

Obadiah: Prophet against Edom

The brief superscription of the book of Obadiah gives us no background for this prophet, stating simply, "The vision of Obadiah" (1:1). Obadiah's vision—like that of Nahum—has a singular theme, that is, to announce Yahweh's judgment on Edom (= Esau), brother of Israel (= Jacob). Edom comprised the high plateau and rugged mountain country below the Dead Sea and east of the Arabah, from the river Zered in the north, 160 kilometers south to the Gulf of Aqaba. In early times, also after the fall of Judah, Edom occupied territory west of the Arabah Valley. An Edomite fortress has been identified at Umm el-Biyara, 300 meters up from the valley floor overlooking Petra. Down the center of Edom ran the King's Highway, an ancient caravan route from Damascus to Elath (Aqaba). Obadiah's prophecy fits into the period following Jerusalem's destruction in 586 B.C.E., when the Edomites became gleeful over Judah's fall (Ps 137:7; Ezek 25:12) and are reported to have aided the Babylonians in destroying the temple (1 Esd 4:45). Obadiah 1-8 parallels closely Jer 49:7, 9-10, 14-16, and opinions differ about dependence one way or the other. Obadiah 9-14, which rejoices over the fall of Jerusalem, has no parallel in Jeremiah and appears to postdate Jeremiah's Edom oracles.

In an opening oracle, Obadiah says the time has come for proud Edom to fall. Yahweh is calling the nations together to do battle against her, but it is Yahweh himself who will bring Edom down from her lofty perch (vv. 1-4). Hubris is blinding, for Edom knows not that it is headed for a fall. From Yahweh there is no safe retreat. Obadiah notes that thieves do not steal everything, only what they want; and grape-gatherers leave the gleanings, but Yahweh's pillage of Edom will be complete. Friends—perhaps allied Arab tribes—will abandon her (vv. 5-7). A Day of Yahweh is coming, when the wisdom for which Edom is known will be no more, because her wise men and mighty warriors will be destroyed. This will happen because of the violence done to brother Jacob (vv. 8-10). The end of the Edomite state is still controverted, but it appears to have come in the middle of the sixth century B.C.E., at the hands of Nabonidus.

Obadiah 11-14 censures Edom even more for standing aloof when foreigners (i.e., the Babylonians) entered Jerusalem and carried off its wealth. The prophet says:

But you should not have gloated over the day of your brother
    on the day of his misfortune.
You should not have rejoiced over the people of Judah
    on the day of their ruin.
You should not have boasted
    on the day of distress.
You should not have entered the gate of my people
    on the day of their calamity.
You should not have joined in the gloating over his disaster
    on the day of his calamity.
You should not have looted his goods
    on the day of his calamity.
You should not have stood at the crossings
    to cut off his fugitives.
You should not have handed over its survivors
    on the day of distress.

(Obad 12-14)

Obadiah then looks ahead to a Day of Yahweh when the evil deeds of nations will come back on their own heads (vv. 15-16). Mount Zion will escape, and Jacob will possess those who possessed him. The house of Jacob will be to the house of Edom like fire consuming stubble (vv. 17-18), and survivors there will not be. Finally, Obadiah looks ahead to the day when the exiles of Israel and Judah will return to repossess their land, and the kingdom shall be Yahweh's (vv. 19-21).

Ezekiel: Prophet of Yahweh's Glory

Ezekiel was a priest taken from Jerusalem to Babylon in the exile of 597 B.C.E. There he took up residence among the exiles at Chebar (1:1) and was happily married (24:16-18). In the fifth year of his exile, he received a vision of the "glory of Yahweh," which became the dominant theme of his preaching. In this vision, he saw a mighty wind coming out of the north, in the midst of which was the likeness of four living creatures (1:4-14). Beside them were four wheels and the likeness of a throne, said to be the likeness of Yahweh's glory (1:28b). The wheels were chariot wheels, about to spirit Yahweh's glory away from Jerusalem (1:15-20; chapters 10–11). Earlier, when Shiloh was destroyed and the ark was captured by the Philistines, Yahweh's glory had departed from Israel (1 Sam 4:21-22). This time the glory is seen rising from the cherubim to the threshold of the temple (10:4), then leaving the threshold to pause briefly at the East Gate (10:18-19), and then heading in an eastward direction. It is last seen resting on the Mount of Olives east of the city (11:23).

Ezekiel in his call is given a scroll of judgment to eat, which he finds to be sweet in his mouth (cf. Ps 119:103) but bitter when it enters his stomach (Ezek 2:8—3:15). Yahweh's word of judgment is known to have such an effect (Jer 15:16-18; Rev 10:8-11). Ezekiel learns, as other prophets had, that the people to whom he must preach will give him stiff opposition (3:4-11).

Ezekiel is made a watchman for Israel, responsible for sounding the alarm when danger is imminent (3:16-17). Four possible situations are envisioned. Yahweh says to the prophet:

> If I say to the wicked, "You shall surely die," and you give them no warning, or speak to warn the wicked from their wicked way, in order to save their life, those wicked persons shall die for their iniquity; but their blood I will require at your hand. But if you warn the wicked, and they do not turn from their wickedness, or from their wicked way, they shall die for their iniquity; but you will have saved your life. Again, if the righteous turn from their righteousness and commit iniquity, and I lay a stumbling block before them, they shall die; because you have not warned them, they shall die for their sin, and their righteous deeds that they have done shall not be remembered; but their blood I will require at your hand. If, however, you warn the righteous not to sin, and they do not sin, they shall surely live, because they took warning; and you will have saved your life. (Ezek 3:18-21)

In chapters 4–5 symbolic acts by the prophet depict siege, death, and exile. Israel's mountains and high places are doomed because of idol worship occurring there (chapter 6). Idolaters will die, and because of them, and also because of the remnant that will be spared, Yahweh says that people "will know that I am Yahweh," a phrase that occurs fifty-four times in Ezekiel. The end is in sight for the entire land (7:2; cf. Amos 8:2), and disaster will come on the heels of disaster (chapter 7). By a vision the prophet is then transported to the temple in Jerusalem, where he sees a host of abominations, even though Yahweh's glory at this time is still there (chapter 8). A carnage in Jerusalem will follow, with only the pious on whom the mark of a scribe is inscribed destined to be spared (chapter 9). Jerusalem's princes will meet up with the sword at Israel's border (11:1-12). While Ezekiel is still prophesying, one of these princes dies, and Ezekiel asks in alarm whether Yahweh intends to make a full end of the remnant (11:13). Yahweh answers that a restoration is planned, and to the remnant Yahweh will give one heart and a new spirit. The covenant also will be renewed among those who obey Yahweh's ordinances (11:14-21).

False prophets and prophetesses are slated for destruction, prophesying as they have about "peace, when there is no peace" (chapter 13; cf. Jer 6:14; 8:11). Elders given over to idolatry are also judged (chapter 14). Intercession will be of no avail; every person must answer to Yahweh for his or her own conduct. If Noah, Daniel, and Job were all present, they would deliver only their own lives by their righteousness (14:14, 20; cf. Jer 15:1). Jerusalem, says the prophet, is a useless vine that must be destroyed (chapter 15).

In chapter 16 Ezekiel gives an allegory of Jerusalem's history. Israel was born in the land of the Canaanites, her parents being of foreign origin: her father was an Amorite and her mother a Hittite. Abandoned on the day of her birth, she was found by Yahweh, who took pity on her, taking her when full grown to be his wife (16:1-14; cf. Hosea 2; Jer 2:2). But then his wife committed adultery with other lovers, provoking him to wrath and making punishment necessary (16:15-43). The allegory is extended so as to make Samaria an elder sister and Sodom a younger sister. Israel must bear the disgrace that came to both of these cities (16:44-52). But Yahweh will restore the fortunes of the disgraced women and will remember his covenant with Israel. It will be an eternal covenant, when Yahweh will forgive her sins (16:53-63). Ezekiel here follows the preaching of Jeremiah about a new and eternal covenant (Jer 31:31-34; 32:40).

With more vivid imagery, Ezekiel indicts the king of Judah—who, though unidentified, must be Zedekiah—for breaking his covenant with the king of Babylon, Nebuchadnezzar. The prophet predicts that Zedekiah will be taken to Babylon to die, which is what happened (chapter 17; cf. Jer 52:1-11). In breaking covenant with the king of Babylon, Judah broke the covenant with Yahweh, and punishment will therefore come from Yahweh (17:19-24).

According to Ezekiel, "the soul that sins shall die," which replaces the age-old retribution formula that the son dies for the iniquity of the father (chapter 18). Ezekiel sees this as a vindication of the justice of God, saying that Israel must get for itself a new heart and a new spirit (18:25-32). Chapter 19 is a lament in poetry over the princes (kings) of Israel, who were caught by enemies and exiled to Egypt and Babylon respectively. Israel now is without a ruler.

Another survey of Israel's past and future relationship with God is given, beginning with the exodus, continuing with Israel's rebellion in the wilderness, and concluding with the present sins of Jerusalem (chapters 20–22). Following is the allegory of the two sisters, Oholah, who is Samaria, and Oholibah, who is Jerusalem (chapter 23; cf. Jer 3:6-11). Oholah played the harlot and was given over to the Assyrians. Oholibah saw this, but went on to do even worse, defiling Yahweh's sanctuary and profaning his Sabbaths. She will therefore be given over to the Babylonians and others, and Yahweh will mete out the punishment reserved for women committing adultery.

Ezekiel gives an allegory of a rusty cauldron that is burned after being emptied of its bones and pieces of flesh so its filth may be consumed (24:1-14). Then Ezekiel's beloved wife dies, and Yahweh tells him not to mourn her. This will be a sign of Yahweh's profanation of the people's beloved sanctuary and the death of sons and daughters left behind in Jerusalem (24:15-27).

Oracles against seven foreign nations come forth from this prophet: Ammon (25:1-7), Moab (25:8-11), Edom (25:12-14), Philistia (25:15-17), Tyre (26:1—28:19), Sidon (28:20-26), and Egypt (29–32). Another prophecy against Edom comes later in chapter 35. Indictments against Tyre and Egypt are developed at length, Tyre probably because it was a giant trading and mercantile nation that exploited Judah to its own advantage, and Egypt because of its great wealth and the evils attending that wealth. The prophet utters a lament over Tyre (27:1-9), and another over the king of Tyre (28:11-19). A lament over the pharaoh is uttered in 32:1-8.

Ammon is judged because it scoffed at the profanation of Yahweh's sanctuary, Israel's land being made desolate, and people being taken into exile (25:3, 6). Moab is judged simply for saying that Judah was like any other nation (25:8). Edom and Philistia incur Yahweh's judgment because they acted vengefully against Judah (25:12, 15). The former was a brother to Israel, and the latter Israel's age-old enemy. Tyre is judged because it was gleeful that Jerusalem's gates were breached, allowing it to enter (26:2). The prince/king of Tyre is censured for being proud and for thinking himself as wise as a god (28:2-10, 17). Tyre and its king are indicted also because of unspecified iniquity and violence carried out in connection with the city's extensive trade (28:15-19). Sidon has been a thorn in the flesh of Israel, treating her with contempt (28:24). Egypt is judged mainly for being proud (30:6, 18; 31:10; 32:12), but also because of boastful lies (29:3, 9b) and wickedness (30:11), and for being a weak reed to Israel when help was needed (29:6-7). Egypt is nevertheless promised a future, but will only be restored as a lowly kingdom (29:13-16).

In chapters 33–48, the final portion of the book, are prophecies of restoration and renewal. Chapters 33–37 contrast past and future. Ezekiel is once again called to be a watchman, responsible for warning people, lest he himself be responsible (33:1-9; cf. 3:16-17). Then follows a word about the justice of God, in whose economy the way to life consists in repenting of one's sins (33:10-20; cf. 18:21-32). Ezekiel now gets word that Jerusalem has fallen, which breaks a period during which he was unable to speak (33:21-22; cf. 24:27). Ezekiel learns also that although people listen to him speak, they do not do what he says. But when Yahweh's word comes to pass, then people will know that a prophet has been among them (33:23-33).

Ezekiel prophesies against Israel's inept shepherds, making judgments also about the flock (34:1-25). Yahweh is introduced as the good shepherd (34:15-16), one who cares for his sheep, searches out the lost, and finds good pasture for the sheep. Yahweh promises a shepherd the likes of David who will rule over Israel in future days (34:23-24). Yahweh promises also to make with Israel a "covenant of peace," and in this new era he will bring upon the people "showers of blessing" (34:25-31). Following Edom's judgment (chapter 35) is promised a transformation of Israel—both its land and its people (chapter 36). Yahweh does this not for Israel's sake but for sake of his holy name, which Israel has profaned among the nations (36:22-23). Israel will be washed clean, and the promise is given once again that Israel will receive a new heart and a new spirit (36:26).

Ezekiel is much remembered for his vision of the Valley of the Dry Bones (chapter 37), in which he sees the whole house of Israel being restored. A king the likes of David will rule a united Israel and Judah. Ezekiel repeats Yahweh's promise of a "covenant of peace" and an "eternal covenant" with his people (37:26), which will be a witness to other nations that Yahweh has sanctified Israel and put his sanctuary in Israel's midst (37:28).

Chapter 38 contains the prophecy against Gog from Magog, which speaks of Yahweh's action against Israel's enemy and his final victory over this enemy (cf. Rev 20:8). Gog is leader of the forces that will launch a final assault on Yahweh's people, but in the end will be defeated.

The final chapters of Ezekiel's book contain a vision of the restored temple and the city in which the temple will reside (chapters 40–48). The temple is described with all its courts (chapters 40–42), and Ezekiel witnesses the return of Yahweh's glory (43:2-5). Chapters 43–46 set forth laws and ordinances for the temple (43:11), with boundaries and divisions of the land being dealt with in chapters 46–48. A stream of water will flow from below the threshold of the temple, an image picked up later in Joel 3:18 and Rev 22:1. The Levites will be assigned menial tasks because they fell into idolatry, and the Zadokite priests, who remained faithful to Yahweh, will be given full status at Yahweh's altar (44:10-16). Then in a climactic word with which the book closes, the prophet says that the name of Jerusalem will henceforth be "Yahweh is there" (48:35).

Second Isaiah: Prophet of the Incomparability of Yahweh

Second Isaiah is the name given to an unknown prophet of the exile who is believed to stand behind the poetry in Isaiah 40–66, although many scholars believe this prophet was responsible only for chapters 40–55; chapters 56–66, in their view, emanate from a postexilic prophet, also unknown, who is given the name Third Isaiah. The background for chapters 40–55 is Babylon, whereas the background for chapters 56–66 is Jerusalem.

The language and themes of chapters 40–66 are different from those of chapters 1–39, e.g., God as Creator and Redeemer and the portrait of the Servant in chapters 40–55, compared to the portrait of the Messiah in 9:1-6 and 11:1-9. The style of chapters 40–66 is more flowing than the terse style of Isaiah of Jerusalem. Second Isaiah's impassioned rhetoric rivals that of any Old Testament prophet. He joyfully anticipates Israel's restoration in the land after a long exile in Babylon, and accompanying this hope is acclaim for the incomparable Yahweh, Creator of heaven and earth and Israel's Redeemer. Second Isaiah's three major motifs are creation, redemption, and history. Yahweh is the living God, mighty in word and deed, totally unlike the gods of the nations and their inert idols, who are nothing and can do nothing (41:23-24, 28-29).

Yahweh is now speaking comfort to his people, tenderly saying that her warfare is ended and her iniquity pardoned. Full payment has been exacted for all her sins (40:1-2). The cry is for a road straight and level in the wilderness on which Yahweh will lead exiles to their homeland (40:3-5; 42:16; 45:2; 49:11). The prophet's collected work begins:

A voice cries:
In the wilderness prepare the way of Yahweh;
    make straight in the desert a highway for our God.
Every valley shall be lifted up
    and every mountain and hill be made low.
The uneven ground shall become level
    and the rough places a plain.
For the glory of Yahweh shall be revealed,
    and all flesh shall see it together.
For the mouth of Yahweh has spoken.
                                    (Isa 40:3-5)

All flesh is grass, but the word of God stands forever (40:6-8). The prophet is told to get up on a high mountain and preach good tidings to Jerusalem and the cities of Judah. Israel's God comes with might and will feed his flock like a shepherd (40:9-11).

The theme of 40:12-31 is the incomparable Yahweh, which recurs throughout the oracles of chapters 40–48. Yahweh alone is God, the first and the last; there is no other. As Creator of heaven and earth (40:12-14), he cannot be compared to the idols, which are beautifully crafted but unable to move (40:18-20). This God directs all affairs on earth because he is great in might and strong in power (40:21-26). Yahweh does not faint or grow weary (40:28), empowering with the same qualities all who wait for him. The prophet says:

He gives power to the faint
    and strengthens the powerless.
Even youths will faint and be weary,
    and young men will fall exhausted.
But those who wait for Yahweh shall renew their strength;
    they shall mount up with wings like eagles.
They shall run and not be weary;
    they shall walk and not faint.
                                    (Isa 40:29-31)

Nations are told to remain silent in a courtroom where Yahweh will render judgment (41:1). Cyrus is the rising star in the east, with victory meeting him at every step (41:2-3; cf. 44:28; 45:1). But other nations and their gods are put on notice that Yahweh is the first and last (41:4; 44:6; 48:12) and is in firm control of world history. The nations have only idols, which cannot move (41:5-7). Israel is Yahweh's servant, chosen and called by him. She is told in these unsettled times not to fear, since Yahweh is with her and will help her. Those warring against her will become nothing. Yahweh is Israel's redeemer, the Holy One of Israel (41:8-14). Israel will thresh and winnow the enemy (41:15-16).

The prophet can therefore give comfort and assurance to Israel. Rivers, streams, and trees in the desert will bear witness to the creative and transformative power of Israel's Holy One (41:17-20). The prophet returns to the court scene, where the nations and their idols are pressed to explain former things or latter things. But they can do neither, for they are nothing (41:21-24). The nations will therefore be judged by the one Yahweh, who is stirring up one from the north, that is, Cyrus (41:25-29).

Yahweh describes his servant as one who has a mission to carry out in the world. The servant here may be an individual, as in chapter 53, and not the nation Israel. Yahweh says:

> Behold my servant, whom I uphold,
>   my chosen, in whom my soul delights.
> I have put my spirit upon him;
>   he will bring forth justice to the nations.
> He will not cry or lift up his voice
>   or make it heard in the street.
> A bruised reed he will not break,
>   and a dimly burning wick he will not quench;
>   he will faithfully bring forth justice.
> He will not grow faint or be crushed
>   until he has established justice in the earth,
>   and the coastlands wait for his law.
>
> (Isa 42:1-4)

Yahweh intends for his servant to be a "light to the nations" (42:6; 49:6; cf. 51:4; 60:1-3), which will open the eyes of the blind and release from prison those who dwell in darkness (42:7; cf. 61:1). All will be released from their bondage. Yahweh has new things to declare, and before they come to pass, he will tell his servant about them (42:9). New things call for a new song, and so all creation and all peoples will join in praising Yahweh (42:10-13). Yahweh has kept silent for a long while, but now he will cry out in full voice. Judgment and salvation will occur simultaneously, and shamed will be those who say to their images, "You are our gods" (42:14-17).

Yahweh interrupts his felicitous word with a censure and judgment on his servant. This servant, who is to be a light to the nations, is said to be deaf and blind (42:18-25). So Yahweh must first turn the servant's darkness into light before the promised redemption can be carried out.

But the future holds great promise, for Yahweh says he has created Israel, redeemed her, and called her by name. He says, "You are mine" (43:1). Yahweh will be with Israel in the trials ahead, for he loves Israel, and he will give other nations as ransom (to Cyrus) for her (43:2-4). Exiles will be brought home from distant places (43:5-7). The nations are again summoned into court to act as witnesses (43:8-9), but they cannot act as witnesses, as they know nothing of former things—also nothing about things to come (cf. 41:22-24). So Yahweh says that the people of Israel will be his witnesses. Yahweh alone is God; there is no other (43:10-13).

Yahweh is preparing to redeem Israel from its Babylonian captivity. The prophet recalls the deliverance from Egypt through the sea, but Israel is told here not to remember former things, as Yahweh is about to perform something infinitely greater. He will make a way—rivers of water, if you will—in the wilderness (43:14-21). But Israel must remember her sinful behavior. Nevertheless, Yahweh will blot out her sins (43:22-28; cf. Jer 31:34).

Reminding Israel again that he is the one who created her, Yahweh promises fertility to the land and his Spirit upon her descendants (44:1-4; cf. Joel 2:28). New people, perhaps foreigners, will be heard saying that they belong to Yahweh as a result of this Spirit's outpouring (44:5; cf. Rom 8:14-17). Yahweh repeats that he is the first and the last; there is no god besides him (44:6-8). Idols and their makers are disparaged; the crafted wonders are nothing (44:9-20). Israel is told again to remember that Yahweh created her and has forgiven her sins. So Israel must return to him, which will cause all creation to sing over Yahweh's redemption (44:21-23).

Yahweh has selected Cyrus as his shepherd. Jerusalem will be rebuilt, and the temple foundations will be laid (44:24-28). Cyrus, as Yahweh's anointed, will subdue the nations and open doors that cannot be closed. Yahweh will go before him; that is, Yahweh will be in the lead, and Cyrus will follow. Cyrus may not know Yahweh, but people from east to west will know that Yahweh is God (45:1-8). People may wonder why Yahweh is bringing deliverance by a foreign ruler, evoking from the prophet the image of a potter, as in Jer 18:1-11. The prophet says:

> Woe to him who strives with his Maker,
>   a vessel with him who formed the earth.
> Does the clay say to him who fashions it, "What are you making?"
>   or "Your work has no handles"?
> Woe to him who says to a father, "What are you begetting?"
>   or to a woman, "With what are you in labor?"
> Thus said Yahweh,
>   the Holy One of Israel, and his Maker:
> Will you ask me of things to come about my children,
>   or command me about the work of my hands?
> I made the earth
>   and created humans upon it.
> It was my hands that stretched out the heavens,
>   and I commanded all their host.
> I have aroused him in righteousness,
>   and I will make straight all his ways.
> He shall build my city
>   and set my exiles free.
> Not for price or reward,
>   said Yahweh of hosts.
>
> (Isa 45:9-13)

A conversion of the nations will follow (45:14-25). They will say, "God is with you only, and there is no other" (45:14). Yahweh has sworn, "To me every knee shall bow, every tongue shall swear" (45:23; cf. Rom 14:11; Phil 2:10-11).

The nations' gods and their idols will fall; Yahweh will bring forth salvation (46:1-13). He has carried Israel from birth and will do the same to old age. Beautiful idols cannot move, having to stand where they are put or needing to be carried on someone's shoulder (46:6-7). If one cries to them, they do not answer or save from trouble. Israel is to remember that Yahweh is God, and there is no other. He will accomplish what he sets out to do, and it will happen speedily (46:8-13).

Second Isaiah speaks a mocking oracle against Virgin Babylon, who must now come down to sit in the dust (chapter 47; cf. Jer 13:18). Yahweh used her to punish Israel, but she mistakenly thought she would be mistress of the kingdoms forever. Not so. Yahweh knows her wickedness, and disaster will come upon her. Her diviners will fail her; none will come to save.

The prophet turns once again to the unique relationship between Yahweh and Israel. But all has not gone well, for which reason Israel's rebelliousness draws from Yahweh another rebuke (48:1-13). Yahweh anticipated her rebelliousness long ago (cf. Deut 31:27). But now Yahweh has new things to declare before they happen, hidden things that people have not known (48:6-8; cf. Jer 33:3). For his own sake he has refined Israel and says, "My glory I will not give to another" (48:11). Israel is thus called to hearken to the God who laid the foundation of the earth and spread out the heavens (48:12-13).

The mission of Cyrus is again told to Israel (48:14-16). Yahweh loves Cyrus, and he will perform his purpose regarding Babylon. Yahweh is Israel's teacher, and had Israel heeded Yahweh's commandments (cf. Ps 81:13), her "peace would have been like a river," not like an unpredictable waterbed that is dry part of the year (48:17-19; 66:12). Exiles are now bid to flee Babylon (48:20-22; cf. Jer 50:8, 28; 51:6, 9); Yahweh has redeemed her. This will mean peace and well-being. "There is no peace," says Yahweh, "for the wicked" (48:22; 57:21).

Chapters 49–55 of Second Isaiah speak about Israel's redemption. In 49:1-6, the servant speaks, telling the nations that Yahweh called him from the womb. The servant, again appearing here to be an individual, thinks that he has labored in vain (49:4). But Yahweh says it is no light matter to receive such a high calling, for he is to be a light to the nations that Yahweh's salvation may reach to the end of the earth (49:6). Yahweh says that nations will come and pay homage to him who has chosen Israel (49:7). Then Yahweh promises Israel the dawn of salvation, which will be a new exodus and a return of the exiles. All creation will be called upon to sing for joy, for Yahweh has comforted his people (49:8-13). Zion is downcast, thinking Yahweh has forgotten her (49:14). But Yahweh answers:

> Can a woman forget her nursing child
>   or show no compassion for the child of her womb?
> Even these may forget,
>   yet I will not forget you.
>
> (Isa 49:15)

Nor has Yahweh forgotten the walls of Jerusalem; he says that builders will outstrip the destroyers. Exiles returning from every direction shall repopulate the city and will be as precious jewels to Yahweh (49:17-18). So many will be the returnees that the place will be too small for them

(49:19-21). Yahweh will raise a banner to the nations, and Israel's children will return home. Israel's enemies shall be brought low (49:22-26).

Yahweh asks Israel about her bill of divorce (50:1), but the question is rhetorical. She does not have one, which means that her break with Yahweh was a separation, a serious one to be sure (cf. Jer 3:1), but not a divorce. Nor did Yahweh sell Israel into permanent slavery. The exile was due to her transgressions, but Yahweh's hand is not so short that it cannot redeem (50:2-3).

The servant in 50:4-9 is Yahweh's disciple, taught to speak in timely fashion and bear the suffering of those persecuting and insulting him. Enemies of the servant will wear out in the end, for Yahweh is present to help his servant (50:9). The servant has discovered that the way to life consists in trusting in the name of Yahweh. Those who kindle fires end up in torment (50:10-11).

In 51:1-11 Israel is told again to reflect on the past in pursuing her future deliverance—to recall Abraham and Sarah and the exodus from Egypt. In this oracle, Second Isaiah combines Yahweh's saving history with an ancient chaos-dragon myth, calling for a new redemptive act that will restore Israel to Zion. Yahweh is addressed:

> Awake, awake, put on strength,
>   O arm of Yahweh.
> Awake, as in days of old,
>   the generations of long ago.
> Was it not you who cut Rahab in pieces,
>   who pierced the dragon?
> Was it not you who dried up the sea,
>   the waters of the great deep;
> who made the depths of the sea a way
>   for the redeemed to cross over?
> So the ransomed of Yahweh shall return
>   and come to Zion with singing.
> Everlasting joy shall be upon their heads;
>   they shall obtain joy and gladness,
>   and sorrow and sighing shall flee away.
>
>   (Isa 51:9-11)

Yahweh will comfort Israel, but Israel must not forget that Yahweh is Creator of heaven and earth (51:12-16; cf. 51:3). Those bowed down in prison will speedily be released, and Yahweh will say to Zion, "You are my people." Jerusalem must awake and stand up. She drank Yahweh's cup of wrath, and no one was able to aid her helpless condition. But now Yahweh has taken this cup from her, and she will drink it no more. It will be passed instead to her tormentors (51:17-23).

In a following oracle, Second Isaiah repeats the call for Zion to awake and put on strength, for she is captive no longer (52:1-2). Yahweh will pay no ransom to Babylon (52:3-6). In a much-loved passage, the prophet says that Yahweh will now be King in Zion:

> How beautiful upon the mountains
>   are the feet of one who brings good news,
> who announces peace, who brings news of good,
>   who announces salvation,
> who says to Zion,
>   "Your God reigns."
> Listen, your watchmen lift up their voices;
>   together they sing for joy.
> For eye to eye they see
>   the return of Yahweh to Zion.
> Break forth together into singing,
>   you waste places of Jerusalem.
> For Yahweh has comforted his people;
>   he has redeemed Jerusalem.
>
> (Isa 52:7-9)

Exiles are bid to leave Babylon and rid themselves of uncleanness, but not in haste, as was the case when the Israelites left Egypt (Exod 12:33; Deut 16:3). This return will be peaceful. Yahweh will go before Israel and will also be her rear guard. It will be a new exodus (52:11-12).

Then follows the moving prophecy of Yahweh's suffering servant (52:13—53:12), which the Christian church has taken to be fulfilled in the person of Jesus. The servant here is not named, only adding to the difficulty of identifying the servant throughout Second Isaiah. In some passages (41:8-9; 43:10; 44:1-2, 21-22; 45:4), the servant is clearly corporate Israel, whereas in others (42:1-4; 49:1-6; 50:4-9?), he appears just as clearly to be an individual. What we seem to have are two servant figures: (1) "the servant Israel," who is the weak, sinful community of exiles in need of constant admonishment to trust Yahweh; and (2) "the servant of Yahweh," who is an extraordinary individual—a prophet, perhaps—seen to be guiltless and sinless, and despite his intense suffering, one who shows an unshakable trust in God. The servant here, though marred in appearance, in the end will prosper and be exalted (52:13-14; 53:2-3, 12). He bears not his own sins but the sins of others, for whom his suffering will bring healing (53:4-12).

The oracle in chapter 54 sings over Israel's consolation (54:1). Once the barren one, Israel will now grow and multiply, making necessary an enlargement of Zion (54:2-3). She will no longer be shamed, because her Maker is again her husband. The marriage has been restored: Yahweh has called back a wife who was cast off (54:4-8). Yahweh says:

> For a brief moment I forsook you,
>   but with great compassion I will gather you.
> In overflowing wrath for a moment,
>   I hid my face from you.
> But with everlasting love I will have compassion on you,
>   says Yahweh, your Redeemer.
>
> (Isa 54:7-8)

Yahweh promises Israel a covenant of peace, as sure as the covenant promised to Noah (54:9-10). Promised also to people who have been tossed about and left uncomforted is a new, glorious, and secure Jerusalem (54:11-17).

The first portion of Second Isaiah's prophecy is climactically ended with the prophet exclaiming over Yahweh's grace to Israel (chapter 55). A lavish banquet is being prepared, and Israel is invited to come and eat without cost. Dining at Yahweh's table will be infinitely better than spending money on what is not bread (55:1-2). In coming to Yahweh, Israel will live, and Yahweh will make with her an eternal covenant (55:3; cf. Jer 32:40). But Israel must come in repentance:

> Seek Yahweh while he may be found;
>   call upon him while he is near.
> Let the wicked forsake his way,
>   and the unrighteous man his thoughts.
> Let him return to Yahweh, that he may have mercy on him,
>   and to our God, for he will abundantly pardon.
> For my thoughts are not your thoughts;
>   neither are your ways my ways, says Yahweh.
> For as the heavens are higher than the earth,
>   so are my ways higher than your ways
>   and my thoughts than your thoughts.
>
> (Isa 55:6-9)

Yahweh is confident about the word going forth from his mouth. He says:

> For as the rain and the snow come down from heaven
> and do not return there, but water the earth,
> making it bring forth and sprout,
> giving seed to the sower and bread to the eater,
> so shall my word be that goes forth from my mouth;
> it shall not return to me empty,
> but it shall accomplish that which I purpose
> and prosper in the thing for which I sent it.
>
> (Isa 55:10-11)

Israel shall go forth from her exile in joy and peace, with the mountains, hills, and trees singing in triumphant chorus before her (55:12-13).

In chapters 56–66 the buoyant optimism of Second Isaiah gives way to a more realistic picture of life in Jerusalem after 538 B.C.E., when the first wave of exiles had returned under Sheshbazzar and were now faced with the monumental tasks of rebuilding a ruined city, a ruined temple, and a ruined Judah. The temple had not yet been rebuilt (66:1), putting a *terminus ad quem* of 515 B.C.E. on these oracles. In this year the rebuilt temple was dedicated; in 520 B.C.E. Haggai was urging people to get on with the rebuilding. A mood of pessimism pervades many of these oracles, dealing as they do with down-to-earth problems of rank wickedness, bloodshed, miscarriages of justice, syncretistic worship, fasting, Sabbath observance, and leaders who are blind, greedy, and drunk on wine. But interspersed with indictments are words of penitence, confession, and pleas for mercy.

This prophet begins by calling on people to do justice and righteousness, for then Yahweh's salvation will come speedily. Blessing will come also upon those who keep the Sabbath and refrain from evil (56:1-2). Eunuchs and foreigners will now be permitted temple access if they keep the Sabbath and hold fast to the covenant (56:3-8), overriding the exclusions of Deut 23:1-8. The prophet says that Yahweh's house shall be a house of prayer for all peoples (56:7; cf. Mark 11:17). But the community struggling for rebirth is plagued by leaders who are blind, ignorant, lazy, greedy, and continually drunk on wine (56:9-12).

The prophet addresses the problem of false worship; syncretistic practices like those that occurred in the time of Jeremiah are again rife (57:3-10; cf. Jer 2:20; 7:31; 19:4-5). The current righteousness is a bogus righteousness, supported by idol worship. Only those who take refuge in Yahweh will possess the land and inherit Yahweh's holy mountain (57:11-13). The prophet echoes 40:3-5 in calling for a way of Yahweh to be prepared. Here, however, it is not a highway in the desert but a way in which the contrite and humble will walk peaceably with Yahweh, and the restless wicked will not be brought along (57:14-21).

The prophet notes that people are worshiping with fasting, but this does not please Yahweh, because with the fasting go oppression and quarreling (58:1-5). Yahweh wants a more elevated form of worship. He says:

> Is not this the fast that I choose:
>   to loose the bonds of injustice,
>   to undo the thongs of the yoke,
> to let the oppressed go free,
>   and to break every yoke?
> Is it not to share your bread with the hungry;
>   and bring the homeless poor into your house,
> when you see the naked, to cover them,
>   and not to hide yourself from your own kin?
> Then your light shall break forth like the dawn,
>   and your healing shall spring up quickly.
> Your vindication shall go before you;
>   the glory of Yahweh shall be your rear guard.
> Then shall you call, and Yahweh will answer;
>   you shall cry for help, and he will say, Here I am.
>
> (Isa 58:6-9)

If people do this, Yahweh will guide them and satisfy them with good things. Their bones will be made strong, and their ruins, about which they are so much concerned, will be rebuilt (58:10-12). People must also keep the Sabbath, and Yahweh will reward them with bounty (58:13-14).

The prophet ticks off a litany of wicked deeds that have separated people from God. The problem is not Yahweh's inability to save (59:1-21). Hands are defiled with blood; people speak lies; there are miscarriages of justice in the courts, with the result that the way of peace and justice is not pursued (59:3-8). The prophet laments on behalf of the community, after which he confesses its sin to Yahweh (59:9-15a). But Yahweh is still displeased with a lack of justice, and because there is no one to intervene (59:15b-16a). Yahweh says that he must act himself to defeat his enemies and redeem those who have repented of wrongdoing in Zion (59:16b-20). He will then make a covenant with his people though the gift of his Spirit (59:21).

In the oracles of chapters 60–62, the prophet becomes almost lyrical in describing Zion's coming glory, a time when prosperity and peace will reign, when the city's inhabitants will be righteous, when good tidings will come to the poor and brokenhearted, and when nations of the world will see Zion's renewal. This future hope reaches a grand climax in the prophecy of a new heaven and a new earth (65:17-25).

In chapter 60 the prophet sees Yahweh's glory coming to Zion. For Israel, it will break the darkness covering the earth, and nations with their kings will come to see this glory:

> Arise, shine, for your light has come,
>   and the glory of Yahweh has risen upon you.
> For darkness shall cover the earth,
>   and thick darkness the peoples.
> But Yahweh will arise upon you,
>   and his glory will appear over you.
> Nations shall come to your light,
>   and kings to the brightness of your rising.
>
> (Isa 60:1-3)

Israel's dispersed will come to Zion, and with them will come the wealth of the nations (60:4-7). Nations east and west shall praise Yahweh and lay gifts on his altar (60:8-9). Foreigners will help rebuild Zion's walls, a sign of Yahweh's mercy, and the city's gates will be open day and night (60:10-11). Those who oppressed Israel will now call Zion the city of Yahweh, the Holy One of Israel (60:14). Israel too shall know Yahweh as her Savior and Redeemer, the Mighty One of Jacob (60:16). Prosperity and peace will reign in the new Zion, with violence no longer being heard (60:17-18). The prophet says:

> The sun shall no longer be your light by day,
>   nor for brightness shall the moon give light to you by night.
> But Yahweh will be your everlasting light,
>   and your God will be your glory.
> Your sun shall no more go down,
>   or your moon withdraw itself.
> For Yahweh will be your everlasting light,
>   and your days of mourning shall be ended.
> Your people shall all be righteous;
>   they shall possess the land forever.

They are the shoot that I planted, the work of my hands,
  so that I might be glorified.

(Isa 60:19-21)

Glad tidings now come to Zion from the prophet himself. He says:

The spirit of Yahweh God is upon me,
  because Yahweh has anointed me.
He has sent me to bring good news to the oppressed,
  to bind up the brokenhearted;
to proclaim liberty to the captives
  and release to the prisoners;
to proclaim the year of Yahweh's favor
  and the day of vengeance of our God,
    to comfort all who mourn;
to provide for those who mourn in Zion,
  to give them a garland instead of ashes,
the oil of gladness instead of mourning,
  the mantle of praise instead of a faint spirit,
that they may be called oaks of righteousness,
  the planting of Yahweh, to display his glory.

(Isa 61:1-3)

Verses 1-2 were later read by Jesus in his hometown synagogue in Nazareth (Luke 4:18-19).

The people of Zion shall be able to build up their ancient ruins, and foreigners will come to do the work. Zion shall thus have spiritual preeminence and material prosperity (61:4-7). The prophet reminds people that Yahweh loves justice and hates robbery and wrongdoing, and so he will make an eternal covenant with them in order that their descendants may be known as a people Yahweh has blessed (61:8-9). The prophet then sings a hymn of thanksgiving and praise to Yahweh, who has caused righteousness and praise to spring forth in the sight of all the nations (61:10-12).

The prophet cannot keep silent about the impact that all this will have on other nations. They shall see Yahweh's salvation of Jerusalem, which, instead of being called "Forsaken" or "Desolate," will be given the new name "Married," for now Yahweh delights in her (62:1-5). Her grain will no longer be food for her enemies, but people will eat and drink what they have labored for (62:6-9). Once again, the call for a "way prepared" is heard. Zion is told, "Behold, your salvation comes." Zion's people shall be called a holy people, the redeemed of Yahweh (62:10-12).

In chapter 63 we are introduced to a victorious conqueror coming forth from Edom, one who has judged the nations (63:1-6). The prophet then launches into a long intercessory prayer in which a familiar story is recounted (63:7—64:12). Yahweh has shown steadfast love toward Israel, has lifted up his people and carried them in days of old (63:7-9), but Israel rebelled, grieving his holy Spirit. Therefore Yahweh became her enemy and fought against her (63:10). Finally, Israel remembered the days of old and Moses, Yahweh's servant, and asked the right questions about the God of the exodus, who led Israel through the depths and the desert. In conclusion, it is affirmed that Yahweh led his people to make for himself a glorious name (63:11-14).

But then the prophet turns suddenly to the tragic conditions of the present, calling upon Yahweh to look down from heaven and see, and asking about Yahweh's zeal and might (63:15). After confessing Yahweh to be Israel's father and redeemer, the prophet lapses into pure lament, wondering why Yahweh hardens the heart of his people so that they do not fear him. He asks Yahweh to return to Israel (63:16-17). The prophet cites the temple in ruins and calls for nothing short of a universal theophany: would that Yahweh rend the heavens and descend to make known his name to his adversaries (63:18-19; 64:1-2). The prophet recalls theophanies of the past but realizes that Yahweh has been angered by Israel's sin. He wonders now if Israel will ever be saved (64:3-5). More confessions of sin and Yahweh's creative work are spoken, and the plea is made that Yahweh not be angry forever (64:6-9). The long prayer ends with the prophet asking whether Yahweh will keep silent, with Zion now a veritable wilderness and the temple lying in ruins (64:10-12).

Yahweh then speaks to his accessibility:

> I was ready to be sought out by those who did not ask,
>   to be found by those who did not seek me.
> I said, "Here I am, here I am,"
>   to a nation that did not call on my name.
> I held out my hands all day long
>   to a rebellious people
> who walk in a way that is not good,
>   following their own devices.
>
> (Isa 65:1-2)

People have provoked him continually by syncretistic worship, the smoke in his nostrils now being smoke of anger (65:3-5). Yahweh will not keep silent but will repay these and the fathers' iniquities (65:6-7). But for the sake of his servant, Yahweh will not destroy all his people but will bring forth descendants from Jacob (65:8-9). There is hope for those who have sought out Yahweh, but those forsaking Yahweh and forgetting his holy mountain will be given over to the sword (65:10-15). The one blessing himself in the land shall bless himself by the God of truth, because former troubles will be forgotten and hid from Yahweh's eyes (65:16).

Then comes the prophet's moving prophecy of new heavens and a new earth (65:17-25), in which "former things" (that is, the "former troubles" of v. 16b) will not be remembered. Yahweh will create a Jerusalem rejoicing, a felicitous event when sounds of weeping will no longer be heard, infants will not die a few days after birth, and men will live into old age. In a flight of imagination, the prophet says that the child shall live to be a hundred, and even the sinner will not be accursed until he reaches a hundred years of age. Covenant curses on house and vineyard will be reversed, with the builders of houses now able to inhabit them, and the planters of vineyards now able to enjoy their fruit. Whereas before Yahweh kept silent because people did not call upon him (65:1-2a; cf. 64:12b), now he will do them one better by answering before they call (v. 24).

The oracle's final verse (v. 25), which is an abridgment of Isa. 11:6-9, speaks of peace and restored harmony in Yahweh's new creation. The wolf and the lamb shall feed together, and the lion shall eat straw like the ox. Future time will be a return to primeval time (Genesis 2–3), but with the difference that the envisioned paradise will be not a new garden of Eden but a new Jerusalem. Yahweh says that the coming peace and harmony will exist on "my holy mountain," namely, Jerusalem.

This oracle becomes the prototype for the prophecy of a new heaven and a new earth by John the Evangelist in the Apocalypse (Rev 21:1— 22:5). But there the old creation is destroyed, which is not envisioned in this prophecy, where former things are only put out of mind. The prophet is speaking here about a transformation of the world as he knows it, of Jerusalem, once a city of wickedness, injustice, false worship, and ruin heaps, now being a city righteous and glorious.

In a final oracle, Yahweh says that heaven is his throne and the earth is his footstool, so what is this house the people intend to build for him? Yahweh looks rather for people who are humble and contrite in spirit (66:1-2). There is corruption in the cult, because when Yahweh called, people did not answer but instead did evil (66:3-4). Yahweh's voice of judgment therefore resounds from the temple (66:5-6). Nevertheless, a wonderful new Zion will be born, and people are called upon to rejoice in the abundance of its glory (66:7-11). Yahweh will extend peace to the city like a river, the wealth of the nations like an everflowing stream. As a mother comforts, so will Yahweh comfort Jerusalem, and indignation will be reserved for Yahweh's enemies (66:12-14). Yahweh is coming to judge the earth, with those entering the gardens and eating swine's flesh being brought to an end (66:15-17).

All nations will be gathered together to see Yahweh's glory; all will come to Yahweh's holy mountain and bring clean offerings to the temple, just as the Israelites do. Some of these Yahweh will take for priests and Levites (66:18-21). Just as the new heavens and new earth will remain before Yahweh, so will Israel's descendants and their names remain. Worship shall continue before Yahweh (66:22-23), but a later editor adds a final unsettling word about people going forth to look on the dead bodies of those who have rebelled against Yahweh (66:24).

Jonah: The Reluctant Prophet

Jonah ben Amittai, from Gath-hepher in Galilee (Josh 19:13), receives mention in the Deuteronomic History as a prophet active during the reign of Jeroboam II (786–746 B.C.E.), at which time he spoke a word from Yahweh in support of Jeroboam's expansionist policy (2 Kgs 14:25). Since Jonah's patronym is the same in 2 Kgs 14:24 and Jonah 1:1, it is reasonable to assume that the two individuals are one and the same. The tale about Jonah in the book bearing his name, however, has little if any connection to Israelite history in the eighth century B.C.E. During the reign of Jeroboam II, Assyria was weak, posing no threat to Israel. Nineveh at the time was not the royal residence. In addition, the term "king of Nineveh" is strange, implying as it does the ruler of a city-state, not a large nation. One would expect "king of Assyria." Having said this, however, what is recounted in 2 Kgs 14:25 about Jonah's nationalistic preaching goes some way toward understanding the reluctant Jonah of the prophetic book, an individual dismayed at Nineveh's repentance and God's decision not to destroy it once it has repented.

Extraordinary features in the story indicate to hearers that it is a folktale, for example, the swallowing of Jonah by a great fish, which later vomits him up on land (1:17; 2:10); the breadth of Nineveh being "a three-day journey for the gods/mighty ones" (3:3), that is, an unbelievably huge place (estimated to be twenty-five to forty miles across, when in fact it was more like three miles across); the dramatic response to Jonah's preaching: all Nineveh—including the king—believing in God, fasting, putting on sackcloth, and turning from evil (3:5-9); and the gourd growing up quickly and dying just as quickly the next day (4:6-7).

The book of Jonah differs from other prophetic books in that it is, in the main, a tale told about a prophet. Three of the four chapters are narrative prose, relating Jonah's (mis)adventures. The prophet's preaching consists of only one proclamation: "Yet forty days and Nineveh shall be overthrown" (3:4). In the center of the book is a prayer of thanksgiving (2:2-9), reported to have been uttered by Jonah when he was in the belly of the fish.

The author of the book of Jonah is unknown, but what seems clear is that his tale of a reluctant, self-pitying, and narrow-minded prophet means to counter particularistic tendencies current in postexilic Judaism. The book has a strident universalism similar to what is found in Second Isaiah, where Israel is called to be a "light to the nations," and people are committed to converting the nations (Gentiles) to the worship of Yahweh God. The book is commonly dated in the postexilic period, at which time Second Isaiah's enthusiasm had given way to the particularism of the Ezra-Nehemiah period. Ezra's reforms are dated c. 444 B.C.E. A *terminus ad quem* for the book of Jonah would be 180 B.C.E., since Sirach (49:10) makes reference to the Book of the Twelve, and Jonah is assumed to be one of the twelve books of the Minor Prophets.

The book of Jonah has numerous links with other Old Testament writings. Some commentators believe that it develops the teaching of Jer 18:8, where God says he will repent of announced evil if people repent of their wickedness (cf. 3:10). The imagery of the fish swallowing its victim and vomiting it up also has a parallel in one of Jeremiah's Babylon oracles (Jer 51:34, 44). Jonah's self-pity in wanting to die (4:3, 8) recalls the "death wish" of Elijah (1 Kgs 19:4, 10).

The tale of Jonah begins with Yahweh calling Jonah to preach against the great city of Nineveh for wickedness that had come before Yahweh—echoes here of the story of Sodom and Gomorrah (Gen 18:20-21). But Jonah took off in the opposite direction, arriving at the port of Joppa, where he boarded a ship going to Tarshish. The author tells us pointedly that Jonah was intent on fleeing from the presence of Yahweh (1:1-3). In rejecting the divine call, Jonah goes further than either Moses or Jeremiah, both of whom put up resistance but did not flee from Yahweh's presence. Nevertheless, Yahweh is seen to be active out in the Mediterranean, pursuing Jonah by calling forth a great wind that threatens to break the ship apart. Pagan sailors on board cry to their gods, while at the same time throwing cargo overboard to lighten the load. Jonah is unafraid, sleeping soundly in the depths of the ship. The captain finds and awakens Jonah, telling him to cry to his god for deliverance (1:4-6). But there is no indication that he did.

A casting of lots reveals that Jonah is responsible for this maritime crisis. The sailors question him and find out, among other things, that he fears Yahweh, God of heaven, who made land and sea. They also learn that Jonah is fleeing from Yahweh. So they ask him what action they should take, and Jonah says they can throw him overboard, for he knows the tempest has arisen on his account. The sailors do not take immediate action, but try valiantly to row the boat to land. But they cannot, and the storm gets worse. So the pagan sailors do what Jonah should have done but did not. They cry to Yahweh, asking also that they be spared the charge of shedding innocent blood for throwing Jonah into the sea. Then they throw him overboard and the sea becomes calm. The effect on the sailors is extraordinary. They fear Yahweh greatly, offer a sacrifice to Yahweh, and make vows (1:7-16). Below in the water, Yahweh then appoints a great fish to swallow Jonah, and the prophet remains in the belly of the fish for three days and three nights (1:17).

The psalm in the center of the book is Jonah's prayer to Yahweh. In it, he now expresses faith and confidence in the God from whom he tried to flee (2:1-9). The demeanor of the prophet changes dramatically. In this prayer, Jonah says that he called to Yahweh in his distress and Yahweh answered him. Now he is grieved to be cast from Yahweh's presence, and he wonders if he will ever again see Yahweh's holy temple. When Jonah was at the bottom of the sea, Yahweh delivered him from the Pit; then he remembered Yahweh, and his prayer was heard in Yahweh's holy temple. The prayer closes with Jonah discrediting those who pay regard to empty idols, and Jonah promises to make a sacrifice to Yahweh and pay vows.

The story then resumes, with Yahweh commanding the great fish to disgorge Jonah on the beach (2:10). Now a second time Jonah is called to preach Yahweh's word to the city of Nineveh, and this time he goes (3:1-3). Yahweh gets his man! The prophet proclaims that Nineveh will be destroyed in forty days. And wonder of wonders, the people of this wicked city—from the least to the greatest—believe God, proclaim a fast, and put on sackcloth. The king too takes off his robe, puts on sackcloth, and sits in ashes. Even the beasts are covered with sackcloth. People cry mightily to God, turn from their evil, and hope that God will repent of the evil planned for the city (3:4-9). God's response is no less dramatic than the response of the Ninevites. He relents from the planned evil and does not carry it out (3:10).

Here the story takes an unexpected turn. One would think that Jonah would be pleased at the extraordinary results of his preaching. But he is not. He is angry that Yahweh shows mercy toward this non-Israelite city, and he makes the lame excuse that he knew Yahweh was a God who repented of evil, which is why he fled in the first place (4:1-2). Then again, maybe he did know all of this and simply did not want to see Nineveh repent. In any case, he now becomes a sulky prophet wanting to die (4:3). We heard something similar from Elijah after his stunning victory over the prophets of Baal (1 Kgs 19:4-8). Jonah's depression is as bad or worse. Yahweh rebukes him for being angry (4:4). Jonah apparently is still holding out hope that Yahweh will destroy Nineveh, and so he goes outside the city, makes a booth for himself, and waits to see what will happen (4:5).

At this point Yahweh appoints a gourd to grow up quickly and relieve Jonah's discomfort from the burning sun. The prophet is now glad (4:6). But then God appoints a worm to attack the plant so it withers and dies, after which an east wind off the desert causes Jonah to languish once more in the sun. Again he wants to die (4:7-8). Yahweh senses that Jonah is angry about the withering of the plant, and he is right, which brings the tale to its grand climax. If Jonah pities the plant that has died, why should not God pity the city of Nineveh in which there are twenty thousand children and many cattle (4:9-11)? The audience is left to answer this question.

Haggai: Prophet for Rebuilding the Temple

Haggai was one of three postexilic prophets who arose in Judah after Persia became the dominant power in the ancient Near East (539 B.C.E.) and the Jews were permitted to return to their homeland. The other two were Zechariah and Malachi. Haggai is securely dated in 520 B.C.E. and is a contemporary of Zechariah, with whom he is associated in the book of Ezra (Ezra 5:1; 6:14). In the LXX, Psalms 145–148 are ascribed to Haggai and Zechariah (the Vulgate assigns only Psalms 145 and 146). Malachi, the third prophet, was active a century later. According to rabbinic tradition, these were the last of the Hebrew prophets, since it was believed that prophecy in Israel came to an end (1 Macc 9:27). Only after a silence of four centuries or more was the prophetic voice heard again in John the Baptist (Matt 11:9-10). Because of the precise dates in his book, Haggai's prophecies can be narrowed down to the three- or four-month period between August and December 520.

Darius I became king of Persia in 522 B.C.E. but was kept busy during his first two years putting down rebellions in the empire. By 520 B.C.E. his rule was consolidated, and the empire was generally peaceful (Zech

1:11). Before 520, Darius had sent Zerubbabel, grandson of the exiled Jehoiachin (Hag 1:1; 1 Chr 3:16-19), to Judah as governor of the territory (Ezra 2:1-2). Some believe that Haggai and Zechariah came to Judah with Zerubbabel, but it has also been argued that Haggai never went to Babylon but was rather a farmer residing in Judah. Early Jewish and Christian writers cited Hag 2:3 in support of the view that Haggai was an old man who remembered the glory of the First Temple, but of this we cannot be sure.

Judah at the time of Sheshbazzar's earlier return (538 B.C.E.) may still have been subordinate to regional authorities in Samaria, but if so, autonomy was achieved soon after. The book of Ezra reports tensions between the Judeans and Samaritans over rebuilding Jerusalem and the temple (Ezra 4:4-5). Sheshbazzar, a son of Jehoiachin (1 Chr 3:17-18) and Judah's first governor, was unable, in eighteen years, to get beyond laying the temple foundations (Ezra 5:14-16). Tensions between the Judeans and the Samaritans had not completely subsided in Zerubbabel's time (Ezra 4:1-5; 5:3-5). Nevertheless, it was Haggai who spurred people on to get the temple rebuilt, and in five years or less, c. 515 B.C.E., the work was completed and the temple dedicated (Ezra 6:14). Zechariah, who prophesied from 520 to 518 B.C.E., added support to the enterprise.

In the second year of Darius, Haggai reported to Zerubbabel and Joshua the high priest that people were not ready to rebuild the temple, so he said to them, "Why not, when you yourselves live in paneled houses?" (1:2-4). This same argument was used earlier by David to Nathan the prophet (2 Sam 7:2). Haggai went on to chide the people on the small yield of their efforts:

> Consider how you have fared. You have sown much, and harvested little; you eat, but you never have enough; you drink, but you never have your fill; you clothe yourselves, but no one is warm; and you that earn wages earn wages to put them into a bag with holes. (Hag 1:5b-6)

Yahweh then said in a divine oracle that the people should go out and fetch wood to build the house so that he may be pleased and honored (1:8). The people were again chided about having high aims that had come to nothing, with Yahweh adding that he had called a drought on the land. The reason for this was that his house lay in ruins (1:9-11).

Zerubbabel, Joshua, and the people promptly obeyed Yahweh's word, after which Yahweh gave them his coveted "I am with you" promise

(1:12-13). Work began on the temple, fulfilling the earlier prophecy of Ezekiel (Ezekiel 40–48).

A month later Yahweh directed Haggai to speak again to Zerubbabel, Joshua, and the people, this time calling attention to the fact that the temple as it was taking shape was not a particularly glorious sight (2:1-9). But Yahweh said not to worry:

> Once again, in a little while, I will shake the heavens and the earth, and the sea and the dry land; and I will shake the nations, so that the treasures of all nations shall come, and I will fill this house with splendor, says Yahweh of hosts. The silver is mine, and the gold is mine, says Yahweh of hosts. The latter splendor of this house shall be greater than the former, says Yahweh of hosts; and in this place I will give prosperity, says Yahweh of hosts. (Hag 2:6-9)

Here one sees a fulfillment of Jeremiah's prophecy that Yahweh would restore the nation's fortunes that had been taken to Babylon (Jer 29:14; 30:3, 18; 31:23; etc.).

Two months later, Haggai delivered another oracle from Yahweh. Of concern now were things clean and unclean. Haggai pointed out that the hands of the people were unclean before the rebuilding began; that is, sacrifices offered before the restoration project were deemed unacceptable to Yahweh. For this reason, the people experienced privation. Now, with the first stones having been laid, things had turned around, and Yahweh says that from this day forward he will bless the people (2:10-19).

On the same day, Haggai received a final word to be communicated to Zerubbabel:

> I am about to shake the heavens and the earth, and to overthrow the throne of kingdoms; I am about to destroy the strength of the kingdoms of the nations, and overthrow the chariots and their riders; and the horses and their riders shall fall, every one by the sword of a comrade. On that day, says Yahweh of hosts, I will take you, O Zerubbabel, my servant, son of Shealtiel, says Yahweh, and make you like a signet ring; for I have chosen you, says Yahweh of hosts. (Hag 2:21-23)

Rebellions occurring at the beginning of Darius's reign may stand behind this passage, but Haggai, more importantly, is looking ahead to a reestablishment of the monarchy. The one wearing Yahweh's signet ring will be Zerubbabel.

Zechariah: Prophet of the Branch

Zechariah was a contemporary of Haggai, beginning his work as a prophet in the eighth month of the second year of Darius I (520 B.C.E.; Zech 1:1). He continued to prophesy until the ninth month of the fourth year of Darius (518 B.C.E.; Zech 7:1). He could have remained in public life longer. Zechariah and Haggai are associated in the book of Ezra (Ezra 5:1; 6:14).

The book of Zechariah gives us minimal information about the prophet, identifying him only as "son of Berechiah, son of Iddo" (1:1, 7). In Ezra 5:1 and 6:4, he is called "Zechariah son of Iddo," where "son" takes on the less precise meaning of "descendant." The book of Zechariah gives the actual order of descent. Zechariah is in a priestly line, the Nehemiah genealogy telling us that Iddo returned from exile with Zerubbabel and Joshua (Neh 12:4, 16). Zechariah, then, was both a priest and a prophet, just as Jeremiah and Ezekiel were. He is clearly sympathetic to the priesthood, to Joshua in particular (3:1-5; 6:11-13), which paved the way for the priesthood becoming prominent in postexilic Judaism. But Zechariah sees the restored Jewish community as having dual leadership: Joshua the high priest, and Zerubbabel the Branch, who is a messianic figure (3:8-10; 4:11-14). The idea of dual leadership survived at Qumran among the Essenes. The background for Zechariah's prophecies, which focus on Yahweh's return to Zion, the rebuilding of the temple, and Yahweh's judgment of the nations, which will mean deliverance and prosperity for Judaism, is the same as the background of the book of Haggai (see above, p. 124, "Haggai: Prophet for Rebuilding the Temple").

Only chapters 1–8 of the book are attributed to the prophet Zechariah. Chapters 9–14 contain different vocabulary and phraseology and are written in a different style—more poetic and showing greater fervor. Moreover, the name of Zechariah vanishes in these chapters. This latter work emanates from one or more authors living at a later time, whose names are unknown. But as is the case with Isaiah, Second Isaiah, and possibly Third Isaiah, here, too, the later work—or works—carries on the tradition of an earlier prophet.

Zechariah's eight visions and their expansions, which form the major portion of the book (1:7—6:15), differ from other prophetic utterances, containing as they do cryptic and figurative language that will come to full flower in genuine apocalyptic, for example, in the book of Daniel in the Old Testament and in Revelation in the New Testament. In these chapters, Yahweh does not speak directly to Zechariah, but rather explains his elaborate revelations through mediating angels. Yahweh is a transcendent God, like the God in Elohistic and Deuteronomic sources of the Pentateuch. Zechariah introduces Satan the accuser (3:1-2; cf. Job 1–2) and is the only prophet to speak of him.

The book begins with the prophet calling for repentance, a clarion bell heard in earlier prophets (Jer 4:1; Joel 2:12; Ezek 33:11; Isa 55:7): "Return to me, says Yahweh of hosts, and I will return to you, says Yahweh of hosts" (1:3). Zechariah points out that former prophets preached this message, but people took no heed. Then judgment came, after which they did repent (1:4-6).

In a night vision three months later (1:7), five months after the temple building had resumed (Hag 1:14-15), Zechariah sees a man riding a red horse among myrtle trees in the valley, and behind him horsemen on horses of different colors (1:8-13). The angel tells him that these horsemen have patrolled the earth and found it to be at rest. So why has Yahweh not shown mercy to Jerusalem and Judah after being angry with them for seventy years? An answer comes in three oracles (1:14-17). Yes, Yahweh is indeed angry with the nations currently at ease, but says he will return to Jerusalem with compassion. Zion will once again be his chosen city. Moreover, the temple will be rebuilt and Judah's cities will overflow with prosperity.

A second vision of four (iron) horns and four smiths follows (1:18-21). The horns represent the powerful nations that have scattered Judah, and the smiths are those who have come to destroy these nations.

Zechariah's third vision, of a man with a measuring cord, which is followed by four oracles, speaks to Jerusalem's future growth and prosperity (2:1-13; cf. Jer 31:38-40). But the man with the cord need not carry out his task, because Jerusalem, with its many people and cattle, will become as a village without walls (2:1-5). Yahweh himself will be as a fiery wall around her. The oracles bid the exiles to flee their distant places, Babylon in particular, and escape to Zion (2:6-13). Yahweh will now come to dwell in the midst of his people. Moreover, many nations will join themselves to Yahweh in this future day, and will become his people (2:11). The prophet concludes with a word reminiscent of Hab 2:20. He says:

> Be silent, all flesh, before Yahweh, for he has
> roused himself from his holy dwelling.
>
> (Zech 2:13)

The fourth vision, about Joshua and his priestly garments (3:1-10), has a few formal characteristics that are different from the other visions, leading some interpreters to believe that it is a later interpolation. Satan here is the accuser, but before he gets to speak, Yahweh rebukes him. Joshua is open to censure for wearing filthy garments. But the angel instructs those present to take the filthy garments off of this brand (Joshua) plucked from the Babylonian furnace. Cleansed from his iniquity, he is to be clothed in a stately robe and have a clean turban placed on his head. Then in a divine oracle the angel charges Joshua to walk in Yahweh's ways and to keep his charge. In so doing, he will rule in Yahweh's temple and enjoy access to the divine council, the latter probably an indication that he will possess the authority of a prophet (cf. Jer 23:18, 22). To Joshua and those with him, Yahweh promises a coming of his servant, "the Branch." The term is messianic (6:12; cf. Jer 23:5; 33:15). Before Joshua there will appear a stone with seven eyes inscribed by Yahweh, and in a single day the guilt of the land will be removed, and Israel will live in peace. It is not known to what the stone refers: a stone in the priestly apparel, or a building stone of the temple (4:7).

The prophet's fifth vision is of a lampstand flanked by two olive trees, the latter supplying oil via pipes to seven lamps atop the lampstand (4:1-14; cf. Rev 11:4). When Zechariah asks what this signifies, he is told that it is Yahweh's word to Zerubbabel: "Not by might, nor by power, but by my Spirit, says Yahweh of hosts" (4:6). The mountain of difficulty looming before him will be reduced to a plain. Zerubbabel shall bring forth the keystone of the temple amid shouts of "Grace, grace to it." Having laid the foundation of the house, he will also complete it (4:7-10). The seven lamps with seven lips atop the lampstand are the eyes of Yahweh, surveying the earth for good and evil (cf. Prov 15:3). The temple work will succeed. The two olive trees—more precisely, two branches of two olive trees—are Yahweh's two "sons of oil": Joshua and Zerubbabel.

Zechariah's sixth vision is of a flying scroll (5:1-4). It contains a curse on anyone who steals and swears falsely by Yahweh's name. The curse will enter that person's house and consume it. It falls upon anyone who breaks the eighth and third commandments.

The seventh vision is of an ephah vessel containing a woman (5:5-11). The ephah is a dry measure, roughly equal to two-thirds of a bushel. Once the leaden circular lid is lifted, the woman appears, who personifies wickedness in the land. But she is quickly thrust down and the weighty lid is put back on the vessel. Two other women with storklike wings then appear and lift the ephah vessel skyward. Zechariah asks the angel where they are going, and he is told that the vessel is being taken to the land of Shinar, that is, Babylon (Gen 10:10). There a house (temple) will be built for it, and it will be set on its base. Judah will now be purified, and evil will reside in Babylon.

The eighth vision is of four chariots pulled by different-colored horses (6:1-8). They come out of two bronze mountains, headed for the four winds of heaven after presenting themselves to Yahweh. The chariots, which are war chariots, are on patrol throughout the earth. The prophet is told by the angel that those going to the north country, that is, Babylon (cf. 2:6), have set Yahweh's spirit at rest there, which is to say that divine anger against Babylon has abated. The vision ends with a return to the world being at rest, as stated in the first vision (1:11).

In a climactic oracle (6:9-15), Zechariah is instructed to make a crown of silver and gold for Joshua and to set it upon his head (6:11). To Joshua is given an oracle announcing "the Branch," who will be the builder of the temple. He shall sit on a royal throne, and the priest shall sit on his throne, and there shall be peaceful understanding between them (6:13). The oracle concludes by saying that others afar off, presumably Judahites still in exile, shall come and help in the temple rebuilding (6:15). Or Zechariah may mean that people of other nations will come and help in the rebuilding. Second Isaiah said that foreigners would help rebuild Jerusalem's walls (Isa 60:10).

Two years after Zechariah received his visions, he was called again to prophesy (chapters 7–8). People residing in Bethel had sent a delegation to Jerusalem asking the priests and prophets whether they should continue mourning and fasting in the fifth month, as they had done in Babylon (7:1-3). The question is then answered in a series of oracles delivered by the prophet.

In the first oracle (7:4-7), the people are told that their fasting (like their feasting) was for themselves, not for Yahweh. This was the teaching of the former prophets. In the second oracle (7:8-14), they are told that true judgments, kindness, and benevolent actions are more important than outward observances, which again is what former prophets taught (Mic 6:6-8; Isa 58:3-9). It was the people's stubbornness and failure to carry out Yahweh's higher teachings that brought the divine wrath, culminating in Judah's exile to distant lands and the homeland being left desolate.

Then in a cluster of oracles (8:1-17) Zechariah speaks about the happy days of holiness and prosperity in store for Jerusalem, in contrast to the difficult days of the past. Yahweh is jealous for Zion and will return to her. Jerusalem will again be a faithful city (cf. Isa 1:26), and Yahweh's mountain will be the holy mountain (8:1-3). Jerusalem's streets will be filled with old men and old women, and boys and girls will be playing there (8:4-5). Will it not be as marvelous a sight to Yahweh as to the remnant (8:6)? Yahweh says that he will bring his people from east and west to Jerusalem and will be their covenant God in faithfulness and in righteousness (8:7-8).

In another oracle, the people are admonished to make their hands strong now that they have heard the prophets urging them to rebuild the temple (8:9-13). It was difficult when the work commenced, with no wages paid for human and animal labor, and no protection from foes. But now things will be different. There will be peace and prosperity, and the remnant will enjoy a productive land. Instead of being a curse among the nations, Yahweh will make them a blessing. They need not fear, but they must also make their hands strong. For good to come to Jerusalem and Judah, people must speak the truth, render judgments that are true and that make for peace, not devise evil against one another, and love no false oath. All of these Yahweh hates (8:14-17).

In three final oracles (8:18-23), Yahweh says that fasts of the various months will be transformed into joyful feasts (8:18-19). People must therefore love truth and peace. In conclusion (8:20-23), Yahweh promises that people from many cities will go to Jerusalem to seek Yahweh's favor. Foreigners, too, will join in the happy pilgrimage, saying to a Jew, "Let us go with you, for we have heard that God is with you."

Second Zechariah: Prophet of Yahweh's Coming King

Second Zechariah is the name given to the unknown prophet responsible for chapters 9–14 of the book of Zechariah. It is possible that these prophecies may emanate from more than one individual. In either case, they carry on the tradition of Zechariah, whose prophecies are preserved in chapters 1–8 (see above, p.127, "Zechariah: Prophet of the Branch"). The prophecies here divide into two groups, each of which is introduced by the title "Oracle" (9:1; 12:1).

The prophet begins by promising the punishment of Israel's enemies: Hadrach, Hamath, and Damascus in Syria, Tyre and Sidon on the Phoenician coast, and the cities of Philistia: Ashkelon, Gaza, Ekron, and Ashdod. A Philistine remnant will come to worship Israel's God and be incorporated into the community of Judah (9:7). At that time Yahweh will encamp and stand guard at his house so that no army can again pass Jerusalem and march to and fro throughout Judah (9:1-8). To Zion, the prophet announces Yahweh's coming king (9:9-17), a prophecy quoted in the New Testament in connection with Jesus' Palm Sunday ride into Jerusalem (Matt 21:5; John 12:15):

> Rejoice, greatly, O daughter of Zion!
>   Shout aloud, O daughter Jerusalem!
> Lo, your king comes to you;
>   triumphant and victorious is he,
> humble and riding on an ass,
>   on a colt, the foal of an ass.
>
> (Zech 9:9)

This humble but triumphant king will bring peace to the nations. And for Israel, because of the covenant, prisoners will be delivered from their dungeons, filling them with hope (9:10-12). Yahweh, using a united Israel as his war instrument, will fight on behalf of the nation and protect it (9:13-15). He will save his people and make them shine like crown jewels. Grain and wine will gladden both young men and maidens (9:16-17).

Attention is then drawn to the source of this grain and wine. The goodness comes not from idols and diviners, but from Yahweh, who makes the storm clouds. Those following the diviners and dreamers are like sheep without a shepherd (10:1-2). Yahweh's anger is kindled against the shepherds, and he will punish them. Out of Judah will come true leaders, who will be victorious in battle because Yahweh will be with them. Judah and Israel will be brought back to their homeland, where they will be strengthened and will increase in numbers. Yahweh has redeemed them. At the time of this new exodus, the pride of "Assyria and Egypt" will be brought down (10:3-12).

In chapter 11 is a more somber prophecy. A devouring foe from the north will descend upon Lebanon and Bashan, coming down also into the lush Jordan Valley to despoil Israel's shepherds, who will wail loudly over their pasture wasteland (11:1-3). In their place, Yahweh has appointed a good shepherd, whom the prophet says is he himself. With two staffs, Grace and Union, he will tend the flock (11:4-7). In the space of one month, three of the evil shepherds are destroyed, but the good shepherd becomes impatient for lack of support, and therefore breaks his Grace staff, annulling his covenant with the people. He tells them they can give him his wages or not, so they pay him a paltry thirty shekels of silver, the price of a slave (Exod 21:32). Scorning the money, the prophet casts it into the temple treasury (cf. Matt 27:3-5). Then he breaks Union, his second staff, annulling the brotherhood between Israel and Judah (11:8-14).

After this Yahweh tells the prophet to take again the instruments of a worthless shepherd, for Yahweh will raise up a shepherd who cares nothing for his people. Oracle 1 ends with a woe upon this shepherd and also a curse that his arm will wither and his right eye be blinded (11:15-17).

The first prophecy in oracle 2 deals with Yahweh's protection of Israel (12:1-9). Yahweh, Creator of heaven and earth, and the one who formed the human spirit, says that he will make Jerusalem a bowl of wrath and a heavy stone for those coming against it and also Judah. The bowl of wrath will make the nations reel, and when they try lifting the heavy stone, they will be gravely injured. On that day Yahweh will make oncoming horses blind and their riders panic-stricken, but Judah and Jerusalem will receive favor and will discover that they have strength through Yahweh of hosts, their God (12:1-5). Jerusalem will become a populous city. Judah will be the first to taste victory, so that the house of David and Jerusalem will not be exalted over the rest of Judah. But the capital city will enjoy divine protection. Nations coming against it will be destroyed (12:6-9).

Yahweh will then pour out upon the house of David and the inhabitants of Jerusalem a spirit of compassion and supplication, so that they will look upon Yahweh whom they have pierced, and will mourn grievously, family by family (12:10-14). But this mourning will bear fruit, for on that day a fountain will be opened for Jerusalem, to cleanse it of its sin and uncleanness. Idols will no longer be remembered, and prophets of an unclean spirit will be removed (13:1-6). Prophets will be ashamed of their visions and will not wear hairy garments in order to deceive. They will say:

> I am no prophet, a tiller of the soil I am; for a man acquired me from my youth. And if one asks him, "What are these wounds on your back?" he will say, "The wounds I received in the house of my friends." (Zech 13:5-6)

The second part of oracle 2 begins with Israel's purification and a renewal of the covenant (13:7-9). Yahweh's shepherd will be stricken and its flock scattered (cf. Matt 26:31). Two-thirds of the people will be cut off, and one-third will be left alive. The third that will be left alive will be refined by fire, as one refines silver and gold. They will then call upon Yahweh's name, and Yahweh will answer them. The covenant will thus be reestablished.

Another future Day of Yahweh has the nations coming against Jerusalem. Half of the city's population will be exiled, but Yahweh with his holy ones will appear to fight on behalf of those who remain. Yahweh will stand on the Mount of Olives, which will be split in two. Unusual natural phenomena will occur—reduced light day and night, and living waters flowing year-round out of Jerusalem. Yahweh will then be king over all the earth, his name being one, even as he is one (14:1-9). The land around

Jerusalem will be transformed, but Jerusalem will remain aloft on its site, inhabited, no longer under a curse, and dwelling in security (14:10-11).

Then will come a plague upon the nations warring against Jerusalem. Even Judah will be fighting against Jerusalem in the panic of war. Jerusalem will end up getting the spoil of the nations (14:12-15). But survivors of the nations will go up year after year to worship Yahweh at the Feast of Booths. Drought and plague will meet any who do not go (14:16-19). On that day one will see a crowning holiness come upon Jerusalem and Judah (14:20-21). "And there shall no longer be a trader in the house of Yahweh of hosts on that day" (14:21; cf. John 2:14-16).

Malachi: Prophet of Yahweh's Messenger

Of this prophet we know nothing. Even his name is in doubt, since Malachi means "my messenger" (3:1; cf. 1:1) and may simply be the title of the book. From internal evidence, the prophecies of this unknown individual are usually dated about 460 to 450 B.C.E., some sixty to seventy years after the prophecies of Haggai and Zechariah, at a time when Judah was under the rule of a Persian-appointed governor (1:8). The temple is rebuilt, worship is formally carried on, and the priesthood has existed long enough to become lax and corrupt (1:6—2:9). Problems in the larger Jewish community—widespread divorce and marriage to foreign women, and abuses in sacrificial worship and tithing—appear to predate the reforms carried out by Ezra and Nehemiah (Neh 13:10-29). Nehemiah arrived in Jerusalem in 445 B.C.E.

Like the preaching of other prophets, Malachi's preaching gains authority by citing what Yahweh of hosts has said, but gone are the "Thus said Yahweh" formulas of the older prophets, and in their place is reasoned argument. Yahweh's "messenger" is now the priest (2:7), pointing to the end of institutional prophecy as it has been known, and the advent of dialectical discourse carried on by priests and scribes. Each topic raised by Malachi opens with a statement followed by a question or two and then developed by argument to make a point.

At the outset, Malachi states that Yahweh loves his people. But the people ask how this can be, with life currently in Judah a far cry from what was promised by visionaries such as Second Isaiah. Yahweh then mentions Esau, Jacob's brother, and says that he loved Jacob more than he loved Esau (cf. Rom 9:13). A recent calamity has befallen the Edomites, who are the descendants of Esau, and Yahweh says that although they may entertain hopes of rebuilding their ruins, he will bring them down

(1:2-5). Yahweh's anger against Edom is ongoing. When the people finally witness this, they will say, "Great is Yahweh beyond the border of Israel." Reference here could be to the destruction of Edom at the hands of Nabonidus in the middle of the sixth century B.C.E. Anticipated also is the conquest of Edom a century or two later by the Nabatean Arabs, who expelled the Edomites from their land.

The prophet then turns to the problem of honor being withheld from Yahweh by priests and laity (1:6—2:9). A son honors his father, and a servant his master, but where is my honor? asks Yahweh. The answer comes back that Yahweh's name is dishonored by priests offering polluted food on the altar. How are the sacrifices polluted? Answer: If animals are blind, sick, and lame, they are polluted. Would the governor be pleased with such offerings? How then can the priests expect favor from Yahweh? Yahweh wants no such offerings; they dishonor his great name (1:11-14). Would that the sanctuary doors be shut and these empty sacrifices not be made! The priests are told that if they fail to bring glory to Yahweh's name, Yahweh will send a curse upon them (2:1-9). They are reminded of the covenant made with Levi (through Phinehas; Num 25:10-13), which was a covenant of life and peace so priests would fear Yahweh. Levi feared Yahweh (2:5). The priest is to guard knowledge and give instruction (Deut 33:10); he is "the messenger of Yahweh" (2:7). But the priests have corrupted this covenant by bad teaching, causing people to stumble. So Yahweh will shame them, making them despised and abased before the people (2:9).

Malachi then addresses the people about the profaning of Yahweh's sanctuary, widespread divorce, and marriage to women who worship foreign gods (2:10-16). He asks, "Have we not all one father? Has not one God created us?" Why then are people faithless to one another, profaning the covenant made with the fathers? Judah has been faithless, profaning the sanctuary that Yahweh loves and marrying daughters of foreign gods. Malachi says that anyone doing these abominations will be cut off (2:11-12). People wonder why Yahweh does not accept offerings made with much weeping and groaning. It is because men have been faithless to wives of their youth. Marriage, after all, is a covenant. God desires godly offspring (2:15). Men are therefore admonished to be faithful to the wives of their youth, for Yahweh says, "I hate divorce." Yahweh also hates violent treatment of wives by their husbands (2:16).

The people are then rebuked for their gross impiety (2:17—3:5). They say that everyone is good in Yahweh's eyes, even those who do evil. They also say, "Where is the God of justice?" (2:17). Yahweh answers that he is sending his messenger to prepare the way of his coming, when he will suddenly appear in his temple. The prophet asks, "Who can endure the day of his coming?" for it will be a day when Yahweh will refine and cleanse the priesthood until priests present right offerings to him, as was the case in former days. On this coming day, Yahweh will also carry out swift judgment against sorcerers, adulterers, those swearing falsely, those oppressing hired workers, and those ill-treating widows, orphans, and sojourners (3:1-5; cf. Deut 24:14-15, 17-18). This answers the people's question, "Where is the God of justice?"

The prophet now turns to the neglect of tithes and offerings (3:6-12). Yahweh reminds people that he does not change, for which reason the people were not consumed altogether (3:6). Israel's disobedience has gone on from time immemorial, so Yahweh says again, "Return to me, and I will return to you" (3:7; cf. Zech 1:3). The people ask how they shall return. The answer is another question: "Will one rob God?" How are they robbing God? Yahweh answers:

> In your tithes and offerings. You are cursed with a curse, for you are robbing me—the whole nation of you! Bring the full tithe into the storehouse, so that there may be food in my house, and thus put me to the test, says Yahweh of hosts; see if I will not open the windows of heaven for you and pour down for you an overflowing blessing. (Mal 3:8b-10)

Yahweh says that he will rebuke any devouring locust so that the earth can bring forth its yield. Then all the nations will call Israel blessed (3:11-12).

The final portion of Malachi's prophecy returns once again to address God's righteous judgment (3:13—4:3). Yahweh says that hard words have been spoken against him. The people ask, "How so?" They question why they should serve God when the arrogant are blessed and evildoers not only prosper but escape after putting God to the test (3:13-15). Some who fear Yahweh, having heard these impious words, speak with one another and Yahweh hears them. As a result, a book of remembrance is made containing their names, a reward to them for fearing Yahweh and thinking on his name (3:16). Yahweh says, "They shall be mine." He will spare them on the day when he makes up his treasure, when the righteous are separated from the wicked, and those who serve him are separated from those who do not (3:17-18). On this day the arrogant and doers of evil will be as straw in the oven. Yahweh will leave them a tree with neither root nor branch. Yahweh continues:

But for you who fear my name the sun of righteousness shall rise, with healing in its wings. You shall go out leaping like calves from the stall. And you shall tread down the wicked, for they will be ashes under the soles of your feet, on the day when I act, says Yahweh of hosts. (Mal 4:2-3)

The book concludes with an admonition and a promise. People are to remember the Law of Moses, Yahweh's servant (4:4), and look forward to a Day of Yahweh before which the returning Elijah will bring about far-reaching reconciliation. The prophet says:

Behold, I will send you the prophet Elijah before the great and terrible Day of Yahweh comes. He will turn the hearts of parents to their children and the hearts of children to their parents, so that I will not come and strike the land with a curse. (Mal 4:5-6)

3

MEASURES OF AUTHENTICITY

AUTHENTICATION WAS A PROBLEM FOR THE PROPHET and his precursors from the very beginning. Always there were people wondering, "Is this prophet for real?" Prophets themselves must have wondered. If they did not wonder about their own authenticity, they surely wondered about the authenticity of others claiming the office. It is one thing to possess the marks of a divine office, but quite another to be thought of as a genuine representative of that office. For this reason certain proofs were called for at various times in order that the prophet's claim to being a prophet might be substantiated.

In this chapter we will look at proofs that the Old Testament itself sets forth. We will also examine measures of authenticity suggested in prophetic preaching. But before we do either, we must ask a preliminary question: Where for the ancient Hebrew people was the real locus of authenticity?

THE LOCUS OF AUTHENTICITY

The Inspirational Event

Authenticity is found, first of all, in the inspirational event. Inspiration is not lifted up in the Old Testament in any official way as a test of true prophecy. It seems simply to be taken for granted. We do learn from the prophets themselves, as they testify to their own experience and as they make judgments about what they perceive to be the experience of others, that the true prophet is possessed by the spirit of Yahweh, whether controlled by fits of ecstasy[1] or moved to a prolonged silence.

138

That Yahweh exercises control over false prophets (1 Kgs 22:22-23; Ezek 14:9), who could be filled with a "lying" or "empty" spirit, should in no way obscure this fact. Micah, after a sharp censure of certain prophets, says this about himself:

> But as for me, I am filled with power,
>   with the spirit of Yahweh,
>   and with justice and might,
> to declare to Jacob his transgression
>   and to Israel his sin.
>
> (Mic 3:8)

Yet how did the Israelite people view inspiration? Abraham Heschel says that inspiration must be understood as an "event," not as a "process." The distinction is basic:

> A process happens regularly, following a relatively permanent pattern; an event is extraordinary, irregular. A process may be continuous, steady, uniform; events happen suddenly, intermittently, occasionally. Processes are typical; events are unique. A process follows a law, events create a precedent. The term "continuous revelation" is, therefore, as proper as a "square circle." . . . Inspiration, then, is not a process that goes on all the time, but an event that lasts a moment.[2]

A correlation exists here with the Hebrew view of God. God is never thought of in terms of "being," or "essence," as would be typical among the Greeks, or even among modern thinkers, for example, Paul Tillich, who spoke of God as "the Ground of All Being."[3] God is known to the Hebrew people through his "acts."[4] These acts continue throughout history, but, as Heschel says, they are "intermittent" or "occasional": "God is not simply available once and for all, to be found whenever man so desires. There is an alternative to God's presence, namely his absence."[5] The prophet, then, does not receive divine inspiration as some kind of permanent possession, which is to say that visions and sounds do not persist all the time. "His experience is a perception of an act that happens rather than a perception of a situation that abides."[6] We see here a relationship between the prophet and Yahweh that is dynamic, not static. This indicates life. It also indicates authenticity.

The Prophetic Act

Authenticity is found in the prophetic act. The prophet achieves authenticity in responding to inspired events or engaging in inspired acts. Authenticity does not have its locus in the prophet's being. Though it is true that certain prophets are consistently seen to be genuine, while other prophets are seen to be consistently disingenuous, we must not think of prophets as possessing some "good essence" making them true, or some "bad essence" making them false. If this were the case, then true prophets would always be true, and false prophets would always be false, which they are not. The prophet is true by virtue of an authentic act or false by virtue of an inauthentic act. Each word and deed comes from a specific inspiration or lack of inspiration, and these we judge true or false.[7]

It is perhaps not by accident that the term "false prophet" never occurs in the Hebrew Bible. It is only in the Greek Septuagint (LXX) that the term *pseudoprophētēs* occurs.[8] Hananiah, for example, is a pseudo-prophet (Jer 28:1; LXX 35:1). Certain Hebrew prophets in Babylon are also pseudo-prophets (Jer 29:1, 8; LXX 36:1, 8). But in the Hebrew Bible every prophet—true or false—is simply a *nābî'*, or "prophet." It may be said of a prophet that he speaks "falsely," meaning that he prophesies "lies," that he utters things "out of his own heart," or that "Yahweh has not sent him." But never are we told that a prophet is fundamentally false.[9] People accusing Jeremiah of speaking falsely still take him to Egypt, which seems to indicate that they otherwise regarded him as a true man of God (Jer 43:1-7).[10]

False prophecy may be compared to sin in Hebrew thought, which is also rooted in acts that one does. Sin may spring from an "evil imagination" (Gen 6:5) or a treasure of evil thoughts (Matt 12:33-37; cf. 5:28); still, sin is neither a condition nor a state of being, although it nearly becomes so in the preaching of Jeremiah (Jer 17:1) and is very much so in the thinking of Paul (Romans 6). But in Hebrew thought one becomes a sinner when committing a sinful act. Again, there are people like Nabal (1 Sam 25:25) who have bad reputations, also entire generations that are remembered as being notoriously evil (Gen 6:5). Nevertheless, evil has its locus in the deed, not in some inward, unalterable condition. The same, of course, holds true for goodness. People are good because they do good deeds (2 Chr 32:32; 35:26-27; Matt 12:35-37). Sometimes seemingly good people do evil deeds, for example, David's sin against Uriah (2 Samuel 11), and sometimes seemingly evil people do good deeds, for example, Rahab the harlot aiding the Hebrew spies (Joshua 2).

There is an unusual story in 1 Kings 13 that shows very well how authenticity resides in the prophetic act.[11] In the short span of one day, a true prophet became false and a false prophet became true. It all began when an unnamed prophet came to Bethel from the southern region of Judah and cried out there against the idolatrous altar of Jeroboam I. This prophet had all the marks of being genuine. He accompanied his word of judgment with a sign, which came to pass almost immediately: The altar was torn down and its ashes poured out. Jeroboam's hand also shriveled. The prophet spoke properly in the name of Yahweh, and his words came true (although the judgment against Bethel would not occur until later). Moreover, he was genuine in that he obeyed Yahweh's command not to remain at Bethel for a meal. Jeroboam, once his hand was restored, had invited the prophet to stay and eat. So this prophet, as he began the journey homeward, was authenticated by virtually every test imaginable. He had had a good day, but the day was not yet over.

An old prophet at Bethel, after hearing what had happened, went out in search of this divine messenger, who by now was on his way home. That the old prophet should rise up in defense of the Bethel sanctuary is understandable, for which reason he is cast at the outset of the story as a disingenuous prophet. When he finds his opposite number on the road, he tells him that a messenger of Yahweh has instructed him to invite the prophet for dinner. At this point the Hebrew text says, "but he lied to him" (1 Kgs 13:18). The words are omitted in the Greek. At any rate, he persuades the younger prophet to stay and eat. But it is a trick, because after they finish eating, the old prophet unleashes holy terror on his guest because he disobeyed the command of Yahweh. His punishment will be death away from the tomb of his fathers. Fulfillment came speedily. As soon as this hapless fellow saddled his ass and resumed the trip homeward, a lion met him and killed him. Thus a true prophet in the morning became a false prophet in the afternoon. But falseness, as we have said, lies in the inauthentic act, which in this case was disobeying Yahweh's command. The other prophet, who began his day defending the idolatrous sanctuary at Bethel, ended the day with an inspired word of judgment. How we are to evaluate the trickery is unclear. The variation between the Greek and Hebrew texts indicates that a problem was seen to exist even in antiquity. In any case, the attack of the lion gives authentication to the old prophet (v. 26).

To try to decide here which prophet is essentially true and which false is to miss the point. Ancient Hebrew people did not think this way. Truth and falsity have their locus in the prophetic act, in the inspired event, and on this particular day each prophet takes a turn at being true and being false. The story concludes in appropriate fashion. The old prophet from Bethel buries the prophet from Judah in his own grave. He also requests that when he dies, he be laid to rest at the prophet's side, for he knows the judgment against Bethel will indeed come to pass. In death, the two will be equalized, even as they were in life.

The Dynamic Message

Authenticity is found in the dynamic message. An authentic prophetic message is one delivered to a specific audience at a particular moment of time. Gerhard von Rad says:

> Here, it is all-important not to read this message as if it consisted of timeless ideas, but to understand it as the particular word relevant to a particular hour in history, which therefore cannot be replaced by any other word. The prophetic word—far more than any of the other forms of speech used by Jahwism—has its origin in an impassioned dialogue; yet the dialogue never tries to climb into the realm of general religious truth, but instead uses even the most suspect means to tie the listening partner down to his particular time and place in order to make him understand his own situation before God.[12]

Such a message we call the dynamic message. The static message is one divorced from the historical situation, or, as von Rad says, one that has "climb[ed] into the realm of general religious truth." People are long-suffering in listening to static messages, even though they have no gripping power whatever. Thus they are often inauthentic. Even the best of prophetic messages do not translate automatically into immutable truths applicable to any situation at any time. True, the same message can be authentic on more than one occasion, in more than one situation, or to more than one audience, but each proclamation must be judged within a specific context. Why? Because the authentic messages of yesterday can become the inauthentic messages of today.

We see what happened when Isaiah's dynamic message to Hezekiah about the inviolability of Jerusalem (2 Kgs 19:32-34) became hardened into dogma in the time of Jeremiah, at which time probably everyone believed it. But that message was now false because Yahweh had something else to say, namely, that Jerusalem and the temple would be destroyed (Jer

7:1-15). In Israel, authentic faith is dynamic.[13] And if the prophetic message is to be authentic, it too must be dynamic.

The Believing Community

Authenticity is found in the believing community. People entering into an inspirational event become a believing community to the extent that they truly appropriate Yahweh's word, and in the believing community one also finds authenticity.

Communities are never totally depraved, however much the impassioned rhetoric of the prophets leads us to believe otherwise. After all, it is the prophets who create the impression that the community knows nothing but untruth. Elijah says, "I, even I only am left, and they seek my life to take it away" (1 Kgs 19:10, 14). But we have only to read on where Yahweh says that there are yet seven thousand in Israel who have not bowed the knee to Baal (v. 18). Exaggeration? You bet! Things were bad, make no mistake about it, but not as bad as the prophet said. Jeremiah, too, sounds at times as though he is the only authentic person left in Judah (Jer 5:4-5; 6:13 = 8:10; 8:6; et passim), but a closer reading of his book turns up others who showed faith in Yahweh, right up until the time Jerusalem fell. There was the good king Josiah (Jer 22:15-16), Baruch the scribe, his brother Seraiah, Ahikam, Ebedmelech, princes and elders who defended and protected Jeremiah at the time of his trial (Jer 26:16-19), and also Jehoiakim's princes, particularly Gemariah, Elnathan, and Delaiah, who protected and defended Jeremiah at the time his scroll was read in the temple (Jer 36:12, 19, 25). There had to be other believers among the more common folk. The message in Jer 5:1-8 about there being not a single righteous person on the streets in Jerusalem is not credible as literal truth. This word from the prophet simply says that a search team, of which Jeremiah was a part, went out in search of a righteous person and did not find one. Because they did not, Yahweh asks how he can pardon Jerusalem. The audience knows the answer, and the prophet's point is made.

In evil times, the numbers of people victimized by deception can be staggering; still, it is within the human community that truth is vouchsafed among the few or many who believe. Communities, just like individuals, cannot be thought of as possessing a false essence. They are false only to the extent that people within them disbelieve Yahweh's word. Further, we must never forget that out of disbelieving communities arose believing communities, ones that decided which prophets spoke Yahweh's authentic word and which prophets did not. To locate authenticity in the human community is essential. Scripture itself shows that there is no other way. Prophets are never authenticated on the basis of their own witness alone. Their witness has to be corroborated at some point by the witness of others, as we pointed out earlier in discussing the call of Amos. Dynamic messages of all the great prophets took root in communities of believers. They, like the prophets, saw judgment coming, watched the nation crumble, and heard the dynamic message of hope and future restoration.

TESTS FOR AUTHENTICITY

Visions and Signs

The problem of authenticity for one later judged to be prophet nonpareil in Israel surfaces in Exod 4:1, where we encounter an anxious Moses who fears that the people will not believe Yahweh has called him to lead them out of Egypt. Moses says, "But, behold, they will not believe me or listen to my voice, for they will say, 'Yahweh did not appear to you.'" Would not people believe Moses when he said he received a vision at a burning bush? Reporting this incident, where the bush burned but was not consumed, should have given Moses all the authentication he needed. Dreams and visions, according to Num 12:6, are what count.[14] But Moses doubts that the vision will persuade them, so Yahweh responds by giving him a sign: a rod turns into a serpent (Exod 4:3). Signs, then, become an early test of prophetic authenticity. But one sign may not be enough, so Yahweh gives Moses another sign. He says:

> "Put your hand into your bosom." And he put his hand into his bosom; and when he took it out, behold, his hand was leprous, as white as snow. And God said, "Put your hand back into your bosom." So he put his hand back into his bosom; and when he took it out, behold, it was restored like the rest of his flesh. "If they will not believe you," God said, "or heed the first sign, they may believe the latter sign." (Exod 4:6-8)

They *may* believe, but then again they may not, in which case Yahweh is prepared with a third sign. Moses will be able to turn the Nile into blood (Exod 4:9).

Throughout the early chapters of Exodus, the words of Moses and Aaron to the people are continually reinforced by signs and wonders. If these signs will not convince the people, they will at least succeed in evoking belief from the Egyptians. The magicians are the first to believe (8:19), then Pharaoh (10:16), and finally all of Egypt, which moves with dispatch after the final sign to hasten the Hebrews' departure (12:33-36).

The "sign" (*'ôt*, אוֹת) and "wonder" (*môpēt*, מוֹפֵת), which have approximately the same meaning, are commonly nature miracles. But they may also predict future events (Exod 3:12; 1 Sam 2:34; 10:1-8; 1 Kgs 13:3). Prophets, as we noted, were from earliest times foretellers of the future.[15] The divine messenger who visited Abraham and Sarah announced the birth of a son (Gen 18:10). Seers also predicted future events, as we learn from traditions about Samuel (1 Sam 9:6). During every period of Israel's existence, prophets and their predecessors made predictions about the future.

Visions and signs in the Bible are an early test of a prophet's authenticity. Both are affirming in nature. They show that Yahweh has really appeared to the prophet, and they give assurances to people of Yahweh's intervention in human affairs. Even during the classical period, when the prophetic word dominates everything else, we hear about visions having occurred and signs being given. Isaiah accompanies his predictions to Ahaz with a sign (Isa 7:14), and the symbolic acts of Ezekiel are taken to be "signs" and "wonders" (Ezek 4:3; 12:6, 11; 24:24, 27). Dreams—which are night visions—come in for later censure by Jeremiah (Jer 23:25-28), and the sign is criticized also by Jesus (Matt 12:38-40; 16:1-4; John 4:48), yet neither completely dies out. The sign plays an important role in the Gospel of John, where it authenticates the prophet to early Christian believers.[16]

The Way of Yahweh

In the first edition of Deuteronomy (chapters 1–28), which is best dated before 700 B.C.E., when Hezekiah was carrying out his reform in Jerusalem, earlier tests for prophetic authenticity appear to have had only limited usefulness. Moses had his own intuition about the value of signs. Now it was necessary to promulgate other tests by which false prophets could be identified.

Deuteronomy contains two tests for prophetic authenticity, or more properly, inauthenticity, since both aim at exposing the prophet who is false. The first is found in Deuteronomy 13, a law in sermonic dress that admonishes people not to go after other gods. In the first point of a three-point sermon (vv. 1-5), attention is focused on the prophet and "dreamer of dreams." The dreamer of dreams may be a seer, but more likely this is a catchall term for any intermediary claiming visual gifts. In any case, should one of these individuals give a sign or a wonder supporting a prediction that comes to pass, people are not to pay heed if that person leads them in the way of other gods. These gods (or goddesses) could be the Baals or Asherahs of Canaan, Chemosh of Moab, Marduk of Babylon, Ishtar of Assyria, or some other deity worshiped in the ancient world. Prophets who lead people in the way of other gods are disingenuous and must be put to death. Yahweh gives these individuals success only so he may test the people to see whether they love him and are committed to walk in his way.

The true prophet is the one who speaks for Yahweh and leads people in Yahweh's way. One should note, however, that the test is put negatively. Its stated aim is not to authenticate the true prophet, but to *discredit* the false one. Israel's problem was with inauthentic prophets.

Even if this test had not been stated before in so many words, it had no doubt been around for a while. Egyptian magicians prior to the exodus performed signs and wonders; dreams and visions, too, were stock-in-trade among practitioners of Egyptian religion. But in the Bible the success of the Egyptian magicians was short-lived (Exod 8:18), which was Yahweh's way of putting them and those looking on to the test. In the end, it was Moses and Aaron, acting on behalf of Yahweh, who were authenticated. Thus it is reasonable to conclude that even in very early times, long before this test was written into the Code of Deuteronomy, Israelite people had learned that only individuals reporting dreams and visions from the God of Israel were genuine.

What brought this test to the fore was the influx of Canaanite religion into northern Israel, which peaked in the mid-ninth century. Ahab (869–850 B.C.E.), spurred on by his Sidonian wife, Jezebel, imported large numbers of Baal prophets from Phoenicia, who posed a serious threat to Yahwistic faith. This led to the celebrated contest on Mount Carmel between Elijah and the prophets of Baal (1 Kings 18), which may be the background for this test in Deut 13:1-5.

Elijah's name means "Yah[weh] is God." When Elijah calls upon the name of Yahweh, and Yahweh answers by fire, the people add their own words of authentication by falling prostrate and crying, "Yahweh, he is God! Yahweh, he is God!" (1 Kgs 18:39). These confessions, as much as the mighty miracle, show Elijah to be the true prophet. The Baal prophets turned up false because they called on Baal and sought to lead people in the way of Baal. The miracle, like the sign, continued to have an authenticating function in Israelite religion, but what mattered now was whether a prophet was a "Yahweh prophet," whether he built altars to Yahweh, called upon Yahweh's name, and led people in the way of Yahweh. Baal prophets were put to death, the punishment prescribed in Deut 13:5.

Sometime later, the last of the ancient Hebrew miracle workers, Elisha ben Shaphat, was called upon to cure Naaman the Syrian, who was a leper. When Naaman came to Elisha, he expected that the good prophet would call upon the name of Yahweh (2 Kgs 5:11). But Elisha did not do that; in fact, he did not even extend this foreign dignitary the common courtesy of coming out of his house. Instead he sent a messenger with instructions for the visitor to carry out, and Naaman was cured. Naaman left, saying that there was no god anywhere like the God of Israel, and that henceforth he would offer sacrifices to none but Yahweh. Here again, what is all-important is the worship of Yahweh and the abandonment of other gods.

During the classical period, prophets representing other gods were branded false. Both Jeremiah and Ezekiel discredited them (Jer 2:8; 23:13; Ezek 13:17—14:11). Yet just how effective the test of Deut 13:1-5 was during these years is hard to say. There is, however, one court case on record showing a prophet who relied on this test for his defense and was then acquitted. That prophet was Jeremiah, and the incident in question is reported in Jeremiah 26.

Jeremiah had just said in an oracle that Yahweh was about to destroy the Jerusalem temple, as he had destroyed the Shiloh sanctuary years earlier. The reaction was spontaneous. Court was hastily called into session, and the priests and prophets charged Jeremiah with a capital offense. Jeremiah's defense was a simple one: Yahweh had sent him with the words he had spoken (26:12, 15). People were told to amend their ways and begin obeying Yahweh. The prophet's words had a salutary effect, for the court concluded: "This man does not deserve the sentence of death, for he has spoken to us in the name of Yahweh our God" (Jer 26:16).

Jeremiah was acquitted because he was a Yahweh prophet, sent by Yahweh to lead people in the way of Yahweh. He was vindicated by the test in Deut 13:1-5, and it is reasonable to assume that both he and others that day were familiar with this test of prophetic authenticity.

Among early Christians, some of the same assumptions about prophetic authenticity were made. For example, it was taken for granted that false prophets could perform signs and wonders (Matt 24:24). What seemed really to matter was a confession of the Name. Prophets confessing the name of Jesus were true prophets, and prophets not confessing the Name were false (1 John 4:1-3).

Fulfillment of Yahweh's Word

So long as it was between prophets of Yahweh and prophets of other gods, the choice was easy. But what do you do when all your prophets are prophets of Yahweh, and there is disagreement among them? One prophet says one thing and another prophet says another. How do you tell the true prophet? Or the false prophet? The problem here is one of prophets purporting to speak Yahweh's word when Yahweh has not sent them, a problem that became particularly acute in Judah's last days (Jer 23:21, 31-32; Ezek 13:6; 22:28). But it surfaced earlier in another classic confrontation that occurred at the end of Ahab's reign, which is recorded in 1 Kings 22.

Elijah's victory was now history, and things are different but not much changed in Samaria. The Baal prophets are gone, and all four hundred prophets sitting at the king's table are prophets of Yahweh (1 Kgs 22:5-6). One might say that Elijah's reform has succeeded remarkably well. Ahab of Israel and Jehoshaphat of Judah are now planning war against the Syrians. While they consult, a leader among the Yahweh prophets named Zedekiah parades with horns of iron to dramatize the coming victory. The four hundred add their support: "Go up to Ramoth-gilead and triumph; Yahweh will give it into the hand of the king" (v. 12).

King Jehoshaphat, however, thinks that a second opinion is needed. So Micaiah ben Imlah is summoned. He too is a prophet of Yahweh, but out of favor with the Israelite king because he does not speak well of him. He may have been in prison. Upon arriving, he says, "As Yahweh lives, what Yahweh says to me, that will I speak" (1 Kgs 22:14). He too is a Yahweh prophet. At first he echoes the prediction given by the other prophets, but that is only a foil for what he really has to say. His word from Yahweh is that Israel will be defeated and Ahab will be killed.

The kings and others in attendance are now faced with a choice different from the one that faced people on Mount Carmel. Who is the true prophet when everyone is speaking for Yahweh, and the word of one contradicts the word of others—here, many others? The test is declared by Micaiah himself in a parting word to Ahab: "If you return in peace, Yahweh has not spoken by me" (v. 28). We are back to fulfillment of the predicted word. Micaiah, who has spoken judgment in Yahweh's name, will be discredited if Ahab returns in peace, and the other prophets will be seen as the true Yahweh prophets. If things turn out differently and Ahab dies, Micaiah will be the true Yahweh prophet, and the others will be discredited. As it happened, Israel was defeated and Ahab was killed. Therefore Micaiah was authenticated as the true prophet, even though nothing more is said in the biblical record about what happened afterward. Nor is anything said about discrediting the other four hundred Yahweh prophets, who, as we suggested earlier, may have been Ahab and Jezebel's former Asherah prophets who had undergone a name change. But the inclusion of this incident in the biblical record is indication enough of what the final conclusion was.

The second test of true and false prophecy, in Deut 18:20-22, is likely the legal residue of this event and ones similar to it. It states:

> But the prophet who presumes to speak a word in my name, which I have not commanded him to speak, or who speaks in the name of other gods, that same prophet shall die. And if you say in your heart, "How may we know the word which Yahweh has not spoken?"—when a prophet speaks in the name of Yahweh, if the word does not come to pass or come true, that is a word which Yahweh has not spoken. The prophet has spoken it presumptuously; you need not be afraid of him.

The older test of Deut 13:1-5 has been incorporated into this new test by the addition of the words "or who speaks in the name of other gods." But at issue here is the problem that surfaced in 1 Kings 22. When prophets of Yahweh speak contrary words, the one (or ones) speaking a word that is not fulfilled is not a true prophet. The assumption of Deut 13:1-5 is here the test of authenticity.

This test is also stated in negative terms, indicating that, like the other test, it aims not so much at authenticating the true prophet as unmasking the pretender. Micaiah framed the test the same way, perhaps for the same reason. Small wonder, when four hundred prophets made up the opposition!

Though this test is formulated in negative terms and aims at discrediting the false prophet, we must not lose sight of its double intent. Micaiah, as the true prophet, is still very much in the biblical writer's mind, a hint of which we get in the concluding words of the test: "you need not be afraid of him" (Deut 18:22). James Crenshaw rightly points out that these words show that the test pertains only to prophecies of judgment.[17] People are not afraid of prophets who predict deliverance and well-being. Micaiah was the Yahweh prophet prophesying judgment, and Ahab was *afraid* of him. So when Deut 18:22 says not to worry about prophets of judgment if their predictions fail to come true, it recalls an Israelite king who had much cause to worry that a judgment spoken against him might be fulfilled.

This test of Deut 18:20-22 was expanded by Jeremiah to include prophecies of peace. It happened in the heat of another confrontation, this one between Jeremiah and Hananiah of Gibeon (Jeremiah 28). Prior to their meeting, Jeremiah had been preaching subservience to the king of Babylon. With a yoke on his neck, he predicted that Judah's servitude would be long and that the temple artifacts, which Nebuchadnezzar had taken from Jerusalem in 597 B.C.E., would not soon be returned. This message had just been given to foreign envoys visiting Jerusalem to discuss revolt, then later to King Zedekiah, and after that to priests and to the people (Jeremiah 27). But Jeremiah's real opponents behind the scenes were the prophets (Jer 27:9, 14-18), whom he had not yet met face-to-face. The opportunity came when Jeremiah met the prophet Hananiah at the temple. Hananiah was the first to speak. He predicted—in the name of Yahweh—that within two years Babylon's yoke would be broken and the temple artifacts would be brought home. Jeremiah, when it came his turn to speak, began as Micaiah did. He agreed wholeheartedly with what Hananiah had said, but only tongue-in-cheek. "However" (the particle 'ak אַךְ is one of emphasis), to this word another must be added. Jeremiah does not repeat what he has said previously to these other audiences. Everyone knows what he said. Instead he reminds Hananiah and the others present that he is not the first prophet in history to preach doom. Moreover, there is a test by which prophets of peace can be authenticated: "As for the prophet who prophesies peace, when the word of that prophet comes to pass, then it will be known that Yahweh has truly sent the prophet" (Jer 28:9).

The test given in Deut 18:20-22 is now expanded to include prophets of peace. When they speak in the name of Yahweh—which is what Hananiah has done—they too must have their word fulfilled. This test is stated in positive terms, which in this situation is necessary if Jeremiah is to be like his predecessors and speak indirectly. Jeremiah's test, of course, is not really new, simply a restatement of the old test about predictive signs, most of which were positive in nature.

Unfortunately—or perhaps fortunately—Hananiah did not live to see himself discredited. But he was made aware of his failing as a true Yahweh prophet. Jeremiah, after leaving the scene, later returned to declare that Hananiah was disingenuous. Yahweh, Jeremiah said, had not sent Hananiah, and he was preaching a lie. He would therefore die before the year was out. And so it happened. The final verse of the chapter says tersely, "In that same year, in the seventh month, the prophet Hananiah died" (Jer 28:17).

With this damning word to Hananiah, and events that later transpired, the Yahweh prophet from Gibeon was shown to be the false prophet according to Deut 18:20-22, and Jeremiah is shown to be the true prophet. Judgment pronounced in Yahweh's name came true. Deliverance pronounced in Yahweh's name did not come true. Temple artifacts did not return to Jerusalem, and instead of Nebuchadnezzar's yoke being broken, it was strengthened, and Israel went into a lengthy exile. For Ezekiel, too, fulfillment of predicted judgment was proof enough that a Yahweh prophet was authentic (Ezek 33:33).

Useful as these tests were, they never became the last word for authenticating Israel's prophets. Other considerations also came into play. In addition, prophets with the best of credentials gave predictions of judgment that went past any point of fulfillment.[18] Most often, however, it was prophecies of peace and salvation that were allowed to go unfulfilled. Only Jeremiah incorporated them into the test of Deut 18:20-22, observing as he did that the peace prophets seemed to disappear into the woodwork as soon as war came. Jeremiah says to Zedekiah, "Where are your prophets who prophesied to you, saying, 'The king of Babylon will not come against you and against this land'?" (Jer 37:19).

But one has the right to ask just how long one must wait for fulfillment. We have been speaking here about days, at most two years. What if fulfillment takes longer? Ezekiel tries to answer those who remain troubled about prophecies delayed in their fulfillment (Ezek 12:21-28). And there are prophecies like Isa 7:14, for example, that were later given messianic interpretation. These and other prophecies of a hopeful nature have been retained in Scripture despite the fact that they were not immediately fulfilled. Some, in fact, could not be fulfilled until a much later time.

The Christian church recognized that prophecies in Scripture were being fulfilled in their midst after a long wait. At the same time, it recognized also that immediate fulfillments were still possible, and that fulfillment could continue to be applied as a test for those claiming to speak a prophetic word (Acts 11:27-30).

One final point regarding fulfillment of the prophetic word. A word of judgment may go unfulfilled if repentance occurs. The book of Jonah is testimony to this. Jonah announced that Nineveh would be destroyed in forty days. But the people of Nineveh repented, and so the prophet's word went unfulfilled. We spoke earlier about words in antiquity having staying power, so much so that once they were spoken they could not be recalled. We said that Yahweh's word also had such power. At the same time, Yahweh is not bound the way human kings are, for which reason words spoken in Yahweh's name may go unfulfilled—if that is what Yahweh desires.[19] Repentance of sin can bring this about. Micah's judgment on Jerusalem went unfulfilled in his time because Hezekiah humbled himself, something that was recalled at Jeremiah's trial. People believed that a similar humility and repentance could keep Yahweh from fulfilling Jeremiah's word of judgment (Jer 26:17-19). But Jehoiakim was not about to repent, and thus Jeremiah had to be protected (Jer 26:24).

One may, of course, argue that nonfulfillment of a given prophecy is only temporary. Micah's prophecy of Jerusalem plowed as a field went unfulfilled in his time, but it was fulfilled in the time of Jeremiah. So also Jonah's prophecy against Nineveh. Though the book of Jonah is dated after the exile, its hero is a prophet in the time of Jeroboam II (2 Kgs 14:25). Nineveh was not destroyed then, but a century and a half later, in 612 B.C.E., by the Babylonians and Medes. According to this view, Yahweh's word, once spoken, will sooner or later come to pass. If there is a cancellation, for example, because of repentance, it may be only temporary.

PROPHETIC INTEGRITY

Scattered throughout the prophetic speeches are charges that other prophets are inauthentic. The sharpest attacks come from Jeremiah, in whose book is a separate collection of oracles devoted "to the prophets" (Jer 23:9-40). Jeremiah makes two basic charges, both of which call into question prophetic integrity. The first has to do with behavior. Some prophets are immoral. The second is related to the first. He says that some prophets are delivering inauthentic messages, which he calls "lies."[20] These may be messages papering over evil or pretending that it does not exist. These lies—also a silence when judgment is called for—make prophets disingenuous.

Messages can never be divorced from the character of those preaching them. There is always a tie-in, whatever people say to the contrary. John Skinner says, "To a false heart no true revelation is vouchsafed."[21] If prophets become such a divided self that they think an evil mind and immoral behavior can be integrated with a seemingly sound message, the end product is a greater deceit. Yahweh will bring such prophets and their messages, also those misled by them, to nought.

Duplicity within the self is an indication of duplicity before Yahweh. Prophets are raised up to restore people to Yahweh, to make them faithful to the covenant, and to bring about obedience to Yahweh's commands.

When they fail in doing these things, they are part of the problem instead of part of the solution. This is why Israel's prophets reserve their harshest criticism for other prophets.

For Hosea, the problems of society were religious in nature (Hos 4:1-10). There was a lack of knowledge of God, resulting in an entire society that was faithless and disobedient. At every turn were swearing, lying, killing, stealing, and adultery. Prophets and priests were no better than anyone else. They were without knowledge. They too behaved immorally. Therefore they forfeited their right to judge those over whom they were called to exercise care.

The true prophet must possess a knowledge of God, and here it needs to be emphasized that knowledge, for the Hebrews, is something personal and intimate. It is not knowledge "about." The prophet needs a "deep experience of God."[22] Lacking that, there will be no inner certainty as to what the prophet is about.[23] False prophets lack divine knowledge and inner certainty. Zedekiah (1 Kings 22) and Hananiah (Jeremiah 28) in their spirited attacks had neither. Zedekiah could only challenge the truth, and Hananiah could only repeat his wishful message of weal. Neither was willing to leave the final decision on authenticity in the hands of those who were listening, something both Micaiah and Jeremiah were able to do, and did do. The prophet having inner certainty believes that others will rise up to corroborate the truth he is proclaiming. Although entire communities can be depraved, within them are always some who know God, and sooner or later they will step forth. In addition, the true prophet is one who can intercede for the people (Jer 27:18)[24] because he knows God.

Moral Behavior

Again and again we hear prophets complain about a lack of personal integrity in prophets they know, referring to immoral behavior of one kind or another. Morality is a prominent theme in the wisdom literature, where immoral behavior is judged to be foolishness. The opposite of foolishness is wisdom, and both wisdom and moral behavior are marks of prophetic authenticity. Zephaniah cites prophets who are reckless individuals, undisciplined and unstable (Zeph 3:4). Jeremiah too observes reckless behavior in prophets he knows (Jer 23:32).

Isaiah impugns prophets and priests who are no better than the drunkards of Ephraim, so incapacitated have they become by wine and strong drink (Isa 28:7-8). It is a pitiful sight, and Yahweh will judge them along with others whose glory has faded. Jeremiah says that he himself has become like a drunken man, but that is because he thinks about Yahweh's holy words, on the one hand, and the immorality of prophets and priests, on the other (Jer 23:9-11). These prophets are guilty of adultery and lies—the latter in some cases, no doubt, being a cover-up for the former. His mention of Sodom and Gomorrah also indicates that sexual perversion is rife in Jerusalem (Jer 23:14; cf. Gen 19:4-5). In a letter to the exiles in Babylon, Jeremiah censures two Hebrew prophets, Ahab and Zedekiah, for committing adultery with their neighbors' wives (Jer 29:21-23). Adultery is often said to be the sin of the upper class,[25] but one finds it also in the lower classes. Jeremiah seems to find it everywhere (Jer 5:1-8). When prophets sink to the level of popular immorality, Jeremiah says that they "strengthen the hands of evildoers" and are scarcely better than prophets who lead people in the worship of Baal (Jer 23:13-14).

Prophets show a lack of integrity when they persecute the upright. It comes a bit late, but one of the laments after Jerusalem had fallen was that the prophets and priests were responsible for shedding the blood of the righteous (Lam 4:13). We remember, too, that it was the prophets and priests—not the royal officials—who called for Jeremiah's death after his oracle that the Jerusalem temple would become like the ruins of Shiloh (Jer 26:11). If inauthentic prophets persecute the upright, authentic prophets can expect persecution from those not upright, and it happens.

Another common charge leveled against prophets is that they are unprincipled in seeking economic gain. Micah says:

Thus says Yahweh concerning the prophets
　who lead my people astray,
who cry "Peace" when they have something to eat
　but declare war against him who puts nothing into their
　　　　mouths.
Therefore it shall be night to you, without vision,
　and darkness to you, without divination.
The sun shall go down upon the prophets,
　and the day shall be black over them.

(Mic 3:5-6)

On another occasion, Micah says that prophets he knows are divining just for the money (3:11). He does not mean that prophets are undeserving of remuneration, or that they must be free of all institutional ties. He is speaking about prophets abusing the prophetic office.[26] Their words have no integrity and are like the words of seers and diviners whom Yahweh will soon discredit (v. 7).

Jeremiah complains about prophets and priests who are "greedy for unjust gain" (Jer 6:13; 8:10). These individuals are preaching peace when there is no peace. Ezekiel made his charge against female prophets wearing magic bands and veils, hunting people down and keeping others alive—just for profit (Ezek 13:17-23). Jeremiah also knows prophets who steal oracles from one another (Jer 23:30), showing a lack of originality but also implying insincerity on their part.[27]

These complaints by Hosea, Isaiah, Micah, Jeremiah, Ezekiel, and others contain a high degree of rhetorical intensity, for which reason we may be led to conclude that the prophets being attacked are totally depraved. But if authenticity resides in the prophetic act, as we have said, then we had best not judge these prophets too harshly. Other actions of theirs were likely commendable. If we knew more about these prophets, our assessment would doubtless be more balanced. And it hardly needs to be said that in every instance we are hearing only one side of the dispute.

Some commentators have suggested that even among the great prophets we find moral standards being compromised.[28] For example, Isaiah walks naked in the streets of Jerusalem, Hosea marries a prostitute, Micaiah and Jeremiah feign the truth in public, and Jeremiah agrees with King Zedekiah not to reveal a private conversation they had but to provide inquisitors with a substitute explanation (Jer 38:14-28). What are we to say about these actions? Are they just borderline, or might some of them be considered immoral like the actions they condemn?

Two of these actions were definitely offensive, and were meant to be so. When Isaiah walked naked and barefoot in Jerusalem for three years, he doubtless offended people's moral sensibilities, although we really do not know the extent of this offense. This action, however, was to dramatize a sober message. Nudity translated into shame, and shame awaited Egypt and Ethiopia for opposing mighty Assyria (Isa 20:1-6). An extreme act of prophetic symbolism? Yes. An immoral act vitiating the prophet's credibility? Probably not. It was remembered as a credible act.

Hosea offended sensible people by marrying Gomer (Hos 1:2). But we misinterpret this act if we judge it to be as immoral as activities he seeks to combat, that is, harlotry and adultery. Marrying an immoral woman is not on a par with violating a marriage, which Hosea did not do. His symbolic action, though offensive to people, was like the symbolic action of Isaiah; it dramatized Israel's violated covenant with Yahweh God. There was another purpose in his action. In taking Gomer back, Hosea communicated the message that Yahweh, in spite of Israel's unfaithfulness, will take her back. People down through the ages have thus recognized Hosea's behavior to be boldly responsible, not recklessly irresponsible.

The other actions, upon closer inspection, are scarcely questionable. Micaiah's and Jeremiah's oracles feigning the truth are simply rhetorical moves aimed at defusing the opposition (1 Kgs 22:14-15; Jer 28:6). Everyone listening—except those totally clueless—knew what these prophets were up to. Not even Ahab was fooled by Micaiah. Jeremiah, for his part, had preached a contrary message to everyone in Jerusalem, and it would be a surprise if anyone did not know what he really thought. Verbal irony has nothing in common with lying, which seeks to hide, refute, or distort the truth.

Nor was Jeremiah's public statement after meeting with Zedekiah a lie, unless a lie consists in not revealing the entire substance of what the two had discussed. The answer given to people who questioned the prophet was no fabrication. Zedekiah told him to say, "I made a humble plea to the king that he would not send me back to the house of Jonathan to die there" (Jer 38:26). Jeremiah had made this plea to the king once before (Jer 37:20), and now when they meet again, he asks not to be put to death (Jer 38:15). Furthermore, if Jeremiah and Zedekiah agreed when concluding their conversation that Jeremiah should not be sent back to Jonathan's prison, which appears to have been the case, this means Jeremiah made the request and Zedekiah granted it. There was no lie here, and no impropriety on the part of either. Only part of a private conversation was made public. In modern courtroom testimony, this could be perjury. But certainly not here, where enemies are waiting to pounce on Jeremiah and the better part of wisdom is to tell only what one has to.

We must conclude that true prophets lived by a much higher standard of morality than the prophets they judged to be false.[29] All the great prophets were individuals of uncommon integrity, living in obedience to the Mosaic covenant, even as they lived in obedience to the divine call. They were not indifferent to evil but spoke out against it, often at great personal risk. Surrounding them and vastly outnumbering them were individuals satisfied to live according to the low expectations of popular religion. There is no need to protect the reputations of Israel's great prophets, which were determined long ago by people of antiquity and have been reaffirmed down through the ages. Had they not risen above their contemporaries, their moralistic preaching would have gone unheeded, for people never listen to individuals who behave no better than they.

Prophets are authenticated, then, by their own personal integrity. It is so in all ages. In the early church, prophets masking deception and lacking in moral principles were judged false (Acts 13:6-12; 2 Peter 2). Jesus, too, said that prophets are known by their fruits (Matt 7:15-20).

PART 2

Poetry, Prose, Rhetoric, and Symbolism
in the Hebrew Prophets

4

Prophetic Discourse in Poetry and Prose

Hebrew Poetry

EVEN BEFORE THE NEW RENAISSANCE IN THE STUDY of the ancient Near East began, in the mid-eighteenth century, important insights had been gained into the nature of Hebrew poetry, for which there was evidence even in antiquity. That poetry or something comparable was spoken and written in ancient Israel could be surmised from the major medieval codices of the Hebrew Bible, the M^A and M^L (tenth and eleventh centuries C.E.), which contained portions of text departing from the normal three-column prose (e.g., Exodus 15; Judges 5; Deuteronomy 32; Psalms; Proverbs; Job). The earlier Dead Sea Scrolls (c. second century B.C.E. to first century C.E.), when they were found, also turned up texts with different formatting, for example, in Deuteronomy 32. Josephus, too, commended Exodus 15 and Deuteronomy 32 to his non-Jewish contemporaries by saying that these were written in hexameter verse.

Modern recognition that Hebrew poetry builds largely on parallelism is credited to Bishop Robert Lowth, who demonstrated this in Lecture XIX of his now-famous *De Sacra Poesi Hebraeorum Praelectiones* (1753), delivered at Oxford commencing in 1741.[1] Parallelism consists of two, sometimes three, successive colons in which an idea is restated, embellished, or contrasted by repetition. Lowth's doctrine of parallelism was based on a sixteenth-century essay by Rabbi Azariah de Rossi, of Ferrara, who discussed Hebrew rhythm in his work *Me'or 'enayim* (1574). Lowth unknowingly had other predecessors, for example, scholars of the late seventeenth century who compared Hebrew parallelism to parallelism in

159

the Finnish epic *Kalevala*.[2] The phenomenon was discussed also in Christian Schoettgen's eighteenth-century work *Horae hebraicae et talmudicae I* (1733),[3] where it was given the name *exergasia*. Although some modern Jewish scholars have expressed doubts about the occurrence of real poetry in the Hebrew Bible, for example, James Kugel,[4] biblical poetry has been acknowledged by every critical methodology since the eighteenth century, and all our modern English Bibles now format poetry as poetry. Rudolf Kittel's 1906 edition of *Biblia Hebraica* was the first to print portions of the Hebrew Masoretic Text as poetry. This and subsequent editions of *Biblia Hebraica* continue to exert a major influence on the scanning of poetic materials in the Bible up to the present day.

Hebrew poetry exhibits many of the features found in poetry generally: terseness; abrupt transitions; and a lack of particles, which in Hebrew consist primarily of the definite article, the relative pronoun (אֲשֶׁר, *ʾăšer*), and the sign of the direct object (אֶת, *ʾēt*). Hebrew poetry also contains uncommon vocabulary and grammar; delayed subjects; postcedents rather than antecedents; parallelisms full and partial; words doing double duty in parallel colons; and inverted syntax, word order, and sequenced actions, which sometimes make a chiasmus. Hebrew poetry also has a sound and rhythm all its own, but this is difficult to quantify, since we lack a knowledge of the original meter and do not always know the pronunciations of ancient Hebrew words. Yet we find an abundance of wordplay in Hebrew poetry, also crescendo and diminution. According to H. L. Ginsberg, the formal elements of Hebrew poetry were largely borrowed from the Canaanites, and William Foxwell Albright traced parallelism back further to Old Akkadian in the third millennium B.C.E.[5]

POETRY IN THE HEBREW PROPHETS

The other major contribution of Lowth is not as well known but is just as important as his discovery of Hebrew parallelism. Lowth showed that large portions of prophetic discourse were in poetry, not prose, as previously thought (Lecture XVIII). The medieval codices of the Hebrew Bible did not format prophetic discourse as poetry, putting it rather in normal three-column prose. But now it was realized that the prophets, beginning with Amos, crafted oracles and other utterances in poetry. Samuel may be an early predecessor (1 Sam 15:22-23), but poetry begins on a major scale with Amos. In Jeremiah, Lowth located poetry at the beginning and end of the book, judging the book to be about evenly divided between poetry and prose. His instincts were correct. The poetic sections were first delineated by Benjamin Blayney in his Jeremiah commentary of 1784. As a result, we now realize that Jeremiah's oracles, confessions, laments, doxologies, prayers, wisdom sayings, and other utterances are carefully crafted in poetry. Only in a few cases is the scanning of material uncertain, for example, in chapter 1, where the discourse appears to be rhythmic prose.

Modern translations of the Bible have followed Kittel's 1906 edition of *Biblica Hebraica* in printing major portions of the prophetic books in poetry. One notable exception is the new *Hebrew University Bible*, which continues to print prophetic discourse in prose.

PROPHETIC ORACLES IN PROSE

One might imagine that prophets also spoke in prose, not just when they were conversing normally, but when they were delivering oracles or making other utterances commensurate with their office. This has not been generally recognized, however, probably because prose material in the prophetic books has been taken to derive from a second hand, and not to be the *ipsissima verba* of the prophet. In the book of Jeremiah, for example, where we have a significant amount of the prophet's discourse in prose, this discourse has simply been lumped together with the contextual narrative, and all of it has been called "sermonic prose."

We cite here just one example from Jeremiah to show how prose oracles in his book have been carefully crafted, suggesting that they, too, like his oracles in poetry, may have been spoken in prose when delivered to their audiences. The passage is Jer 7:3-14. Earlier scholars saw in 7:1-15 a "temple sermon" delivered by Jeremiah in 609 B.C.E., a summary of which appears with background information in Jer 26:4-6. The term *sermon*, however, is a misnomer. These verses do not contain a unified sermon, but rather three self-contained oracles brought together in a cluster: vv. 3-7, vv. 8-11, and vv. 12-14. The biblical text is as follows:

> ³Thus said Yahweh of hosts, the God of Israel:
> Make good your ways and your doings and I will let you dwell in this place. ⁴Do not trust for yourselves in the deceptive words, "The temple of Yahweh, the temple of Yahweh, the temple of Yahweh are these." ⁵For if you really make good your ways and your doings, if you really act justly each man toward his fellow, ⁶the sojourner, the orphan, and the widow you do not oppress, and the blood of the innocent you do not shed in this place, and after other

gods you do not go, to your own hurt, ⁷then I will let you dwell in this place, in the land that I gave to your fathers for all time.

⁸Look, you trust for yourselves in the deceptive words to no avail. ⁹Do you think you can steal, murder, and commit adultery, and swear to the Lie, and burn incense to Baal, and go after other gods that you have not known, ¹⁰and then come and stand in my presence, in this house upon which my name is called, and say, "We are safe!"—only to keep doing all these abominations? ¹¹A robber's den is this house upon which my name is called in your eyes? As for me, Look! I have seen!—oracle of Yahweh.

¹²Go indeed, would you, to my place that was in Shiloh, where I first made my name dwell, and see what I did to it because of the evil of my people Israel. ¹³Now then, because you have done all these doings—oracle of Yahweh—when I spoke to you—constantly I spoke—but you did not hear, and I called you but you did not answer, ¹⁴I will do then to the house upon which my name is called, in which you trust, yes, to the place that I gave to you and to your fathers, as I did to Shiloh.

Criteria used to delimit three separate oracles are the following: (1) section markings, (2) messenger formulas, and (3) the rhetorical device of inclusio. The Hebrew text contains section markings, the *setumah* and the *petumah*, which are now known to be very old. They have turned up in the Dead Sea Scrolls, including the *Temple Scroll*, and are present also in the Samaritan Pentateuch. Here in the present verses, the three main medieval codices, M^L, M^A, and M^P, have a *setumah* before v. 3, marking the beginning of Oracle I; M^L and M^P have a *setumah* after v. 11, marking the end of Oracle II; and M^L has a *setumah*, M^A and M^P a *petuuah*, and 4QJer^a a section after v. 15, marking the end of the larger unit.

Each of the oracles contains a messenger formula. Oracle I is prefaced with an embellished "Thus said Yahweh of hosts, the God of Israel" (v. 3); Oracle II concludes with "oracle of Yahweh" (v. 11); and Oracle III has "oracle of Yahweh" in the middle (v. 13). The different locations of the formulas are probably intentional, particularly if the oracles were spoken as a cluster.

Looking to rhetorical form, we see that all three oracles employ the inclusio, which is a verbal tie-in between beginning and end. The repeated words and phrases in the three oracles in Jer 7:1-15 are as follows:

I	*I will let you dwell in this place*	v. 3
	I will let you dwell in this place	v. 7
II	*Look! hinneh*	v. 8
	Look! hinneh	v. 11
III	*my place . . . in Shiloh*	v. 12
	the place . . . to Shiloh	v. 14

The inclusio in Oracle III supports a bracketing out of v. 15 as a later addition, the purpose of which is to render a comparison between Judah and Ephraim (= northern Israel).

What we have, then, in 7:1–15 is an introduction (vv. 1–2), three separate oracles (vv. 3–14), and a later add-on (v. 15). The first oracle is hortatory preaching like that found in Deuteronomy, although it calls for correction (v. 3: "Make good [= amend] your ways and your doings"), making it suit the milieu of the Josianic reform; the second oracle is indictment; and the third oracle is riveting judgment. The three messages can be reduced to the following:

Oracle I: A people making good its ways and its doings, acting justly each man toward his fellow, not oppressing the sojourner, the orphan, and the widow, not shedding innocent blood, and not going after other gods, will be permitted by Yahweh to remain in the land.

Oracle II: You steal, murder, commit adultery, swear to the Lie, burn incense to Baal, and go after other gods.

Oracle III: Because you have done all these things, Yahweh will make this place like (the ruined) Shiloh.

Another offshoot of this revised reading is that we discover in the text a rudimentary form of logic when all three oracles are taken as a unit. The three messages can be reduced to a syllogism, which is customarily credited to Aristotle and the Greeks:

Major premise: A people not violating the covenant can remain in the land.

Minor premise: This people has violated the covenant.

Conclusion: Yahweh will bring (this people and) this land to ruin.

Earlier scholars were troubled by a lack of coherence in their so-called sermon, particularly between vv. 3-7 and vv. 12-14.[6] Oracle I, as we mentioned, is simply a call for covenant obedience, prophetic only in the sense that it calls people to amend their behavior. The hope, nevertheless, is that the nation will escape judgment and remain in the land. Then comes a strident indictment of evils already committed, and finally unequivocal judgment, making one wonder why people were told in the early verses that they could remain in the land if they "made good their ways and their doings." Now with the recognition that we have three self-contained oracles, the problem is much reduced, if not eliminated altogether. Each oracle is seen to have an integrity of its own, and only when all three are brought together is there movement from warning to judgment.

It could be that this three-oracle cluster is a later editorial creation. But when we compare the three oracles with the narrative in chapter 26, we see in the preaching summary (26:4-6) and in Jeremiah's defense (v. 13) segments drawn not from just one oracle, but from all three.[7] It appears, then, that all three oracles were spoken on this one celebrated occasion as a cluster, and that the prophet is intentionally moving from general principle, to a violation of principle, to judgment. If so, we have not only evidence of Jeremiah the prophet delivering oracles in prose to his temple audience, but evidence of what I would call rudimentary logic in the preaching of Jeremiah.

5

RHETORICAL DISCOURSE
IN THE PROPHETS

RHETORIC IN THE ANCIENT NEAR EAST

IF THE CLASSIC PROPHETS EMANATE FROM ANCIENT Israel, the classic orators and teachers of rhetoric hail from ancient Greece and Rome. The names of Aristotle, Cicero, and Quintilian spring immediately to mind, but there were others, many others. Rhetoric in the modern West is therefore conceptualized and measured in large part against what we know about classical rhetoric, and many do not even think of looking at cultures predating the Greeks and Romans to find a rhetorical tradition more ancient than the one they know best.

We have, of course, the Hebrew Old Testament, and teachers in church, synagogue, and academy have long noted a rhetorical excellence in this document of Holy Writ. Its excellence was carried over into the New Testament and, not infrequently, better explains the richness of discourse there than classical rhetoric taught in Hellenistic schools of the time. Today, Hebrew rhetoric is being much studied, and we are learning a considerable amount by simply reading the biblical text with an eye for the rhetorical nature of its discourse. But we have no textbook on the subject. As a result, we must depend on classical handbooks for definitions and functions of rhetorical figures. Research is also being carried on in the broader field of ancient Near Eastern rhetoric, inasmuch as we have at our disposal thousands of excavated texts from the ancient Near East. Decipherment and translation of these texts have gone on for 150 years, opening up a whole new world more ancient than the classical world of

165

Greece and Rome. The rediscovery of this ancient Near Eastern world is nothing short of a new renaissance.

HEBREW RHETORIC

Hebrew rhetoric developed from an ancient preclassical rhetorical tradition going back to the beginning of recorded history. Sumerian scribal schools, called "tablet houses," produced a literate class that has left behind a rich legacy of rhetorical discourse from early Mesopotamian society (c. 3000 B.C.E.). The Sumerians wrote poetry having repetition, parallelism, epithets, and similes.[1] Cuneiform texts of the third and second millennia show that this rhetorical tradition survived in Old Babylonia, Assyria, and Ugarit. A rhetorical tradition doubtless developed during the same period in Egypt, where scribal schools are known to have existed from the early third millennium, and where poetry also was written, but about this tradition little is known.

Israel's oldest literature, to judge from its earliest poems (Exodus 15; Deuteronomy 33; Judges 5) and other writings, contains works of fine art. A simplified twenty-two- to thirty-letter alphabet introduced at Ugarit two to three centuries before Israel's entry into Canaan (thirteenth century), which is the prototype of the Hebrew alphabet, created new possibilities for oral and written discourse as words began replacing older cuneiform signs. Ancient Hebrew rhetoric survives largely in the Hebrew Bible / Old Testament, from which it may be concluded that during the eighth to sixth centuries B.C.E. it experienced its "golden age," a full three centuries and more before the art achieved classical expression by Aristotle in Greece, and by Cicero, Quintilian, and others in Rome.

Hebrew rhetorical tradition produced no theoretical work the likes of Aristotle's *Rhetoric* (322–320 B.C.E.), nor handbooks such as the *ad Herennium* (c. 86–82 B.C.E.) and Quintilian's *Institutes* (c. 90 C.E.). Nevertheless, in the Bible are to be found an array of figures of speech performing the same or similar functions as in classical rhetoric, as well as modes of argumentation known and classified by later Greek and Roman authors. Prophets embellish their discourse with metaphor, simile, comparison, euphemism, epithet, chiasmus, asyndeton, alliteration, rhetorical question, hyperbole, paronomasia, and irony both dramatic and verbal. Amos is the prophet of the rhetorical question; Hosea is the prophet of vivid metaphors and oracles with split bicolons (i.e., bicolons split so that one colon begins the oracle and one colon ends it), also the prophet with an extraordinary capacity for expressing pathos;

Isaiah is the master of verbal irony; and Ezekiel is the prophet of the extended metaphor, or allegory. But the prophet possessing the greatest rhetorical skill is unquestionably Jeremiah, who can hold rank with the best of the Greek and Roman rhetors, anticipating them as he does in style, structure, and modes of argumentation. His indebtedness is to Hosea and the sermonic prose of Deuteronomy. The latter might be expected, since Deuteronomy is a seventh-century book, and Jeremiah a prophet of the late seventh and early sixth century. Moreover, Deuteronomy is widely conceded to be the rhetorical book par excellence of the Old Testament.

The preachers of Deuteronomy appear to have been Levitical priests, some of whom were trained scribes and went by the name of "scribe" (2 Chr 34:13). How they received their schooling is not known, but it is reasonable to assume that they attended a Jerusalem school where writing and rhetorical skills were taught. Isaiah, Jeremiah, Ezekiel, and other Judahite prophets would have attended this school, receiving the same training as the Levitical priests before venturing forth as heralds of the divine word. Although we know nothing of a Jerusalem school, one would have been required in the time of David and Solomon (tenth century B.C.E.), when scribes first began appearing at the royal court as high officials.[2] In Jeremiah's time, this school would have been headed by Shaphan the scribe and would have been attached to the palace or the temple, as in neighboring societies (cf. 2 Kgs 22:8-10).

PROPHETIC RHETORIC

In this chapter I want to provide a window into the world of Hebrew rhetoric as it appears in oracles and other discourse emanating from the prophets. Particular attention will be paid to rhetorical moves in the discourse of Jeremiah. Although Israel's prophetic movement began with Samuel, who, together with Nathan, Elijah, Micaiah ben Imlah, and others, burst in early upon the scene and delivered Yahweh's word with a power that still commands our admiration, the real rhetors of preexilic Israel were the so-called writing prophets, that is, Amos and Hosea in northern Israel, and Micah, Isaiah, perhaps Joel, Nahum, Habakkuk, Obadiah, Zephaniah, and Jeremiah in Judah a century and a half later. Ezekiel was born and reared in Judah, but his prophecies were given in Babylon to Judahites who were taken there in the exile of 597 B.C.E. The great prophet of the exile is a nameless individual we call Second Isaiah, the one responsible for the lofty poetry in Isaiah 40–66. Postexilic prophets are Haggai, Zechariah, and Malachi, all of whom possessed rhetorical skills that are worthy of our attention.

Repetition

Repetition is the single most important feature of ancient Hebrew rhetoric,[3] being used for emphasis, wordplays, expressing the superlative, creating pathos, and structuring both parts and wholes of prophetic discourse. Its importance can hardly be overestimated. Repetitions can be sequential or placed in strategic collocations to provide balance. In both, they can also bring about closure: repeated terms can be intentionally broken at the end of a series, and repeated words and/or split bicolons can form a tie-in beginning and end (inclusio).

The Superlative. Repeated words can function as a periphrasis for the superlative:

Isa 6:3:	*holy, holy, holy*
Joel 3:14:	*multitudes, multitudes*

Isaiah is acclaiming Yahweh to be "the holiest"; Joel means "multitudes upon multitudes."

Geminatio. Many repetitions are simply for emphasis (*geminatio*), for example:

Jer 4:19:	*my innards, my innards*
Jer 6:14 [= 8:11]:	*peace, peace*
Jer 7:4:	*the temple of Yahweh, the temple of Yahweh, the temple of Yahweh*
Jer 22:29:	*land, land, land*
Ezek 21:27:	*ruin, ruin, ruin*

An echo effect is created when repetitions occur in succession:

Jer 46:20:	*A beautiful, beautiful* heifer was Egypt,
	a horsefly from the north *came, came.*

Anaphora. Anaphora is the repetition of a word or words at the beginning of two or more successive colons, lines, or poetic verses. This figure serves to heighten pity, disdain, fear, joyful anticipation, or other emotional state. This type of repetition often creates *onomatopoeia*.

In Jer 5:15-17, a fourfold repetition of "nation" is answered by a four-fold repetition of "it/they shall consume," where the latter simulates an enemy who eats without stopping. The initial stanza has *epiphora* in the center ("it is"), and predications in the latter stanza form a chiasmus (see p. 177):

Look! I will bring upon you
    a nation from afar, house of Israel . . . ,
    a nation well established it is,
    a nation from antiquity it is,
    a nation whose language you do not know,
and what it says you will not understand.

. . . .

It shall consume your harvest and your food;
    they shall consume your sons and your daughters;
    it shall consume your flocks and your herds.
It shall consume your vines and your fig trees.
It will beat down your fortified cities—
    in which you trust—by the sword.

In Jer 50:35-38, a fivefold repetition of "sword" simulates the repeated stabbing of victims, but at the end is a climactic *paronomasia* with the similar-sounding "drought."

A sword [*ḥereb*, חֶרֶב] upon Chaldeans . . . and to the inhabitants of
    Babylon . . .
A sword [חֶרֶב] to the diviners, that they become foolish.
A sword [חֶרֶב] to her warriors, that they be broken.
A sword [חֶרֶב] to his horses and to his chariots, and to all the
    mixed races . . . , that they become women.
A sword [חֶרֶב] to her treasures, that they become booty.
A drought [*ḥōreb*, חֹרֶב] to her waters, that they be dried up.

In Jer 51:20-23, a ninefold repetition of "with you I smash" simu-lates the sense by creating the sound of a hammering club (onomato-poeia). The tedium of repetition is lessened with the terms of predica-tion, naming the hapless war victims, arranged into a chiasmus:

You were a club for me, a weapon of war:
   with you I smashed nations . . . and kingdoms,
     with you I smashed horse and his rider,
      with you I smashed chariot and its rider,
       with you I smashed man and woman,
        with you I smashed old and young,
       with you I smashed young man and maiden,
      with you I smashed shepherd and his flock,
     with you I smashed farmer and his team,
    with you I smashed governors and commanders.

In Jer 31:4-5, Jeremiah simulates the resumption of city life in Zion with this anaphora:

Again I will build you, and you shall be built.
Again you'll deck yourself with your hand-drums
   and go forth in the dance of merrymakers.
Again you'll plant vineyards on Samaria's mountains;
   planters shall plant and eat the fruit.

Zephaniah is particularly fond of anaphora:

Zeph 1:2-6: *I will utterly sweep away* everything
           from the face of the earth, says Yahweh.
        I will sweep away man and beast;
        I will sweep away the birds of the air
          and the fish of the sea

        . . . .

        those who bow down on the roofs
          to the hosts of heaven,
        those who bow down and swear to Yahweh
          and yet swear by Milcom,
        those who have turned back from following Yahweh,
          who do not seek Yahweh or inquire of him.

The repetitions in vv. 5-6 echo the repetitions of vv. 2-3 (cf. Jer 5:15-17). There is also deviation in that the final line uses another verb.

Zeph 1:15: *A day* of wrath is that day,
        a day of distress and anguish,
        a day of ruin and devastation,

> *a day* of darkness and gloom,
> *a day* of clouds and thick darkness,
> *a day* of trumpet blast and battle cry
> *against* the fortified cities
> *and against* the lofty battlements.

This poetry compares structurally with Jeremiah's chaos vision in Jer 4:23-26. More anaphora occurs in Zeph 2:2: *before . . . before . . . before.* The "woe . . . therefore" structure of Isa 5:8-25 and the "woe" structure of Hab 2:6-17 are anaphora on a large scale.

Epiphora. Epiphora (Lat.: *conversio*) is the repetition of a word or words at the end of two or more successive colons, lines, or poetic verses. In Jeremiah:

Jer 4:19: My innards, my innards, let me writhe,
> the walls of *my heart*;
> it roars to me, *my heart*,
> I cannot be still.

In one of his three-stanza poems, Jeremiah shifts from epiphora to anaphora:

Jer 8:22–9:2: Is there no balm in Gilead?
> Is there no healer there?
> Indeed, so why has it not arisen,
> healing for *my dear people?*

> *Who* can make my head waters
> and my eyes a well of tears,
> so I might weep day and night
> for the slain of *my dear people?*

> *Who* can make for me in the desert
> a traveler's lodge,
> so I might forsake my people
> and go away from them?

A large-scale epiphora occurs in Amos 4:6-11, where the fivefold repetition of "yet you did not return to me" becomes a virtual refrain.

Alliteration. Alliteration is the repetition of consonants in succession, usually occurring at the beginning of two or more consecutive words, or in words near to one another. This is a figure of sound, not meaning. Quite often there will also be *paronomasia*. In Jeremiah:

Jer 17:12-13a:	The consonant *k* (כ) begins two words, and immediately following are five successive words beginning with the *m* (מ) consonant.
Jer 48:15:	The combination *bû* repeats three times (paronomasia).
Jer 49:15:	The *b* (ב) consonant repeats three times.

Inclusio. The inclusio structures poetic and prose discourse by repeating at the end of a given discourse, or portion of discourse, words or phrases occurring at the beginning. Sometimes the end terms will be synonyms or fixed equivalents of the beginning terms. Classicists call this figure "ring composition." The inclusio commonly functions to effect closure, although it can simply give emphasis and have other functions. This inclusio appears in Amos:

Amos 2:9:   Yet I destroyed *the Amorite* before them,

whose height was like the height of the cedars
    and who was as strong as the oaks.
I destroyed his fruit above
    and his roots beneath.
Also I brought you up out of the land of Egypt
    and led you forty years in the wilderness,

to possess the land of *the Amorite.*

Amos 5:2:   Fallen, no more to *rise,*
        is the virgin Israel.
    Forsaken on her land
        with none to *raise her up.*

Other inclusios occur in Amos 5:10-12 (*gate . . . gate*) and Amos 8:9-10 (*day . . . day*).

Hosea crafts oracles with split bicolons containing keyword repetitions, for example:

Hos 4:11-14: New wine takes away the mind of *my people.*

> They inquire of their thing of wood,
>   and their staff gives them oracles.
> For a spirit of whoredom has led them astray,
>   and they have gone a-whoring out from under
>   their God.
> On the tops of the mountains they sacrifice,
>   and on the hills they burn offerings.
> Under oak, poplar, and terebinth
>   because their shade is good!
> Therefore your daughters play the whore,
>   and your sons' brides commit adultery.
> I will not punish your daughters when they play
>   the whore
>   nor your sons' brides when they commit
>   adultery.
> For those men over there go aside with whores
>   and sacrifice with sacred prostitutes.

> *A people* without sense will be thrust down!

Hos 8:9-13: For *behold they* have gone up to Assyria.

> A wild ass off by himself,
>   Ephraim has hired lovers.
> Even though they hire among the nations,
>   now I will gather them up,
> so that they soon writhe under the burden
>   of the officials' king.
> Indeed, Ephraim has multiplied altars;
>   he uses them for sinning,
>   altars for sinning.
> Though I write for him multitudes of my laws,
>   they are regarded as something strange.
> Sacrifices they love, so they sacrifice
>   flesh, and they eat.
>   Yahweh takes no delight in them.
> Now he will remember their iniquity
>   and punish their sins.

> *Behold they* will return to Egypt!

Another keyword inclusio in Hosea:

Hos 5:3-4: *I know* Ephraim,
    and Israel is not hid from me,
    for now, Ephraim, you have played the harlot;
    Israel is defiled.
    Their deeds do not permit them
    to return to their God.
    For the spirit of harlotry is within them,
    and *they know not* Yahweh.

The prophetess Huldah framed her celebrated Josiah oracle with an inclusio:

2 Kgs 22:16-20: *I will bring / evil / upon this place*

. . . all the evil / that I will bring / upon this place

Nahum's preaching contains this inclusio:

Nah 1:9-11: What do you *plot against Yahweh?*
    He will make a full end;
    he will not take vengeance twice on his foes.
    Like tangled thorns they are consumed,
    like dry stubble.
    Did one not come out from you
    who *plotted* evil *against Yahweh*
    and counseled villainy?

Jeremiah makes liberal use of the inclusio, reflecting as one might expect the rhetoric of Deuteronomy, where the inclusio is the controlling rhetorical structure of the First Edition (chapters 1–28). A single word creates this inclusio in a double bicolon:

Jer 5:21: *Hear* this, would you please,
    stupid people without heart.
    They have eyes but do not see;
    they have ears but do not *hear.*

There is also irony here: The prophet asks a people to hear who cannot hear.

Jeremiah points up one of many incongruities with this inclusio, where also epiphora occurs at the center:

Jer 4:22:   For my people are fools;
             me *they do not know*;
                stupid children are **they**;
                not discerning are **they**;
             wise are they to do evil,
        but to do good, *they do not know.*

Jeremiah's three Temple Oracles all make use of the inclusio:

Jer 7:3-7:   *and I will let you dwell in this place . . .*
             then I will let you dwell in this place
Jer 7:8-11:   *Look!*
             Look!
Jer 7:12-14: *my place . . . in Shiloh . . .*

             the place . . . to Shiloh

Jeremiah's defense before the court begins and ends:

Jer 26:12-15: *Yahweh sent me . . . all the things . . .*

             . . . Yahweh sent me . . . all these things

Entire poems in Jeremiah have inclusio structures (3:1-5; 10:6-7; 20:7-10, 14-18; 51:11-14).

In Joel is this inclusio:

Joel 1:19-20: *For fire has devoured*
             the pastures of the wilderness,
        and flame has burned
            all the trees of the field.
        Even the wild beasts cry to you
            because the water brooks are dried up.
        Yes, fire has devoured
            the pastures of the wilderness.

Chiasmus. Chiasmus is an inversion of words, word cognates, fixed pairs, syntactic units, and even sounds in the bicolon, the verse, and the larger composition. In larger structures, the center of the chiasmus is the turning point, also frequently the climax.[4] This figure occurs in both the poetry and the prose of the prophets. These keyword chiasms from Amos:

Amos 2:11-12:   And I raised up some of your sons for *prophets*
and some of your young men for *Nazirites*.
Is it not indeed so, O people of Israel?
But you made the *Nazirites* drink wine
and commanded the *prophets*: You shall not
prophesy.

Amos 5:4-6a: *Seek me and live,*
but do not seek *Bethel,*
and do not enter into *Gilgal*
or cross over to *Beersheba,*
for *Gilgal* shall surely go into exile
and *Bethel* shall come to nought.
Seek Yahweh and live.

Another keyword chiasmus occurs in Amos 2:14-16.

From the prophet Hosea:

Hos 12:4-5a: In the womb he took his brother by the heel,
and in his manhood *he strove* with God;
yes, *he strove* with an angel and prevailed.
He wept and sought his favor.

Here keywords in the center repeat the account of Jacob's wrestling at the Jabbok (Gen 32:22-32). The first and last colons recount Jacob's relationship with his brother Esau.

An entire keyword chiasmus in Hosea is the following:

Hos 13:14:   Shall I ransom them from the power of *Sheol*?
Shall I redeem them from *Death*?
O Death, where are your plagues?
O Sheol, where is your destruction?

Isaiah makes a keyword chiasmus with fixed word pairs:

Isa 5:7:   For the *vineyard* of Yahweh of hosts
is the *house of Israel*,
and the *men of Judah*
are his *pleasant planting*.

This keyword chiasmus turns up in the preaching of Micah:

Mic 3:2-3:   who tear the *skin* from off my people
   and their *flesh* from off their bones,
   who eat the *flesh* of my people
   and flay their *skin* from off them.

Jeremiah crafts an array of chiastic structures. This one is laden with irony:

Jer 2:27b-28a: But *in the time of their trouble* they say,
   "*Arise and save us*,"
   but where are your gods which you made
   for yourselves?
   Let them *arise* if they can *save* you
   in your time of trouble.

At the center Yahweh interrupts the people's cry to pose a question of his own.

This keyword chiasmus in Jeremiah has long been noted:

Jer 9:4:   Each person beware of his *fellow*,
   and every *brother* do not trust,
   for every *brother* is a "Jacob,"
   and every *fellow* goes about slandering.

Large keyword chiasms in whole poems occur in Jer 2:5-9; 5:1-8; 8:13-17; and 51:34-45.

From the prophet Joel is this chiasmus using both repetition and fixed word pairs:

Joel 2:28-29: And it shall be afterwards: *I will pour out my spirit*
   on all flesh;
   your *sons* and your *daughters* shall prophesy,
   your *old men* shall dream dreams,
   and your *young men* shall see visions;
   even upon the *menservants* and *maidservants*,
   in those days, *I will pour out my spirit.*

Peter quotes this prophecy at Pentecost (Acts 2:17-18) but inverts the center colons.

Zechariah crafts this keyword chiasmus:

Zech 9:5:   *Ashkelon* shall see it, and be afraid;
            Gaza too, and shall writhe in anguish.
                Ekron also, because its hopes are confounded.
            The king shall perish from *Gaza*;
            Ashkelon shall be uninhabited.

Another type of chiasmus is made by inverted syntax. From Isaiah:

Isa 11:1:   It shall come / a shoot from the stump of Jesse
            and a branch from his roots / it shall grow.

Jeremiah's poetry teems with syntactic chiasms, where verbs are typically placed at the extremes. A few examples:

Jer 2:19:   It will chasten you / your wickedness
            and your apostasy / will reprove you.
Jer 4:7:   It has gone up / a lion from the thicket
            and a destroyer of nations / has gone forth.
Jer 4:9:   And they shall be appalled / the priests
            and the prophets / shall be astounded.
Jer 20:6:   You shall go / into captivity
            and Babylon / you shall enter.

Only rarely does Jeremiah place verbs in the center:

Jer 2:36:   So by Egypt / you will be shamed
            as you were shamed / by Assyria.
Jer 51:38: Together like lions / they shall roar;
            they shall growl / like lion's whelps.

Multiclinatum. Multiclinatum is the repetition of verbal roots in succession, occurring often in Jeremiah, where it is a virtual signature of the prophet:

Jer 11:18: Yahweh made me know, and I knew.
Jer 15:19: If you return, then I will let you return.
Jer 17:14: Heal me, Yahweh, and I shall be healed.
Jer 20:7:   You enticed me, Yahweh, and I was enticed.

Accumulation

The celebrated rhetorical prose in Jeremiah and the Deuteronomic literature is largely accumulation (*accumulatio*). It is heavy and stereotyped, with nouns heaping up in twos, threes, and fours, and longer phrases balancing rhythmically in parallelism. Accumulation is found also in poetry. Hebrew rhetoric, says James Muilenburg, strives after totality.[5]

Accumulatio. Accumulatio turns up most often in the Jeremiah prose. Some examples:

> *the cities of Judah . . . the streets of Jerusalem* (Jer 7:17, 34; 11:6;
>   33:10; 44:6, 17, 21)
> *the voice of joy and the voice of gladness, the voice of groom and the
>   voice of bride* (Jer 7:34; 16:9; 25:10; 33:11)
> *the(ir) dead bodies . . . will be food for the birds of the skies and the
>   beasts of the earth* (Jer 7:33; 16:4; 19:7; 34:20)
> *disgrace, proverb . . . taunt and curse* (Jer 24:9; and variously in Jer
>   19:8; 25:9; 29:18; 44:12)

Often nouns appear in triads:

> *into a fortified city, and into an iron pillar, and into walls of bronze,
>   against its princes, against its priests, and against the people of the
>   land* (Jer 1:18)
> *by sword, and by famine, and by pestilence* (Jer 14:12; 21:9; 24:10;
>   27:8)

Some examples of accumulatio in the Jeremianic poetry:

Jer 1:10:   *to uproot and to break down,*
                   to destroy and to overthrow,
                       to build up and to plant
Jer 12:7:   *I have forsaken my house,*
                   I have abandoned my heritage,
               I have given the beloved of my soul
                   into the hand of her enemies.

Accumulatio turns up also in the poetry of Joel:

Joel 2:19:   *grain, wine, and oil*

Asyndeton. Asyndeton is the rapid accumulation of verbs, with or without connectives, in both prose and poetry. Classical authors used asyndeton to heap up praise or blame. Jeremiah uses the figure to heap up blame (7:9), press home a message of divine judgment (51:20-23), or emphasize the joy attending Israel's future salvation (31:4-5). Other examples:

Jer 4:5:   *Blow* . . . *cry out, pour it out,* and *say* . . .

Jer 5:1:   *Go back and forth* in the streets of Jerusalem, *look,* please, and *take note,* and *search* her squares.

From Jeremiah's Foreign Nation Oracles:

Jer 46:3-4:   *Ready* buckler and shield!
                  and advance to battle!
              Harness the horses!
                  and *rise up,* O horsemen!
              Stand ready with helmets!
                  Polish lances!
                      Put on scale armor!

Jer 49:8:   *Flee! Be gone! Go deep to dwell.*

Jer 49:30:   *Flee! Wander all about! Go deep to dwell!*

Chain Figure. This figure, which lacks a better name, occurs in Joel's locust parade:

Joel 1:4:   What the *cutting locust* left,
                  the *swarming locust* has eaten;
              what the *swarming locust* left,
                  the *hopping locust* has eaten;
              and what the *hopping locust* left,
                  the *destroying locust* has eaten.

The function of this figure is to express totality. It is not to be confused with the *sortie,* which came with the infusion of Greco-Roman rhetoric into postexilic Jewish life in the fourth century B.C.E.[6] The sortie (Gk.: *klimax;* Lat.: *gradatio*) appears in the Jewish writings of *Pirqe Aboth* (1:1; 4:12) and the Wisdom of Solomon (6:17-19). It, too, is a catalogue of statements, each word picking up from a preceding word, but its function is to lead to a climax. The sortie was used often by Paul, for example, in Rom 5:3-5: "More than that we rejoice in our *sufferings,* knowing that *suffering* produces *endurance,* and *endurance* produces *character,* and *character* produces *hope,* and *hope* does not disappoint us"; and in Rom 8:29-30: "For those whom he foreknew he also *predestined* to be conformed to the image of his Son . . . and those whom he *predestined* he also *called*; and those whom he *called* he also *justified*; and those whom he *justified* he also glorified."

Tropes

Tropes are words or expressions used to mean something other than what they normally mean, yet having a connectedness to normal meanings—sometimes through a link term—so as to give an idea of freshness or emphasis.[7] Prophets, like all good orators, embellished their oracles and other speeches with tropes, which strengthened the discourse and kindled audience imagination. Common tropes are the metaphor, simile, allegory, metonymy, synecdoche, *abusio*, epithet, and irony, all of which are well represented in discourse of the prophets.

Metaphor. Metaphors are tropes in which figurative terms or descriptions are superimposed over literal terms or descriptions, creating a vivid mental likeness of objects or ideas. In lowering the level of abstraction, metaphors make ideas more concrete. At the same time, they appeal to the imagination. Prophetic discourse teems with metaphors, some of the more common drawing from the family, animals, sex, the wilderness, the hunt, cooking, agriculture, and the military. Animal metaphors occur very often. Amos, Hosea, and Jeremiah sometime combine metaphors with similes or literal equivalents, which, according to modern tastes, weakens the figure.

One of the most striking metaphors in the Old Testament is Amos's use of "lion" for God:

Amos 3:8:   *The Lion has roared,*
           who will not fear?
        Yahweh God has spoken,
           who will not prophesy?

"Lion" here is a pure metaphor for God, a coinage without parallel in the Hebrew Bible. Another striking metaphor from Amos:

Amos 4:1:   Hear this word, you *cows of Bashan*.

Here the prophet follows with a clarifying word, identifying the "cows of Bashan" as the women of Samaria who oppress the poor and whine to their husbands for something more to drink.

Some of the most memorable metaphors emanate from Hosea, who describes the covenant as a relationship between "father and son" or between "husband and wife" (Hosea 2; 11:1, 3). Other metaphors from Hosea:

Hos 7:8:   *Ephraim is a cake not turned.*
Hos 10:1:   *Israel is a luxuriant vine.*
Hos 10:11:   *Ephraim was a trained heifer that loved to thresh.*

In the following examples, Hosea combines metaphors with literal equivalents:

Hos 8:9:   *A wild ass wandering alone,*
              Ephraim has hired lovers.
Hos 9:16:   Ephraim is stricken;
                  their root is dried up;
                      they shall bear no fruit.
Hos 12:7:   *A trader in whose hands are false balances,*
                  he loves to oppress.
Hos 13:12-13: The iniquity of Ephraim is bound up;
                  his sin is kept in store.
              The pangs of childbirth come for him
                  but he is a dumb son,
              for now he does not present himself
                  at the mouth of the womb.

Jeremiah's preaching owes a great debt to the preaching of Hosea. His metaphors describe Yahweh, the false gods, kings, the nation, the enemy, and even the prophet himself. One of his more memorable metaphors for God:

Jer 2:13:   They have forsaken me, *the fountain of living waters.*

The false gods, says Jeremiah, are *broken cisterns, which do not hold water* (Jer 2:13).

Jeremiah's most disparaging metaphors are reserved for his own nation:

Jer 2:20:   *you broke your yoke*
                  you tore away your straps
Jer 2:23-24: *a swift young camel crisscrossing her tracks*
                  a wild ass . . . in her desirous craving sniffing the
                      wind
Jer 5:8:   *well-endowed early-rising horses*

Like Hosea, Jeremiah will sometimes combine a metaphor with a clarifying statement:

Jer 3:3:   The *brow of a whore-woman* you have;
            you refuse to be disgraced.
Jer 4:7:   *A lion has come up from the thicket,*
            a destroyer of nations set out.

Simile. The simile is a metaphor with "as" or "like," resulting in an imaginative comparison.

Hosea's preaching contains an abundance of similes.

Hos 4:16:   *Like a stubborn heifer, Israel is stubborn.*
Hos 5:14:   *For I will be like a lion to Ephraim*
            and like a young lion to the house of Judah.
Hos 6:4:   *Your love is like a morning cloud,*
            like the dew that goes early away.
Hos 7:11:   *Ephraim is like a dove,*
            silly and without sense.
Hos 7:16:   *They are like a treacherous bow.*

Similes, like metaphors, are sometimes combined with clarifying statements:

Hos 7:7:   *All of them are hot as an oven,*
            and they devour their rulers.

Jeremiah's similes cover much the same ground as his metaphors:

Jer 4:13:   *Look, like clouds he comes up,*
            and like the whirlwind his chariots.
Jer 4:17:   *Like keepers of a field they are against her round about.*
Jer 4:31:   *distress like one bearing her first child*
Jer 6:24:   *pain like a woman in labor*
Jer 8:6:   *Everyone turns into their course*
            like a horse plunging headlong into battle.
Jer 9:22:   *The human corpses shall fall*
            like dung in the open field,
            like grain stalks after the reaper.

Second Isaiah uses a simile that compares God to a mother:

Isa 42:14:   *Now I will cry out like a woman in travail;*
              I will gasp and pant.

Abusio. One of the harsher tropes is the abusio, which is an implied metaphor. This type of metaphor behaves somewhat extravagantly, in that a word is taken from one usage and put to another. Abusios can be made from either nouns or verbs.

This abusio occurs in both Amos and Joel:

Amos 1:2:   Yahweh *roars* from Zion.
Joel 3:16:   Yahweh *roars* from Zion.

In Hosea are these abusios:

Hos 8:7:   They *sow* the wind,
                 and they shall *reap* the whirlwind.
Hos 10:13:   You have *plowed* iniquity,
                 you have *reaped* injustice,
                     you have *eaten* the fruit of lies.
Hos 12:1:   Ephraim *herds* the wind.

Jeremiah's most memorable images are abusios:

Jer 4:4:   Remove the foreskins of *your hearts.*
Jer 5:8:   each man *neighing* for his neighbor's wife
Jer 7:28:   Truth *perished; it was severed* from their mouth.
Jer 18:18:   Come, let us smite him with *the tongue.*
Jer 51:44:   Nations no longer *stream* to him.

In the following example, Jeremiah combines an abusio with a clarifying statement:

Jer 6:10:   Look! *Their ear* has foreskin;
                 they are unable to take heed.

Euphemism. Another example of "language at a stretch" is the euphemism, which is the substitution of a milder term or one with adjunct meaning for a term deemed too harsh or too explicit. In Jeremiah:

Jer 13:22:   For your great sin, *your skirts* were exposed;
                 your heels were violated.

He really means the "private parts" of a personified nation. The same indelicacy is alluded to in another euphemism:

Jer 13:26:   Your *disgrace* was seen.

Parable. Jesus, like the rabbis generally, taught in parables, but some can be found also in the Old Testament. Hosea says, "I spoke to the prophets; it was I who multiplied visions, and through the prophets *I give parables*" (Hos 12:10).

Nathan uses a parable to trap King David regarding his sin against Uriah the Hittite:

> There were two men in a certain city, the one rich and the other poor. The rich man had very many flocks and herds; but the poor man had nothing but one little ewe lamb, which he had bought. And he brought it up, and it grew up with him and with his children; it used to eat of his morsel, and drink from his cup, and lie in his bosom, and it was like a daughter to him. Now there came a traveler to the rich man, and he was unwilling to take one of his own flock or herd to prepare for the wayfarer who had come to him, but he took the poor man's ewe lamb, and prepared it for the man who had come to him. (2 Sam 12:1-4)

Then Nathan points the finger, saying, "You are the man!" (v. 7), after which the parable is explained.

An unnamed prophet traps King Ahab in similar fashion with a disguise and a parable:

> Your servant went out into the midst of the battle; and behold a soldier turned and brought a man to me, and said, "Keep this man; if by any means he be missing, your life shall be for his life, or else you shall pay a talent of silver." (1 Kgs 20:39)

Ahab concurred with the judgment, at which point the prophet threw off the bandage on his eye and applied the judgment to the king. Isaiah's well-known Song of the Vineyard (Isa 5:1-7) is a parable with a built-in interpretation.

Allegory. An allegory is an extended metaphor in which a series of actions is symbolic of other actions, and in which the symbolism frequently—but not always—involves personification.

Jeremiah's oracle on the Fallen Sisters is an allegory:

And Yahweh said to me in the days of Josiah the king: Have you seen what she did, Rebel Israel, that woman going up on every high hill and under every leafy tree and whoring there? And I thought, after she has done all these things she will return to me, but she did not return. And Faithless, her sister Judah, saw it. And she saw that precisely because Rebel Israel committed adultery I sent her away—handed her a bill of divorce. Yet Faithless Judah, her sister, was not afraid, and went and played the whore—she too! And she took her whoring casually, polluted the land, and committed adultery with the stone and with the tree. And yet for all this Faithless, her sister Judah, did not return to me whole-heartedly, but falsely—oracle of Yahweh.

And Yahweh said to me: Rebel Israel is herself more righteous than Faithless Judah! (Jer 3:6-11)

Ezekiel is the prophet of the allegory, as we know best from his "faith-less wife" allegory in chapter 16 and his Oholah and Oholibah allegory in chapter 23. Zechariah, too, gives us an allegory, on Grace and Union (11:4-14).

Epithet. An epithet is an honorific or disparaging title giving character to a name. Isaiah and Jeremiah are particularly fond of epithets:

Isa 30:7:	Egypt is called "Rahab Who Sits Still."
Jer 3:23:	Baal is called "Noise of the Mountain."
Jer 17:13:	Yahweh is called "The Hope of Israel."
Jer 30:17:	Jerusalem is called "The Zion Whom No One Cares About."
Jer 46:17:	Pharaoh is called "Loud Noise, Who Lets the Deadline Pass."
Jer 50:7:	Yahweh is called "The Righteous Pasture" and "Hope of Their Fathers."

Metonymy. Metonymy is the substitution of a word for another it suggests, usually the abstract for the concrete. From Jeremiah:

Jer 4:29:   *Every city* is fleeing.

"Every city" here means "the people of every city."

Jer 26:2:   *all the cities of Judah* who come to worship in the house of Yahweh

"All the cities of Judah" means "all the people of the cities of Judah."

Jer 32:24:   Look, the *siege ramps* have come to the city to take it.

"Siege ramps" means "the Babylonian army that has built the siege ramps."

Jer 33:4:   toward the *sword*

"Sword" here means "the Chaldeans wielding the sword."

Jer 50:6:   *Mountains* led them astray.

"Mountains" refer in this case to the "fertility worship taking place on the mountains."

Synecdoche. Synecdoche is a type of metonymy in which a part is substituted for the whole, or the whole for a part. From Jeremiah:

Jer 4:20:   Suddenly my tents are devastated; in a moment *my curtains.*

"My curtains" represents all the home furnishings.

Jer 14:2:   [Judah's] *gates* languish.

Judah's "gates" are Judah's cities.

Jer 32:4:   *His mouth* shall speak with *his mouth.*

Nebuchadnezzar and Zedekiah will meet personally.

Merismus is a form of synecdoche in which a totality is expressed by contrasting parts or extremes.

Jer 51:22:   *old and young*

Reference here is to "everyone."

Comparison

Speech that carries over elements of likeness from one thing to another thing yields a comparison (Lat.: *similitudo*). The figure is used to clarify or reprove. Metaphors are commonly expanded into comparisons, being more general and less vivid than similes. Jeremiah contains the following comparisons using *kĕ . . . kēn* (כְּ . . . כֵן) and *'ākēn . . . kēn* (אָכֵן . . . כֵן) constructions:

Jer 2:26:	*Like* the shame of a thief when found out,
	so the house of Israel is deeply shamed.
Jer 3:20:	*Surely as* a woman faithless to her companion,
	so you have been faithless to me, house of Israel.
Jer 5:27:	*As* a cage is full of birds,
	so their houses are full of loot
Jer 6:7:	*As* a well keeps fresh its water,
	so she has kept fresh her evil
Jer 18:6:	*Like* clay in the hand of a potter,
	so are you in my hand, house of Israel

Second Isaiah compares God to a comforting mother:

Isa 66:13:	*As* one whom his mother comforts,
	so I will comfort you

Contrast

Prophets also make contrasts, a figure in classical rhetoric called the *antithesis*. The antithesis is an opposition created by contrasting words, phrases, or ideas. From Isaiah comes this well-known contrast:

Isa 1:3:	The ox knows its owner
	and the ass its master's crib.
	But Israel does not know;
	my people do not understand.

Jeremiah's preaching is filled with contrasts, most of them with rhetorical questions used as a foil. The following example does not use rhetorical questions but is nevertheless a contrast of the "But my people" type:

Jer 8:7:   Even the stork in the skies
         knows her seasons.
     The turtledove, swift, and swallow
         keep the time of their coming.
     But my people do not know
         the order of Yahweh.

See also the contrast between the "cursed and blessed man" in Jer 17:5-8, and the contrast of the "two ways" in Jer 21:8-9.

Oxymoron. An oxymoron is the juxtaposition of incongruous or contradictory terms. From Jeremiah:

Jer 25:9:   Nebuchadrezzar, the king of Babylon, *my servant*

"My servant" in the mouth of Yahweh is otherwise a term of endearment.

Argument

While prophets speak with divine authority, they also use argument, particularly Jeremiah, whose rhetoric comes closer to Greek dialectic than that of any other prophet, including Haggai, Zechariah, and Malachi, who use question and answer to great effect.

Authority. In Hebrew rhetoric, the driving force behind the assertive discourse of one speaking for God is *authority*, which substitutes for *ethos* in classical rhetoric. Elijah speaks thus to Ahab:

1 Kgs 17:1: As Yahweh the God of Israel lives, before whom
         I stand, there shall be neither dew nor rain these
         years, except by my word.

Enthymeme. The enthymeme, as was pointed out earlier, is a syllogism lacking one premise, usually the major premise.[8] In prophetic preaching, the major premise can be supplied from Deuteronomic preaching. In Jeremiah, the enthymeme often takes the following form:

[A Judah not listening to Yahweh's word will be punished.]
Judah—or its king, priests, prophets, people—has not listened
    to Yahweh's word.
Judah—or its king, priests, prophets, people—will be punished.

Protasis–Apodosis. The protasis–apodosis form ("If . . . then . . .") is at home in legal discourse, but one finds it in the preaching of Jeremiah:

Jer 4:1-2:   *If* you return, Israel—oracle of Yahweh—
     to me you return.
And if you remove your wretched things from me
     and do not waver about,
then you can swear, "By Yahweh's life,"
     in truth, in justice, and in righteousness.
Then nations shall bless themselves in him,
     and in him they shall boast.

Jer 31:36-37:   *If* these statutes depart
     from before me—oracle of Yahweh—
then the seed of Israel shall cease
     from being a nation before me—all the days.

If the heavens above can be measured
     and the foundations of the earth explored to the
          depths,
then I, I will reject all the seed of Israel
     because of all that they have done—oracle of
          Yahweh.

Arguments a minori ad maius. The argument *a minori ad maius* (Hillel: *qal vechomer*) is from the lesser to the greater. In the New Testament, it is expressed with the phrase "how much more." In Jeremiah we encounter these examples of the *a minori ad maius* argument:

Jer 3:1:   Look, *if* a man sends away *his wife*
     and she goes from him
and becomes wife to another man,
     will he return to her again?
Would not that land
     be greatly polluted?
But you, you have whored with *many companions*,
     and would you return to me?

Jer 12:5:   *If* with men on foot you have run and they wearied you,
     how then will you fare in a heat with horses?
And *if* in a peaceful land you have fallen down,
     how then will you do in the jungle of the Jordan?

Jeremiah uses this same argument in addressing the nations:

Jer 25:29:   Look, *if* I am beginning to work evil in the city
upon which my name is called, *then* for you, shall
you assuredly go unpunished?

In one case, Jeremiah poses the argument and then answers it:

Jer 49:12:   Look, *if* those for whom there is no judgment to
drink the cup must surely drink, are you *then* one
who will surely go free? You will not go free, for
you will surely drink!

Haggai uses an argument *a minori ad maius* in order to get the temple rebuilt:

Hag 1:4:   Is it time for you yourselves to dwell in your paneled houses, while this house lies in ruins?

Rhetorical Question. This is a question posed for which there is only one answer, but because the answer is self-evident or self-condemnatory, the addressee will not give it. Rhetorical questions function as emphatic statements and are often used to intimidate. All the prophets employ the rhetorical question. One comes to Saul from Samuel, which the prophet then answers:

1 Sam 15:22:   Has Yahweh as great delight in burnt offerings
and sacrifices
as in obeying the voice of Yahweh?
Look, to obey is better than sacrifice,
and to hearken than the fat of rams.

Prophets used rhetorical questions as foils for preferred subjects. Nothing quite matches the string of rhetorical questions in Amos 3:3-8:

Do two walk together
unless they have made an appointment?
Does a lion roar in the forest
when he has no prey?
Does a young lion cry out from his den
if he has taken nothing?

Does a bird fall in a snare on the earth
   when there is no trap for it?
Does a snare spring up from the ground
   when it has taken nothing?
Is a trumpet blown in the city
   and the people are not afraid?
Does evil befall a city
   unless Yahweh has done it?
. . . .
The Lion has roared;
   who will not fear?
Yahweh God has spoken;
   who will not prophesy?

Isaiah follows up these rhetorical questions with a bit of irony:

Isa 10:15:   Shall the ax vaunt itself over him who hews
               with it
            or the saw magnify itself against him who
               wields it?
        As if a rod should wield him who lifts it
            or as if a staff should lift him who is not wood!

Jeremiah uses rhetorical questions as much as Amos does, but they are not as mechanical. His setup questions in almost every case contain a word or thought link to the preferred subject, which comes next. Jeremiah puts the rhetorical question to two specialized uses, both aimed at exposing an incongruity. In one, a single or double question lifts up some paradigmatic behavior, a common happening, or something built into the natural order, which the prophet then contrasts to the nation's behavior, judged to be scandalous:

Jer 2:11:   Has a nation exchanged gods
        even though they are no-gods?
      But my people has exchanged its glory
        for No Profit!
Jer 2:32:   Can a maiden forget her ornaments,
        a bride her knotted cords?
      But my people have forgotten me
        days without number.
Jer 18:14-15: Can it leave the mountain highland,

the snow of Lebanon?
Can foreign waters dry up
the cool flowing streams?
But my people have forgotten me;
they burn incense in vain.

The second type is a threefold question in the form *ha-* . . . *'im* . . .
maddûaʻ? (‏מַדּוּעַ‎ . . . ‏אִם‎ . . . ‏הֲ‎), commonly translated "Is . . . is . . . so why?"
or "If . . . if . . . so why?" This form is a signature of Jeremiah. Here two
rhetorical questions are a foil for the third, which states the troubling
vexation that Jeremiah really wants to address. Some examples:

Jer 2:14:	Is Israel a slave?
	Is he a house-born?
	So why has he become plunder?
Jer 2:31:	Have I become a wilderness to Israel,
	Or a land of thick darkness?
	So why do my people say, "We are free to roam;
	we will no longer come to you?"
Jer 8:4-5:	If [people] fall down, do they not get up?
	If one turns away, does he not return?
	So why has this people turned away, Jerusalem, the
	rebel perpetual?
Jer 8:22:	Is there no balm in Gilead?
	Is there no healer there?
	Indeed, so why has it not arisen,
	healing for my dear people?

Hypophora. Sometimes Jeremiah will answer his own rhetorical question,
which in the classical rhetorical handbooks was given the name *hypophora*:

Jer 6:20:	Why is it frankincense comes to me from Sheba
	and the good cane from a distant land?
	Your offerings are not acceptable;
	your sacrifices are not pleasing to me.
Jer 31:20:	Is Ephraim my dear son,
	the child of my delight?
	For as often as I speak of him
	I certainly remember him still.
Jer 46:7-8:	Who is this that rises like the Nile,
	like the great river, its waters swell?

> Egypt rises like the Nile;
> and like the great river, the waters are swollen.

Jer 49:7: Is there no longer wisdom in Teman?
> Counsel has perished from people of
> understanding;
> their wisdom stinks!

Surrender. "Surrender" (Gk.: *epitropē*; Lat.: *permissio*) is a veiled argument in which one yields a matter to the will of another. This argument was commonly used in court cases. An example from the *ad Herennium*:

> Since only soul and body remain to me, now that I am deprived of everything else, even these, which alone of many goods are left me, I deliver up to you and to your power. You may use and even abuse me in your own way as you think best; with impunity make your decision upon me, whatever it may be; speak and give a sign—I shall obey. (*ad Herennium* iv 29; LCL)

In his celebrated trial of 609 B.C.E., Jeremiah spoke thus to the court:

> But as for me, look! I am in your hands. Do with me as seems good and right in your eyes. Only know for sure that if you put me to death you will bring innocent blood upon yourselves and on this city and its inhabitants; for in truth Yahweh sent me to you to speak in your ears all these things. (Jer 26:14-15)

Descriptio. In classical rhetoric, *descriptio* was an argument used by either the prosecution or the defense to describe adverse consequences of possible court action. The *ad Herennium* proposes this descriptio for a defense:

> For if you inflict a heavy penalty upon the defendant, men of the jury, you will at once by a single judgment have taken many lives. His aged father, who has set the entire hope of his last years on this young man, will have no reason for wishing to stay alive. His small children, deprived of their father's aid, will be exposed as objects of scorn and contempt to their father's enemies. His entire household will collapse under this undeserved calamity. But his enemies, when once they have won the bloody palm by this most cruel of victories, will exult over the miseries of these unfortunates, and will be found insolent on the score of deeds as well as of words. (*ad Herennium* iv 39; LCL)

Jeremiah in his defense before the court says:

> Only know for sure that if you put me to death, then you will bring innocent blood upon yourselves and to this city and to its inhabitants; for in truth Yahweh sent me to you to speak in your ears all these things. (Jer 26:15)

Distributio. A speaker will sometimes say, "Not this . . . but that . . . ," which is an argument that classical rhetoricians called the *distributio*. This figure does more than compare; it apportions. Jeremiah used a distributio in his exchange with the prophet Hananiah:

> Jer 28:8-9:   The prophets who were before me and before you, from ancient times, yes, they prophesied to many lands and against great kingdoms of war and evil and pestilence. The prophet who prophesies peace, when the word of that prophet comes to be, the prophet whom Yahweh has truly sent will be known.

A "broken distributio" destroys a distinction widely held to be true, arguing for inclusiveness. These turn up in successive Jeremiah oracles:

> Jer 23:23-24: Am I a God nearby—
> oracle of Yahweh—
> and not a God far off?
>
> If a person hides himself in secret places,
> do I myself not see him?—
> oracle of Yahweh.
>
> The heavens and the earth
> do I not fill?—
> oracle of Yahweh.

Exaggerated Contrast. Hebrew rhetoric contains a type of distributio to which has been given the name "exaggerated contrast." This idiom juxtaposes statements solely to emphasize the one occurring second, having the practical effect of making the second statement more important than the first. The first statement negates an idea, but the speaker does not really mean to deny it, for it is otherwise valid or true. If the negation were to stand alone, it would be false. Some modern examples of the exaggerated contrast:

You're not getting older, you're getting better. (greeting card)

The church is not a building; the church is people. (theology)

Not he who has died is dead; dead is rather the dead among the living. (Arab proverb)

Discrimination is not unfair; it is illegal. (civil rights slogan)

Prophets use the exaggerated contrast in argument. From Amos and Jeremiah:

Amos 7:14:   I am no prophet, nor a prophet's son, but I am a herdsman and a dresser of sycamore trees.

Jer 7:22-23:   For I did not speak to your fathers nor did I command them in the day of my bringing them out of the land of Egypt about such things as burnt offerings and sacrifices. But this word I commanded them: Hear my voice, and I will be for you God; as for you, you will be to me a people.

Jer 22:10:   Do not weep for the dead, and do not condole for him; weep bitterly for him who goes away, for he will not return again to see the land of his birth.

Humor and Irony

Humor is difficult—some would say impossible—to define, yet we know it when we hear it. Correction: Some people know it when they hear it. Prophets in both relaxed and stressful contexts were playful with their audiences, sharing with them sudden flashes of insight and quick wit by the use of wordplay, hyperbole, and understatement, all of which would doubtless have put smiles on the faces of their hearers. It is widely conceded that irony was well known in ancient Israel. In ancient Greek culture, of course, it was developed into a fine art. Irony there was conceived originally as feigned ignorance or agreement meant to provoke one's antagonist ("Socratic irony"); an *eirōn* was someone who said less than what he meant. More commonly, irony was saying with subtlety or ambiguity the opposite of what one meant (verbal irony). Irony addresses a double audience, one that hears but does not understand, and another that perceives more than what meets the ear as well as the outsider's incomprehension. All the prophets possessed a sense of humor, and there is evidence aplenty that they were skilled in the use of irony. Wordplays emphasize and threaten; hyperbole is a countermeasure for audience resistance; and irony is but another way of telling the truth.

Paronomasia. Broadly defined, paronomasia is either a play on multiple meanings of identical or cognate words, or else a play on different words close enough in sound so as to make *assonance* (near-rhyme), or puns. Paronomasia more generally is called "wordplay." Paronomasia of both sound and meaning is everywhere present in the Old Testament, even in laments. The prophets used it to enliven discourse and facilitate audience attention.

Nathan, in an oracle to King David, conveys an important theological message by playing on the word "house":

> Thus says Yahweh, would you build me a house to dwell in? I have not dwelt in a house since the day I brought up the people of Israel from Egypt to this day. . . . Moreover Yahweh declares to you that Yahweh will make you a house. (2 Sam 7:5-11)

David wanted to build Yahweh a house of cedar and stone, that is, a temple, but Yahweh comes back with a promise to build David a permanent "house" of descendants.

From the later prophets we have an array of wordplays:

Amos 8:1-2:	"summer fruit" (*qāyiṣ*, קָיִץ) and "the end" (*qēṣ*, הַקֵּץ)
Mic 1:10:	"Tell it not in Gath, weep not at all" (*bĕgat 'al-taggîdû, bākô 'al-tibkû*, בְּגַת אַל־תַּגִּידוּ בָכוֹ אַל־תִּבְכּוּ).
Jer 1:11-12:	"almond" (*šāqēd*, שָׁקֵד) and "watching" (*šōqēd*, שֹׁקֵד)
Jer 2:12:	"Be appalled, Heavens" (*šommû šāmayîm*, שֹׁמּוּ שָׁמַיִם).
Jer 2:20:	"high hill" (*gib'â gĕbōhâ*, גִּבְעָה גְבֹהָה)
Jer 5:13:	"wind" (*rûaḥ*, רוּחַ), meaning both "spirit" and "hot air"
Jer 22:22:	"All your shepherds [*rō'ayik*, רֹעַיִךְ] the wind shall shepherd [*tir'eh*, תִּרְעֶה]."
Jer 49:30:	"Flee! Wander all about!" (*nūsû nūdû*, נֻסוּ נָדוּ)
Jer 51:44:	"Bel in Babylon" (*bēl bĕbābēl*, בֵּל בְּבָבֶל)

Like the classical poets, the Hebrew prophets enjoyed playing on both personal names and place names:

Amos 5:5:	"Gilgal shall surely go into exile" (*haggilgāl gālōh yigleh*, הַגִּלְגָּל גָּלֹה יִגְלֶה).

Zeph 2:4:	"Gaza shall be deserted" (*'azzâ 'ăzûbâ tihyeh*, עַזָּה עֲזוּבָה תִהְיֶה).
Jer 4:15:	"the voice of one declaring from Dan" (*qôl maggîd middān*, קוֹל מַגִּיד מִדָּן)
Jer 6:1:	"In Tekoa blow the trumpet" (*bitqôa' tiqě'û šôpār*, בִּתְקוֹעַ תִּקְעוּ שׁוֹפָר).
Jer 9:3:	"a supplanting Jacob" (*āqôb ya'qōb*, עָקוֹב יַעְקֹב)
Jer 9:4:	"In Heshbon they planned" (*běḥešbôn ḥāšěbû*, בְּחֶשְׁבוֹן חָשָׁבוּ).

Hyperbole. Hyperbole is a deliberate exaggeration of the truth where something is represented as greater or less, better or worse, than is possible. Its purpose is to magnify or minimize before an audience disinclined to listen. Rabbi Simeon ben Gamaliel (early second century c.e.) noted exaggerated language in Deut 1:28, where the returning spies said, "The people are greater and taller than we; the cities are great and fortified up to heaven; and moreover we have seen the sons of the Anakim there" (*Sifre Deuteronomy* §25). Heschel says of the prophets: "[They] were unfair to the people of Israel. Their sweeping allegations, overstatements, and generalizations defied standards of accuracy. Some of the exaggerations reach the unbelievable."[9]

An example of hyperbole in Isaiah:

Isa 10:19:	The remnant of the trees of the forest will be so few that a child can write them down.

Jeremiah uses hyperbole to heighten divine affirmations and respond to gross evil. In the case of the latter, he must address audiences who are unwilling to listen, exhibit shame, or repent.

Jer 1:5:	Before I formed you in the belly, I knew you, and before you came forth from the womb, I declared you holy, a prophet to the nations I made you.
Jer 2:20:	Indeed, on every high hill and under every leafy tree, you bend backward, you whore.
Jer 2:28	For as many as your cities are your gods, O Judah.
Jer 3:2:	Lift up your eyes to the bare heights and see; where have you not been laid?

Jer 4:13:	Look, like clouds he comes up,
	    and like the whirlwind his chariots.
	His horses are swifter than eagles;
	    woe to us, for we are devastated!

Jer 37:10:	Even if you should strike down the entire army of the Chaldeans who are fighting against you, and there remained among them only wounded men, each man in his tent, they would rise up and burn this city with fire.
Jer 50:20:	In those days and at that time . . . iniquity shall be sought in Israel and there shall be none, and sins in Judah, and they shall not be found. For I will pardon those whom I left remaining.

Jeremiah follows up this hyperbole with a clarifying statement:

Jer 5:3:	They have made their faces harder than rock; they refuse to repent.

Litotes. Understatement for rhetorical effect was called *litotes* by the classical rhetoricians. This figure does not occur often in the Old Testament, as Hebrew rhetoric is more given to overstatement than understatement. But prophetic discourse does contain a few litotes.

In one Hebrew manuscript, Elijah is quoted by the king's messenger as having said to those who came to him: "Go back to *the man* who sent you, and say to him" (2 Kgs 1:6), whereas the Masoretic Text reads: "Go back to the king who sent you, and say to him." To refer to the king as simply a "man" is understatement, which may be the better and original reading.

Huldah similarly substituted "man" for "king" in 2 Kgs 22:15, clearly an understatement.

From Jeremiah are these examples of litotes:

Jer 8:14:	Let us be silent (= Let us die)
Jer 18:23:	their counsel (= their murderous plots)

Dramatic Irony. The prophet Micaiah used dramatic irony when summoned by Jehoshaphat and Ahab to prophesy the outcome of a battle upon which the kings were about to embark. A company of four hundred prophets had already predicted success, but a contrary word was anticipated from Micaiah, who did not like Ahab. In order to defuse the situation, Micaiah begins by feigning agreement with the four hundred prophets: "Go up and triumph; Yahweh will give it into the hand of the king" (1 Kgs 22:15). But Ahab is not fooled, and he tells the prophet to speak the truth, which he then proceeds to do.

Jeremiah in his encounter with the prophet Hananiah acted similarly. Knowing that Hananiah and some in the audience were hostile to Jeremiah's message calling for subservience to Nebuchadnezzar, Jeremiah at first feigned agreement with his opposite number. He said:

> Amen! So may Yahweh do! May Yahweh confirm your words that you have prophesied—to bring back the vessels of the house of Yahweh and all the exiles from Babylon to this place!

But then the prophet followed with these words:

> But do hear this word that I speak in your ears and in the ears of all the people: The prophets who were before me and before you, from ancient times, yes, they prophesied to many lands and against great kingdoms of war and evil and pestilence. The prophet who prophesies peace, when the word of the prophet comes to be, the prophet whom Yahweh has truly sent will be known. (Jer 28:6-9)

Verbal Irony. Speakers resort to irony when straight talk fails, making ironic language desperate and extravagant. Isaiah is said to be the master of verbal irony. Irony appears early in the account of his call, in which appears also a keyword chiasmus:

Isa 6:9-10: Go say to this people:
　　　　　　Hear and hear, but do not understand;
　　　　　　　see and see, but do not perceive.
　　　　　　Make the **heart** of this people fat
　　　　　　　and their **ears** heavy,
　　　　　　　　and shut their **eyes**,
　　　　　　　　lest they see with their **eyes**
　　　　　　　and hear with their **ears**
　　　　　　and understand with their **hearts**
　　　　　　and turn and be healed.

Isaiah uses irony in describing how to teach people given to hard drink:

Isa 28:10, 13: For it is precept upon precept, precept upon
precept,
line upon line, line upon line,
here a little, there a little.

On another occasion Isaiah advocates something worse than drunkenness, then explains:

Isa 29:9-10: Stupefy yourselves and be in a stupor;
blind yourselves and be blind!
Be drunk, but not with wine;
stagger, but not with strong drink.
For Yahweh has poured out upon you
a spirit of deep sleep
and has closed your eyes, O prophets,
and covered your heads, O seers.

Jeremiah is every bit Isaiah's equal in this subtle art, using irony to address incongruities with razor sharpness. The great incongruity for Jeremiah is Israel's abandonment of Yahweh and the covenant, while at the same time showing enormous devotion to idols and idol worship.

Jer 2:33: *How well you make your way
to seek love.*
So even you can teach
your wicked ways.
Jer 5:30-31: A frightful and horrible thing
has happened in the land.
The prophets, they prophesy by the Lie,
and the priests, they rule at their sides.
And my people, they love it so!
But what will you do at the end of it?
Jer 14:10: *So they have loved to wander;*
their feet they did not restrain.

Sexual preferences are mocked when Jeremiah reverses the sexes in Baal fertility worship, making the tree masculine and the stone feminine:

Jer 2:27: Who say to a tree, "You are my father,"
and to a stone, "You gave me birth."

Epitrophe. Epitrophe is the granting of permission for an action of which one disapproves. It is advice given "tongue in cheek." Some examples:

Elijah:	Cry aloud, for he is a god; either he is musing, or he has gone aside, or he is on a journey, or perhaps he is asleep and must be awakened. (1 Kgs 18:27)

Amos:	Come to Bethel and transgress
	    to Gilgal and multiply transgressions.
	            (Amos 4:4-5)

Hosea:	Ephraim is joined to idols; let him alone. (Hos 4:17)

Micah:	If a man should go about and utter winds and lies, saying,
	  "I will preach to you of wine and strong drink,"
	    he would be the preacher for this people!
	            (Mic 2:11)

Jeremiah:	Your burnt offerings add to your sacrifices, and eat meat. (Jer 7:21)
Jeremiah:	Whoever is to death—to death, and whoever is to the sword—to the sword, and whoever is to famine—to famine, and whoever is to captivity—to captivity. (Jer 15:2)

Jeremiah:	Go up to Lebanon and scream,
	    and in the Bashan raise your voice!
	And scream from Abarim
	    because all your lovers are broken. (Jer 22:20)

Jeremiah:	Well, then, confirm your vows! Go ahead and perform your vows! (Jer 44:25)

Drama

Drama is also found aplenty in prophetic preaching. The Foreign Nation Oracles of Amos, Isaiah, Obadiah, Nahum, Jeremiah, and Ezekiel are all dramatic actions, in that they address audiences too far distant to hear. Amos's oracles to the nations (Amos 1–2) have even more drama because of his strategy of circumlocution. Eight nations are addressed in all. Here the prophet will have no difficulty bringing his audience along as he thunders judgment on Damascus, Gaza, Tyre, Edom, Ammon, and Moab. A northern Israelite audience might also assent to the next judgment, on Judah. But when Amos comes to indict and judge Israel, which is what he really wants to do, the audience, having given hearty assent to judgments on six or seven other nations, will find it difficult to stop the momentum and refrain from judging Israel. The prophet has trapped his audience into making a judgment they are disinclined to give, and his objective has been achieved.

Jeremiah's preaching contains much drama. He uses simulated dialogue, also employing the classical figures of onomatopoeia, aposiopesis, apostrophe, personification, pathos, and diminution, which is a rhythmic device.

Simulated Dialogue. Jeremiah alternates voices in his poetry, which simulates dialogue. This real or imagined speech occurs between the prophet and others, among other people, or between others—including the prophet—and God. Sometimes Jeremiah is heard speaking to himself (4:19; 5:4-5).

In Jer 6:4-5 words of the enemy frame the frightened cry of besieged Jerusalem:

Enemy:	Sanctify war against her; *up, let us attack at noon.*
Jerusalem:	Woe to us, for the day has turned away, for the shadows of evening have stretched out.
Enemy:	*Up, let us attack at night;* let us destroy her citadels.

In Jer 8:18-21 is a poem with an elaborate speaker chiasmus:

Jeremiah:	My joy is gone, grief is upon me, my heart is sick.
People:	Listen! a voice . . . "Is Yahweh not in Zion?" "Is her king not in her?"
Yahweh:	So why have they provoked me to anger with their images, with their foreign nothings?
People:	The harvest is past, the summer is ended, and we are not saved!
Jeremiah:	For the brokenness of my dear people I am broken, I mourn; desolation has gripped me.

The climax comes at the center, where Yahweh interrupts the questions of the people with a more important question of his own.

Open-Ended Conclusions. Two speeches of Jeremiah are left open-ended, containing questions from Yahweh that the audience must answer for itself. In Jer 3:1-5, the pressing question is posed at the beginning:

> Jer 3:1:   But you, you have whored with many companions,
> and would you return to me?

In Jer 5:1-8, it is posed at the end:

> Jer 5:7:   Why then will I pardon you?

Onomatopoeia. Onomatopoeia is the sound of a word or its repetition imitating natural sounds or simulating the sense. Jeremiah contains numerous examples of this figure, as we saw earlier in Jer 5:17; 50:35-38; and 51:20-23.

Aposiopesis. In classical rhetoric, aposiopesis (Lat.: *praecisio*) is the sudden and intentional breaking off of discourse in mid-sentence. There seems to be evidence of this figure in Jeremiah:

> Jer 10:18:   Jeremiah stops short of stating what effect the
> impending distress will have on the people, saying
> simply, "so they may find out . . ."
> Jer 46:5:   Jeremiah leaves unfinished a vision of Egyptians
> being overrun by Babylonians on the battlefield,
> saying, "so why have I seen . . . ?"

Apostrophe. Apostrophe is a turning away from one's audience to address a person, city, nation, or other inanimate object. It is used to emphasize a point, heighten grief, or express indignation. This figure often includes personification. The person may also be purely imaginary, absent, or dead.

> Jer 2:12:   Jeremiah addresses the heavens, which cannot hear.
> Jer 15:10:   Jeremiah addresses his mother, who is absent.
> Jer 22:29:   Jeremiah addresses the land, which cannot hear.
> Jer 22:30:   Jeremiah addresses an imaginary scribe.
> Jer 31:16-17: Jeremiah addresses Rachel, who is long dead.
> Jer 47:6:   Jeremiah addresses the sword, which cannot hear.

Pathos. Pathos in Greek rhetoric is an emotional appeal to awaken feelings of pity and sorrow. Hebrew rhetoric only occasionally appeals to the emotions, but one does find pathos in the preaching of Hosea and Jeremiah:

Hos 11:1-4: When Israel was a child, I loved him,
  and out of Egypt I called my son.
The more I called them,
  the more they went from me.
They kept sacrificing to the Baals
  and burning incense to idols.
Yet I, I taught Ephraim to walk,
  taking them up by his arms,
    and they did not know that I healed them.
I led them with cords of human kindness,
  with the bands of love.
And I became to them like those
  who lift infants to their cheeks;
    yes, I bent down to them and fed them.

Hos 11:8-9: How can I give you up, O Ephraim!
  How can I hand you over, O Israel!
How can I make you like Adman!
  How can I treat you like Zeboiim!
My heart recoils within me;
  my compassion grows warm and tender.
I will not execute my fierce anger;
  I will not again destroy Ephraim.
For I am God and no mortal,
  the Holy One in your midst,
    and I will not come in wrath.

Jeremiah combines "father-son" and "husband-wife" imagery in this moving oracle:

Jer 3:19-20: And I, I said to myself,
  How will I treat you among the children?
I will give you a fine land,
  a heritage—beauty of beauties—among the
    nations.
And I said, You will call me "My Father"
  and will not turn back from following me.

> Surely as a woman faithless with her companion,
> > so you have been faithless to me, house of
> > > Israel—
> > > > oracle of Yahweh.

Even more moving is this confession in which Jeremiah curses the day of his birth. He says:

Jer 20:14-18: Cursed be the day
> on which I was born,
> > the day my mother bore me.
> Let it not be blessed.
> Cursed be the man
> > who brought my father the news:
> "A male child is born to you,"
> > making him very glad.
> Let that man be like the cities
> > which Yahweh overthrew and did not pity.
> Let him hear a cry in the morning
> > and an alarm at noontime.
> [. . . . . . .]¹⁰
> > because he did not kill me in the womb,
> so my mother would have been my grave,
> > and her womb eternally pregnant.
> Why this: from the womb came I forth
> > to see hard times and sorrow,
> > > and my days end in shame?

Other examples in Jeremiah:

Jer 31:15: The voice of lament is heard in Ramah,
> > bitterest weeping.
> Rachel is weeping over her sons;
> > she refuses to be comforted over her sons,
> > > because they are not.
Jer 31:16-17: Restrain your voice from weeping
> > and your eyes from tears.
> For there is a reward for your labor—
> > oracle of Yahweh—
> > > and they shall return from the land of the enemy.

> And there is hope for your future—
>> oracle of Yahweh—
>>> and sons shall return to their territory.

Jer 31:18-19: I can indeed hear,
> Ephraim rockin' in grief.
> You disciplined me, and I was disciplined
>> like a young bull not trained.
> Bring me back so I can come back,
>> for you are Yahweh my God.
> For after my turning away,
>> I repented.
> And after I came to understand,
>> I hit upon my thigh.
> I was ashamed and also disgraced,
>> for I bore the reproach of my youth.

Jer 31:20: Is Ephraim my dear son?
> Is he the child of my delight?
> For more than all my speaking against him
>> I will assuredly remember him still.
> Therefore my innards moan for him;
>> I will assuredly have mercy on him—
>>> oracle of Yahweh.

Diminution. Jeremiah decreases colon length in his moving chaos vision, simulating a cessation of life in the entire creation:

Jer 4:23-26: I saw the earth, and look! it was waste and void,
> and the heavens, their light was not there.
> I saw the mountains, and look! they were quaking,
>> and all the hills were tossing about.
> I saw, and look! the human was not there,
>> and all the birds of the sky had fled.
> I saw, and look! the garden land was a desert,
>> and all its cities were ruined.
>>> before Yahweh,
>>> before his burning anger.

6

PROPHETIC SIGNS, WONDERS, AND SYMBOLIC BEHAVIOR

WE HAVE BEEN TALKING THUS FAR ABOUT WORDS used by the prophets to convey their message, and prophets are, to be sure, messengers of the spoken word. But the prophets also make statements not consisting of words, or other types of statements that supplement the words that they speak. The prophets and their predecessors, being men and women of the "spirit," were from earliest times given to dramatic behavior. For them, the prophetic message was more than words, even though words in the ancient world were believed to be invested with sufficient power to bring about their actualization. The earliest Hebrew prophets, also some later ones, gave signs and wonders pointing to later fulfillment. For Elijah and Elisha, the sign was the mighty work itself (1 Kgs 17:8-24; 2 Kgs 2:19-24; 4:1-44; 5:1-27). Already at the end of Solomon's reign, we begin to see the spoken word supplemented by symbolic action, where the latter works the same as the former, having itself sufficient power to bring about its actualization.

SIGNS AND WONDERS

Samuel gives Saul signs that confirm his anointment and commission to be prince over all Israel (1 Sam 10:1-16). In the last of these, he predicts that Saul will meet up with a band of ecstatic prophets and be "turned into another man." It takes place that very day (vv. 5-9).

Early "messengers of Yahweh" who rove about in Canaan, where Abraham is sojourning, give signs to support their divine words (Gen

208

18:10). Moses, too, who later becomes Israel's prophet par excellence (Deut 34:10-12), is remembered prior to the exodus as having given a number of signs, some of which were miracles of a most extraordinary sort (Exod 3:12; 4:1-9, 17; 9:8-11 et passim). But in Deut 13:1-5, as we pointed out, signs and wonders are no sure indication that Yahweh has sent the prophet. Prophets and dreamers serving other gods are not to be followed. Yahweh allows them their day in the sun only to test people's loyalty to him.

In these precursors to Israel's great prophets, the Old Testament shows no interest in personal characteristics. These may even be repressed. One does not need to know from where the divine messenger comes, or whither he will go after his visitation. In fact, sudden appearances and sudden departures are indications that the divine messenger is authentic. Typically, the divine messenger will not give his name or remain long enough to eat a meal (Judg 13:6, 15-18; 1 Kgs 13:7-32).

SYMBOLIC ACTS

In the later prophets, we begin to see a different sort of dramatic behavior, although older features may continue to be present and the behavior too may be interpreted as a sign or wonder, as happened with Ezekiel. In an important article, H. Wheeler Robinson pointed out how Israel's later prophets went beyond their predecessors in dramatizing the spoken word with symbolic action.[1] He called this "prophetic symbolism," a phenomenon noted earlier by Richard G. Moulton.[2] Symbolic acts, like the spoken word in all its fullness, were efficacious in bringing things to pass. Symbolic action was therefore a natural extension of the prophetic preaching. At the same time, it would count for nothing, just as the prophetic word would count for nothing, if Yahweh was not behind it.

Ahijah the Shilonite

Prophetic symbolism appears first in the Old Testament after Solomon's long reign had ended. Robinson points to the early symbolic act by Ahijah the Shilonite, who, before announcing the breakup of the Solomonic kingdom, tears a new garment into twelve pieces and then gives ten of them into the hand of Jeroboam son of Nebat, king-designate of the northern tribes. The twelve northern tribes will follow Jeroboam; the other tribe (reduced from two tribes), for David's sake, will follow Solomon's son Rehoboam (1 Kgs 11:29-39).

Elijah and Elisha

With Elijah and Elisha comes more symbolic action, perhaps because both were bigger-than-life figures, and more interest was now being taken in individual characteristics. Scholars of the Wellhausen era took the prophets to be towering individuals, and while this view has come under criticism for building too much on psychological analysis, there is considerable truth in the claim. Elijah the Tishbite was no ordinary individual. The same, to a lesser degree, can be said of Elisha. Legend preserves stories of extraordinary individuals, and the stories about Elijah and Elisha in the Old Testament are legends. With the later prophets, beginning with Amos and Hosea, and continuing with Micah, Isaiah, Jeremiah, and Ezekiel, we meet up again with individuals who stand taller than the bulk of their contemporaries, although biblical tradition preserves the legacy of these prophets in a different type of literature. Stories about these prophets are not legends.

Elijah, after his stunning victory over the prophets of Baal on Mount Carmel, now waiting for the drought to break, crouches on the ground with his face between his knees, and continues in this position until a small cloud is reported to be rising out of the sea (1 Kgs 18:42-44). Some years later, when all the prophets in Samaria had become prophets of Yahweh, we see their lead man, Zedekiah ben Chenaanah, predict victory for Kings Ahab and Jehoshaphat by making horns of iron and prophesying to the assembled: "Thus said Yahweh, With these you shall push the Syrians until they are destroyed" (1 Kgs 22:11). Then at Jehoshaphat's request but against the wishes of Ahab, another Yahweh prophet, Micaiah ben Imlah, is brought in, who prophesies a different outcome. The battle was lost, and Ahab was killed, showing the symbolic action of Zedekiah to be nothing more than an empty gesture. Yahweh was not in it.

Elijah ends his prophetic career with more symbolic acts. In the first of two legendary episodes in 2 Kings 1–2, we see him making a statement against royalty and opulence by the clothes that he wears: a haircloth garment and leather girdle about his loins (2 Kgs 1:8; cf. John the Baptist in Matt 11:7-9, 14). His dress is a symbolic act. More important yet is the symbolism dramatizing the prophecy he gives to Ahaziah, king of Israel. Ahaziah has fallen sick and is sending to inquire of Baalzebub (= Baalzebul), god of Ekron, to see if he will recover.[3] The entire legend plays on the "up and down," with Elijah now being apprised of the king's solicitation. He declares that Ahaziah will not *come down* from the *upper* chamber to which he has *gone up*, but will surely die (2 Kgs 1:4). To dramatize this word, Elijah goes *up* to the top of a mountain and refuses to *come down*. A captain of fifty sent by the king commands him, "*Come down*" (v. 9). Elijah answers the captain, "If I am a man of God, let fire *come down* from heaven and consume you and your fifty" (vv. 10-11). Fire comes down. The sequence of events repeats a second time, with a similar result. It then repeats a third time, which is common in legends, but with the difference that this captain of fifty wisely falls on his knees before Elijah, pleading for his life. At a divine messenger's bidding, Elijah then *goes down* from the mountain to speak directly to the king (v. 16). This "messenger of Yahweh" who appeared at the beginning of the account (v. 3) may well be Elisha, who is no longer incognito when the first legend of chapter 2 begins.

Elisha, in miraculously bringing the son of a Shunammite woman back to life, lies on the boy's cold body, rises to walk backward and forward in the house, and then stretches himself again on the boy, at which point the boy sneezes, opens his eyes, and regains body warmth (2 Kgs 4:32-37). The symbolic action here is done in conjunction with a mighty work.

As Elisha lay sick and was soon to die, he, like his master, performed a final symbolic act, only in this case it was carried out by the king at Elisha's direction. The prophet tells King Joash to take in hand a bow and a supply of arrows, and then, with the prophet's own hands on the king's hands, Elisha tells Joash to shoot eastward an "arrow of victory" over the Syrians. The king does this. Then the prophet tells the king to strike the ground with the arrows remaining. Joash strikes the ground three times, but Elisha becomes angry, saying that if Joash had struck the ground five or six times, he would have brought about the end of Israel's troublesome foe (2 Kgs 13:14-19). The symbolic act here determined the future outcomes of wars with the Syrians. Had the Israelite king been more vigorous in his action, the result would have been more Israelite victories, and the Syrian menace would have ended for good.

Amos

The prophet Amos performed a symbolic act in his eight oracles against the nations (Amos 1–2). Nils W. Lund proposed a number of years ago that these oracles form a simple crosswise pattern following the points on a compass.[4] The first four nations, more distant from the prophet, make an X; the four closer nations, located on either side of the Jordan, complete the figure. These are addressed in clockwise fashion, beginning with Ammon and ending with Israel, at which point the climax is reached, the drama ends, and the audience is shocked to learn the outcome. The pattern is the following:

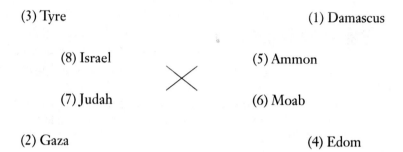

(3) Tyre	(1) Damascus
(8) Israel	(5) Ammon
(7) Judah	(6) Moab
(2) Gaza	(4) Edom

If Amos can be imagined as standing somewhere between Jerusalem and Samaria (the X in the diagram)—perhaps at Bethel, the one location where he is known to have preached (Amos 7:10-13)—his recitation of oracles while facing each nation would constitute drama of a high order. Amos begins by facing the Aramean (Syrian) city of Damascus to the northeast, then turns 180 degrees to face the Philistine city of Gaza to the southwest. He then faces northwest to address the Phoenician city of Tyre, after which he makes another 180-degree turn to address Edom in the southeast. In the sweep of nations closer to home, Amos first addresses Ammon in the near northeast, then Moab in the near southeast. Turning west, he then addresses Judah in the near southwest, and finally Israel in the near northwest. The masterful survey ends right where the prophet intends: in Israel. If the audience has given hearty assent to the judgment on seven other nations—which doubtless it has—it cannot now stop the momentum and refrain from judging Israel, which it would like to do. The northern Israelite audience has been trapped, and the prophet's objective has been achieved. It may also have been the case, even though there is no evidence for this, that Amos smashed some pottery as he was reciting each judgment. Judgment oracles in Egypt are known to have been accompanied by the smashing of pottery.[5] In any case, we see here symbolic action occurring simultaneously with the preaching of the divine word.

Isaiah

Isaiah, for three years before Assyria took Ashdod in 711 B.C.E., went "naked" ('ārôm, עָרוֹם) and barefoot in Jerusalem to dramatize the fate of

Egyptian captives and Ethiopian exiles (Isa 20:2). It has been suggested that the Hebrew term may mean simply "half clad," that is, with only a loincloth,[6] although elsewhere *'ārōm* (עָרוֹם) or *'ērōm* (עֵירֹם) means "bare naked" (Gen 3:7, 10-11). The LXX has *gymnos*, which can mean "half-clad," that is, without an outer garment. But Isa 20:4 says that the prophet's "buttocks" were uncovered (cf. 2 Sam 10:4), which is probably naked enough. Isaiah's reduced attire was to symbolize a captive's attire—or lack of the same—on the way into exile. The prophet wished to send a message to Judah, which at the time was relying on Egypt for help. In v. 3 the dramatic action is called a "sign and wonder," which Robinson says shows that it was divinely ordered.

Jeremiah

Jeremiah supplemented his preaching with a number of symbolic acts. Early in his ministry, Yahweh commanded him to purchase a linen loincloth and to put it on but not to wash it. Then after wearing it for a time, the prophet was to go to nearby Parah and hide the loincloth in a rock. Parah was also the name for the Euphrates, a symbol of Assyria, which, at the time, was a waning world power but still one to be reckoned with. Then after many days, Yahweh told Jeremiah to retrieve the loincloth, which he did, only to find it ruined. The two oracles following indicate that this act was to symbolize the ruined pride of Judah and Jerusalem, which at the time were pinning hopes on Assyria rather than listening to Yahweh's voice and obeying his commands (Jer 13:1-11).

On another occasion, Jeremiah bought an (empty) decanter at the potter's shop, and after delivering two oracles at the Potsherd Gate above Jerusalem's Ben Hinnom Valley, he broke it in the presence of those accompanying him. Two more oracles followed. This act was to symbolize Yahweh's determination to punish Jerusalem for covenant violations, the worst of which was child sacrifice in the Ben Hinnom Valley; to "make empty" the counsel of those planning Jerusalem's future; and to break both city and people so neither could be mended, leaving Ben Hinnom a heap of unburied bodies and making Jerusalem unclean like the Topheth dump because of roof sacrifices to astral deities and other gods (Jer 19:1-13).

Jeremiah performed one symbolic act in a vision (Jer 25:15-29). The prophet saw Yahweh hosting a banquet for the nations, where he had been appointed server of the wine. Yahweh told him to take the wrath-filled cup from his hand and make the nations around the table drink. All would become thoroughly drunk, retch, and go mad, after which they would be easy prey before the sword Yahweh was sending upon them. Jeremiah did as instructed, making the nations drink. First to drink was Jerusalem and the cities of Judah, and last was Babylon. The oracles following repeat the message of the symbolic act.

With a fringe group of Rechabites living in Judah, but trying to preserve their ascetic way of life, Jeremiah went to the temple to test their resolve not to drink wine. Before them, he placed full pitchers of wine and cups and told them to drink the wine. They refused, saying that Jonadab their father had commanded them not to drink wine, and they would obey his command. This symbolic act, and the oracles following, were to give Judahites a lesson on turning from evil and obeying Yahweh's command, which they had failed to do. Judgment would therefore come (Jeremiah 35).

Some years later, when the Babylonians were poised to exercise imperial rule over nations of the eastern Mediterranean, Jeremiah was commanded by Yahweh to wear yoke bars and straps on his neck. These were to symbolize the submission Judah and neighboring nations must render to Nebuchadnezzar, king of Babylon (Jeremiah 27). The prophet sent these miniature symbols also to foreign kings, via envoys who were visiting Jerusalem to discuss rebellion against Nebuchadnezzar. This put him in opposition to another Yahweh prophet, Hananiah son of Azzur, who, when the two met face-to-face, broke the yoke bar off Jeremiah's neck and prophesied that Nebuchadnezzar's yoke would be broken in two years (Jeremiah 28). Hananiah, too, was capable of a symbolic act! Jeremiah later returned and said that Yahweh would replace the yoke of wood with a yoke of iron, and to Hananiah he said that Yahweh had not sent him, and that he would die. In two months Hananiah died. Jeremiah, because he delivered the right message, was vindicated in his symbolic act. The symbolic act of Hananiah came to nothing; Yahweh was not in it.

A year before the fall of Jerusalem, Jeremiah, from his place of confinement in the court of the guard, was instructed by Yahweh to redeem a field at Anathoth from his cousin Hanamel. He carried out the transaction in the presence of witnesses and then gave the deed to his scribal friend Baruch for safekeeping. This symbolic act was to point ahead to the day when Yahweh would restore his people to the land and cut an eternal covenant with them, also when houses, fields, and vineyards would once again be bought and sold in the land (Jeremiah 32).

Jeremiah's final symbolic act took place in Egypt, where he was taken with survivors after Jerusalem had fallen and the remnant community at Mizpah had dissolved following the murder of Gedaliah, its governor. Soon after his arrival in Egypt, Jeremiah buried large stones with mortar in the brick pavement before Pharaoh's palace at Tahpanhes. This was to symbolize Nebuchadnezzar's future arrival in Egypt and the erection of his throne on the site (Jer 43:8-13).

Ezekiel

Jeremiah's younger contemporary, Ezekiel, who was taken to Babylon in 597 B.C.E. and carried out his entire ministry in that distant land, was another prophet given to symbolic behavior. His symbolic acts, which were many, have been variously assessed. Hermann Gunkel thought that in the modern day they would be regarded as signs of mental illness, or at least nervous derangement.[7] But this prophet is nevertheless a credible figure acting under the inspiration of God. Soon after his call to be Israel's "watchman," the spirit enters Ezekiel and directs him to remain in his house. Ezekiel even submits to being bound with cords so he cannot go outside. In confinement, Yahweh makes him dumb so that he cannot rebuke a rebellious people, but after a time, the prophet's tongue is loosed, and he is able to reprove them (Ezek 3:22-27).

Soon after, Ezekiel carries out a series of symbolic acts to portray the upcoming siege of Jerusalem and the exile of its people. First, he draws a plan of Jerusalem on a clay tablet and builds a miniature siege-works around it. Then he places an iron plate, commonly used in baking, between himself and the city. This miniature iron wall, as it is meant to be, represents the barrier currently existing between Yahweh and Jerusalem. Assuming the role of Yahweh, Ezekiel then sets his face toward the city and proceeds to press the siege against it. This symbolic act is to be a sign for the house of Israel (Ezek 4:1-3).

After this, the prophet is instructed to lie on his left side for 390 days (LXX: 190 days), which is to symbolize Yahweh's punishment in years for the house of Israel. Then he is to lie on his right side for forty days, which is to symbolize Yahweh's punishment in years for the house of Judah. The prophet's own punishment represents Israel and Judah's punishment. Then Ezekiel is to face a besieged Jerusalem with arm bared, representing a wrathful divine warrior, and to prophesy against the city. Once again he allows himself to be bound with cords, this time so he cannot turn from one side to the other (Ezek 4:4-8). The present symbolic act is to dramatize the captivity of Israel's northern and southern kingdoms in their respective places of exile.

More actions symbolizing siege and exile follow (Ezek 4:9-17). Ezekiel is instructed to weigh out a small quantity of grains and vegetables, to put the mixture into a pan, and to bake it in the sight of the exiles. He is then to eat his barley cake once a day while lying on his side. Once a day he is to drink a measured quantity of water. Yahweh wants the barley cake baked over a fire of human excrement, but this scandalizes the prophet, who, as a priest, is unaccustomed to defiling himself. Yahweh then agrees to have the cake baked over a fire of cow excrement. This is to symbolize the meager rations of food and water to be expected in a besieged Jerusalem, and the detrimental effect it will have on the bodies of those besieged.

Ezekiel on another occasion was commanded by Yahweh to shave his hair and beard with a razor and then divide the hair into three parts by weighing it on a scale (Ezek 5:1-17). One part was to be burned in the midst of the city; another was to be cut up and spread about the city; and a third was to be scattered to the winds. This treatment of the three portions of the prophet's hair was to symbolize what would happen to an evil-ridden Jerusalem once the siege was brought to a successful conclusion: judgment within the city (cannibalism); judgment around the city (sword, famine, and pestilence); and judgment on those fleeing the city (a pursuing sword).

Yahweh told Ezekiel to clap his hands and stamp his feet in an exultation of scorn over Yahweh's judgment on Israel for rank abominations. People will fall by the sword, by famine, and by pestilence, and the land will become a desolate waste (Ezek 6:11-14).

Ezekiel carried out one symbolic action while in a trance. In 592 B.C.E., while sitting before the elders of Judah in his house, he was transported by the forelocks to the inner gate of the Jerusalem temple. After observing an image deemed highly offensive to Yahweh, he was taken to the door of the court and commanded there to dig a hole in the wall, through which he would see even greater abominations. He saw these and more, which led Yahweh to say that his wrath would be spent on such a people (Ezek 8:1-18).

On another occasion, Ezekiel was commanded to dig a real hole in the wall of the place where he was staying, and through it to carry an exile's baggage on his shoulder—in the light of day, and in the dark of evening—to another place (Ezek 12:1-16). In the evening, he was to cover his face so as not to look upon the land. This was to dramatize Jerusalem's coming exile, although included in this interpretation are clear allusions to Zedekiah's escape from Jerusalem, his capture at Jericho, his blinding at Riblah, and his journey in chains to Babylon (cf. 2 Kgs 25:4-7; Jer 52:7-11). A pursuing sword will scatter other hapless souls to the four winds. Ezekiel in this symbolic act was to be a "wonder" to the house of Israel (Ezek 12:6, 11): as he did, so Jerusalem will do.

Perhaps soon afterward, Ezekiel was commanded to eat bread and drink water with fear and trembling (Ezek 12:17-20). Here again, he was representing Jerusalem's inhabitants, who would so eat and drink when their land was stripped bare and made a desolate ruin.

In another prophecy, Ezekiel was commanded to face the south, that is, Jerusalem, and to sigh deeply as he preached Yahweh's judgment against the city and forestland to the south. Yahweh's destroying fire would consume both green tree and dry, that is, both righteous and wicked from south to north (Ezek 20:45—21:7). Ezekiel was then to cry, wail, and smite his thigh over Yahweh's fateful sword, sharpened and polished as it was in the hand of a slayer who remains unnamed. He was then to clap his hands and maneuver the sword to come down two, yes, three times on those about to be slain, cutting to the right, then to the left. Yahweh too will clap his hands in satisfying his fury (Ezek 21:8-17).

In another symbolic act, Ezekiel marks out two ways for the sword of the king of Babylon to go, putting at the crossroads a signpost pointing to Rabbath Ammon and to Jerusalem. When the king comes to the parting of the ways, he will use divination to determine in which direction to go. The lot will fall on Jerusalem, where the Babylonian king will besiege the city and eventually capture it, Yahweh saying that its guilt must be brought to remembrance (Ezek 21:18-23).

Ezekiel's final symbolic act turns the corner to express a grand hope. The prophet is told to write on two sticks "Judah" and "Joseph" (= northern Israel), and then to join them in his hand into one stick. This is to symbolize the gathering of Israelite exiles from all nations, the reunion of the two kingdoms in their own land, the placing of one Davidic king over them, and the brokering of an everlasting covenant of peace that will cleanse them from sin and idolatry (Ezek 37:15-28).

THE PROPHET AS SYMBOL

J. G. Herder saw the fullest expression of divine prophecy as being when the life of the prophet itself became the symbol.[8] T. K. Cheyne, too, said of Jeremiah that "the greatest poem is his life."[9] Hosea became himself the symbol in a marriage that was broken and then reestablished (Hosea

1–3). Hosea married a prostitute, had children with her, and gave his children symbolic names to dramatize Israel's broken covenant with Yahweh. Then in taking the faithless Gomer back, he symbolized Yahweh's decision in future days to take Israel back.

Jeremiah became himself the symbol by not marrying (Jer 16:1-4), also by absenting himself from mourning and joyful feasts (Jer 16:5-9). But it was the prophet's suffering in the final days prior to Judah's collapse, when the nation was tumbling headlong into ruin, that the focus was taken almost entirely off the prophetic word and symbolic act to be rather on the prophet himself (Jeremiah 37–39). Jeremiah's entire being had now become the message—a dual message about a suffering nation and a suffering God in whose service the prophet remained steadfast to the very end.[10] Messages of such a grand scope were later repeated in the Suffering Servant of Isaiah 53, and again in the New Testament Gospels, where the divine message became acted out in the passion of Jesus Christ. Paul, too, writes to the Roman church: "Present your bodies as a living sacrifice, holy and acceptable to God, which is your spiritual worship" (Rom 12:1).

On the eve of Jerusalem's destruction, Yahweh told Ezekiel that his wife, "the delight of his eyes," would die, and that he should not weep or engage in any of the usual mourning rites. He could only sigh inwardly (Ezek 24:15-27). His wife died, and Ezekiel did as commanded. This all-encompassing symbolic act was to be a "wonder" to all who looked on (vv. 24, 27). When the people would hear of the destruction of Jerusalem and the temple, which was "the delight of their eyes," and of sons and daughters left behind becoming victims of the sword, they too were not to mourn in the usual fashion. The prophet's mouth would eventually be opened, and he would then be able to speak to the people (v. 27; cf. 3:27).

In conclusion we return to Elijah, who, like Jeremiah, became himself the symbol at the end of his life. He too was not the primary actor but rather the one acted upon by Yahweh God. Elijah's final wonder was a chariot ride to meet his death, one preserved in tradition as a chariot ride into heaven.[11] From heaven, Elijah would return to usher in the coming Day of Yahweh (Mal 4:5-6). Jesus said that Elijah did return in the person of John the Baptist (Matt 11:14-15). Elijah's chariot ride also became the prototype for Jesus' death, resurrection, and ascent into heaven.

CONCLUSION

OUR EXAMINATION OF THE HEBREW PROPHETS HAS revealed a rather complex picture—both of the individuals themselves and of the messages they proclaimed. Prophets were seen to have a number of distinguishing marks, yet not all prophets possessed all the marks. What is more, some of those who boasted of certain marks, for example, being able to speak the divine word, being the recipient of a divine vision, and being filled with the spirit, turned out to be false. Some prophets reported a call to the prophetic office. Other prophets, particularly Jeremiah, were great men of prayer. Other tests existed whereby a prophet was judged to be true or false. The prophet had to speak in Yahweh's name and lead people in the way of Yahweh, and words spoken about the future had to come true. Prophets also seem to have had sufficient personal integrity so as to commend them to the Israelite community. Bad character figured into the evaluation, discrediting certain individuals claiming to be prophets.

What seemed to have mattered most was whether these individuals were truly spokespersons of Yahweh God, and, as we have seen, this was sometimes difficult to determine. Yet a determination was made. The mark of a genuine prophet turned finally on the question of faith, whether the individual had a true faith in the God of Israel, and whether the community had faith in the one acting as a prophet. When Jeremiah, in his trial of 609 B.C.E., rested his defense on the fact that Yahweh had sent him with the message he was preaching, people had to believe him, even though he came with a message they did not want to hear.

Might not some of these same marks be looked for in prophets said to exist in the present day? One would think that they might possess at least some of these marks. They might be able to relate a call to their office, although it need not be made public. They will, to be sure, speak with authority on issues of the day, expressing not just opinions but censuring and judging people and life as they see it being carried on. Do their words ring true? Do predictions they make come true? Will they not also have

219

vision? They could even report visions bringing them revelations from God. Some will perform mighty works; most will be spirit-filled and will have to give evidence of being filled with the spirit of God. And they should be individuals given to prayer—praying for themselves, praying on behalf of others, praying for the church, praying for the communities in which they live, and praying for the nation.

What are we to say about Billy Graham's disclaimer of being a prophet? Amos made a disclaimer, and people still took him to be a prophet. Billy Graham has spoken to huge crowds over a number of years about irresolute living, and he has censured it, saying that it is disobeying God's commands. Yes, he is a conservative, but the Hebrew prophets were conservatives. And yes, Graham's message has been directed more toward personal wrongdoing than ills in the society. Nevertheles, he has addressed sin and evil with great clarity. Billy Graham has also said a considerable amount about the need of people to repent of their sins, but he has not been candid with the many presidents he has come to know personally. By anyone's standard, however, he has been an uncommonly moral and upright person. What will be the final assessment of him?

And what is one to say about the great civil rights leader Martin Luther King Jr., against whom there have been countless charges of moral lapses—great moral lapses? His close associate Ralph Abernathy has stated in a book that King had numerous extramarital affairs, some said to have taken place on the very night he was assassinated. Wiretaps, said to contain more damaging information on King's adventurism with women, are presently sealed up and will not become public until 2026. Do these and other character flaws in an otherwise extraordinary man, who changed forever life in America for the good, have any bearing on his being called a modern-day prophet?

We learned also that even the best of prophetic messages had to fit into a specific historical context. Prophets could not be "dealers in used oracles." An authentic message on one occasion could become an inauthentic message on another. Prophets preaching Isaiah's message a hundred years later in Jeremiah's time ended up being false prophets, for now Yahweh had a different word to proclaim. Today one might well ask, for example, if the civil rights messages of the 1960s can be recycled to apply to same-sex intercourse and same-sex marriage, which is what is taking place. The former, civil rights, was a justice issue, but is the latter? Many would say the latter is a moral issue, in which case the message of the 1960s simply cannot be recycled to fit the situation today.

Towner's four great themes in the prophetic messages are seen to hold up rather well:

1. calls for justice, particularly for the poor, weak, and powerless;
2. indictments of corruption among society's powerful, even at personal cost;
3. calls for purifying the religious community;
4. expressions of hope for redemption, peace, and obedient living.

To these I would simply add that the Hebrew prophets went beyond indicting the corrupt; they announced harsh judgment upon them. The Sinai covenant not only warned against disobedience; it also stated what would happen if the people disobeyed: a multitude of curses would fall. At the same time, obedience to the covenant would bring blessing and well-being and would be the road to life itself. Prophets also called for repentance, and if this happened, punishment could be rescinded.

We learned that prophets were very able speakers, having exceptional command of language and the ability to mount compelling arguments. Even Amos, who was a shepherd and dresser of vines, was extraordinary with words. Jeremiah was a master of argument. All the later prophets were articulate. Are we to expect, then, that today's aspiring prophets be babblers in nonsense, unable to think clearly, and unable to make a clear case for God and against the things that God hates? And should we not expect to find in prophets a keen wit and a robust sense of humor? One needs humor to see the incongruities in human behavior and in community life generally. Some modern-day preachers of judgment are humorless souls, leading one to wonder if they are correctly perceiving others and, yes, correctly perceiving themselves.

There is an abundance of symbolic behavior in our modern world, much of it said to be of a prophetic nature. How also are we to evaluate street marches, signs held aloft, and other actions aimed at dramatizing a message? In ancient Israel, both genuine and ingenuine prophets carried on symbolic action.

The biblical prophets were certainly not perfect individuals, nor were their messages precise assessments of the present or perfect predictions about the future. Their messages were credible in the main, and what they said about the future was basically on target. If such were not the case, they would never have been taken as authentic spokespersons of

Yahweh God, and would never have been accepted and honored by a believing community. Believing communities today must make similar judgments about men and women claiming to be prophets, or who are taken by others to be prophets. Issues today remain complex, and decisions will continue to be difficult, but if genuine prophets and genuine prophetic messages are to be identified, decisions will nevertheless have to be made.

NOTES

INTRODUCTION

1. W. Sibley Towner, "On Calling People 'Prophets' in 1970." *Interpretation* 24 (1970): 492–509.

2. Ibid., 497, 505–9.

3. Ernest T. Campbell, "An Open Letter to Billy Graham," and "Billy Graham Answers His Critics," in *A.D.* 2/3 (March 1973): 6–8, 10–11.

4. Campbell, "Billy Graham Answers His Critics," 11.

CHAPTER 1

1. See Herbert B. Huffmon, "The Origins of Prophecy," in *Magnalia Dei, the Mighty Acts of God: Essays on the Bible and Archaeology in Memory of G. Ernest Wright*, ed. Frank Moore Cross et al. (Garden City, N.Y.: Doubleday, 1976), 171–86.

2. William F. Albright, *From the Stone Age to Christianity: Monotheism and the Historical Process*, 2nd ed. (New York: Doubleday, 1957), 303. See also G. Ernest Wright, "The Nations in Hebrew Prophecy," *Encounter* 26 (1965): 225.

3. Albright, *From the Stone Age to Christianity*, 303.

4. M. Gilula, "An Egyptian Parallel to Jeremia I 4-5," *VT* 17 (1967): 114.

5. "Oracles Concerning Esarhaddon" (*ANET*³ 605, ii 30).

6. William F. Albright, *Samuel and the Beginnings of the Prophetic Movement*, Goldenson Lecture 1961 (Cincinnati: Hebrew Union College Press, 1961), 13. Max Weber (*The Sociology of Religion*, 4th ed., trans. Ephraim Fischoff [Boston: Beacon, 1963], 46) says: "The personal call is the decisive element distinguishing the prophet from the priest."

7. Elijah is probably getting food from the palace at Samaria, which would explain his intimate association with the royal steward Obadiah (1 Kgs 18:7). Micaiah, too, is getting food from Ahab, although his rations will be cut back significantly after predicting the king's defeat (1 Kgs 22:27). Amos is believed by some to be receiving board as a prophet back in Judah (Amos 7:12), and Jeremiah gets food from Zedekiah until the fall of Jerusalem (Jer 37:21).

8. Albright, *Samuel and the Beginnings of the Prophetic Movement*; see also Huffmon, "Origins of Prophecy," 176–77.

9. Ibid., 177.

10. Robert H. Pfeiffer, *Introduction to the Old Testament* (New York: Harper & Bros., 1948), 55.

11. James M. Muilenburg, "The 'Office' of the Prophet in Ancient Israel," in *The Bible in Modern Scholarship: Papers Read at the 100th Meeting of the Society of Biblical Literature, December 28–30, 1964*, ed. J. Philip Hyatt (Nashville: Abingdon, 1965), 74–97.

12. Martin Noth, "History and the Word of God in the Old Testament," *BJRL* 32 (1950): 197–200; Herbert Huffmon, "Prophecy in the Mari Letters," *BA* 31 (1968): 101–24; and James F. Ross, "The Prophet as Yahweh's Messenger," in *Israel's Prophetic Heritage: Essays in Honor of James Muilenburg*, ed. Bernhard W. Anderson and Walter Harrelson (New York: Harper & Bros., 1962), 98–107. The recognition of the prophet as Yahweh's messenger was seen already by Hermann Gunkel; see his "The Israelite Prophecy from the Time of Amos," in *Twentieth Century Theology in the Making*, ed. Jaroslav Pelikan, trans. R. A. Wilson, 3 vols. (London: William Collins; New York: Harper & Row, 1969–70), 1:67–68.

13. Alfred Haldar, *Associations of Cult Prophets among the Ancient Semites* (Uppsala: Almqvist & Wiksells, 1945), 128–30. Albright hints at the same idea; see his *Samuel and the Beginnings of the Prophetic Movement*, 7.

14. Albright (*Samuel and the Beginnings of the Prophetic Movement*, 7) says that *nābî'* is equivalent to "man of God." See also Raphael Hallevy, "Man of God," *JNES* 17 (1958): 237–44, who says that the nondifferentiation comes with later writers.

15. Jack R. Lundbom, "Elijah's Chariot Ride," *JJS* 24 (1973): 40–43. The modern prophet William Wade Harris of West Africa (1910–1929) appears to have understood this "angel" as an extraterrestrial being known to Elijah in a trance, a state into which he entered as a prophet; see David A. Shank, *Prophet Harris, the 'Black Elijah' of West Africa*, abridged by Jocelyn Murray, Studies on Religion in Africa 10 (Leiden: Brill, 1994), 122.

16. The title may or may not be a personal name.

17. Jack R. Lundbom, "Jeremiah 15, 15–21 and the Call of Jeremiah," *SJOT* 9 (1995): 143–55.

18. H. H. Rowley, "The Nature of Prophecy in the Light of Recent Study," *HTR* 38 (1945): 22.

19. Henry George Liddle and Robert Scott, *A Greek-English Lexicon*, rev. Henry Stuart Jones, 2 vols. (Oxford: Clarendon, 1951), 1538.

20. Abraham Joshua Heschel, *The Prophets* (New York and Evanston, Ill.: Harper & Row, 1962), 406.

21. Huffmon, "Origins of Prophecy," 182–83.

22. Theophile J. Meek, *Hebrew Origins* (New York: Harper & Bros., 1950), 150.

23. Thorleif Bowman, *Hebrew Thought Compared with Greek*, trans. Jules L. Moreau (Philadelphia: Westminster, 1960), 206.

24. Huffmon, "Origins of Prophecy," 72.

25. Harry M. Orlinsky, "The Seer in Ancient Israel," *Oriens Antiquus* 4 (1965): 164.

26. Huffmon ("Origins of Prophecy," 179) says that there was no difference basically between the seer and the prophet.

27. Only in the New Testament (2 Pet 2:15-16) is he called a prophet. Joshua 13:22 calls him a "soothsayer."

28. Robert R. Wilson, *Prophecy and Society in Ancient Israel* (Philadelphia: Fortress Press, 1980), 149. Samuel presides over the sacrifice in 1 Samuel 9 to which Saul is invited. For the seer as an institutional figure whose activities overlap with those of the priest, see Orlinsky, "Seer in Ancient Israel," 157–58.

29. Wilson, *Prophecy and Society in Ancient Israel*, 132, 149.

30. So Elijah, according to Huffmon, "Origins of Prophecy," 182.

31. Shank, *Prophet Harris*, 177–88; Bengt G. Sundkler, *Bantu Prophets in South Africa* (London: Lutterworth, 1948), 186.

32. Huffmon, "Origins of Prophecy," 178.

33. On ecstasy in modern religious figures, particularly in Scandinavia, see J. Lindblom, *Prophecy in Ancient Israel* (Philadelphia: Fortress Press, 1965).

34. James L. Crenshaw (*Prophetic Conflict: Its Effect upon Israelite Religion*, BZAW 124 [Berlin and New York: Walter de Gruyter, 1971], 28 and 94) thinks that this remark is rather made by the people.

35. Weber (*Sociology of Religion*, 46) considers the prophet to be a "bearer of charisma."

36. Heschel (*Prophets*, 315–17) calls it "divine pathos."

37. Hermann Gunkel, "The Secret Experiences of the Prophets," *The Expositor*, 9th ser., 1 (1924): 364–65.

38. Heschel, *Prophets*, 9–10.

39. Lundbom, "Elijah's Chariot Ride," 47–50.

40. A. R. Johnson (*The Cultic Prophet in Ancient Israel* [Oxford: Oxford University Press, 1944], 52–53) says that he may have had special quarters in the temple.

41. Joseph Blenkinsopp, *A History of Prophecy in Israel* (Philadelphia: Westminster, 1983), 62.

42. James Muilenburg, "Old Testament Prophecy," in *Peake's Commentary on the Bible*, ed. Matthew Black and H. H. Rowley (London and New York: Thomas Nelson, 1977), 476; Wilson, *Prophecy and Society in Ancient Israel*, 150–51.

43. Elijah, and perhaps Elisha as well, is a possible exception; see Johnson, *Cultic Prophet*, 27–28.

44. Ibid., 50–51, 63.

45. See Samuel E. Balentine, "The Prophet as Intercessor: A Reassessment," *JBL* 103 (1984): 161–73.

CHAPTER 2

1. Hermann Gunkel, "The Secret Experiences of the Prophets," *The Expositor*, 9th ser., 1 (1924): 433; idem, "The Israelite Prophecy from the Time of Amos," in *Twentieth Century Theology in the Making*, ed. Jaroslav Pelikan, trans. R. A. Wilson, 3 vols. (London: Collins; New York: Harper & Row, 1969–70), 1:69.

2. James M. Muilenburg, "Old Testament Prophecy," in *Peake's Commentary on the Bible*, ed. Matthew Black and H. H. Rowley (London and New York: Thomas Nelson, 1977), 476.

3. Abraham Joshua Heschel, *The Prophets* (New York/Evanston, Ill.: Harper & Row, 1962), 23.

4. See J. Lindblom, *Prophecy in Ancient Israel* (Philadelphia: Fortress Press, 1965), 329–30.

5. Thomas M. Conley, "The Enthymeme in Perspective, *Quarterly Journal of Speech* 70 (1984): 168–87.

6. Jack R. Lundbom, "Hebrew Rhetoric," in *Encyclopedia of Rhetoric*, ed. Thomas D. Sloane (Oxford: Oxford University Press, 2001), 326.

7. See John M. Powis Smith, "The Conservatism of Early Prophecy," *AJT* 23 (1919): 290–99; Edmond Jacob, "The Biblical Prophets: Revolutionaries or Conservatives?" trans. James H. Farley, *Interpretation* 19 (1965): 47–55. Peter Berger ("Between Tyranny and Chaos," *Christian Century* 85 [October 30, 1968]: 1370) observed that the prophets had a message that was both "radical" and "conservative."

8. John Barton, "History and Rhetoric in the Prophets," in *The Bible as Rhetoric: Studies in Biblical Persuasion and Credibility*, ed. Martin Warner, Warwick Studies in Philosophy and Literature (London and New York: Routledge, 1990), 56.

9. Heschel, *Prophets*, 284.

10. Reinhold Niebuhr, "The Test of True Prophecy," in *Beyond Tragedy* (New York: Charles Scribner's Sons, 1937), 93–110.

11. John Skinner, *Prophecy and Religion: Studies in the Life of Jeremiah* (1922; repr., Cambridge: Cambridge University Press, 1963), 193.

12. Sheldon Blank, *Of a Truth the Lord Hath Sent Me: An Inquiry into the Source of the Prophet's Authority*, Goldenson Lecture 1955 (Cincinnati: Hebrew Union College Press, 1955), 9.

13. Skinner, *Prophecy and Religion*, 187.

14. Hans Walter Wolff, *Joel and Amos: A Commentary on the Books of the Prophets Joel and Amos*, trans. Waldemar Janzen et al., Hermeneia (Philadelphia: Fortress Press, 1977), 124.

15. John Bright, *A History of Israel*, 3rd ed. (Philadelphia: Westminster, 1981), 255.

16. Jack R. Lundbom, "The Lawbook of the Josianic Reform," *CBQ* 38 (1976): 293–302.

17. *ANET*³, 287–88.

18. See the earlier discussion above under "Second Moses: Prophet of the Song," which compares this portion of the oracle with verses from Deuteronomy 32.

CHAPTER 3

1. Ecstasy by itself is no test for authenticity; see A. B. Davidson, "The False Prophets," *The Expositor*, 5th ser., 2 (1895): 4–5; James L. Crenshaw, *Prophetic Conflict: Its Effect upon Israelite Religion*, BZAW 124 (Berlin and New York: Walter de Gruyter, 1971), 54.

2. Abraham Joshua Heschel, *The Prophets* (New York and Evanston, Ill.: Harper & Row, 1962), 431.

3. Paul Tillich, *Systematic Theology*, vol. 1, *Reason and Revelation; Being and God* (Chicago: University of Chicago Press, 1951), 211–89.

4. Heschel, *Prophets*, 264; G. Ernest Wright, *God Who Acts: Biblical Theology as Recital*, Studies in Biblical Theology 8 (London: SCM, 1952). The theology of "God's mighty acts" has recently come under attack for not being inclusive enough in appropriating the entire Old Testament witness. It does not, for example, take into sufficient consideration the wisdom literature. See Werner E. Lemke, "Revelation through History in Recent Biblical Theology: A Critical Appraisal," *Interpretation* 36 (1982): 34–46. At the same time, "act" is still the important category in ancient Hebrew thought, not "being."

5. Heschel, *Prophets*, 431.

6. Ibid., 432.

7. Davidson, "False Prophets," 1.

8. The term occurs in the LXX a total of ten times: Jer 6:13; 33:7, 8, 11, 16 [MT 26:7, 8, 11, 16]; 34:9 [MT 27:9]; 35:1 [MT 28:1]; 36:1, 8 [MT 29:1, 8]; Zech 13:2.

9. Davidson, "False Prophets," 1. The same conclusion is reached by Thomas W. Overholt, who emphasizes that falsity, at least in the book of Jeremiah, lies in the prophetic message; see Overholt, *The Threat of Falsehood: A Study in the Theology of the Book of Jeremiah*, Studies in Biblical Theology, n.s., 16 (Naperville, Ill.: Alec R. Allenson, 1970), 85.

10. Davidson, "False Prophets," 1–2.

11. This passage is discussed in some detail by Crenshaw in his *Prophetic Conflict*, chapter 3, where he comments on an earlier treatment by Karl Barth.

12. Gerhard von Rad, *Old Testament Theology*, vol. 2, *The Theology of Israel's Prophetic Traditions*, trans. D. M. G. Stalker (Edinburgh and London: Oliver & Boyd, 1965), 129.

13. Overholt, *Threat of Falsehood*, 94; see also Paul D. Hanson, *Dynamic Transcendence: The Correlation of Confessional Heritage and Contemporary Experience in a Biblical Model of Divine Activity* (Philadelphia: Fortress Press, 1978); and James A.

Sanders, "Hermeneutics in True and False Prophecy," in *Canon and Authority: Essays in Old Testament Religion and Theology*, ed. George W. Coats and Burke O. Long (Philadelphia: Fortress Press, 1977), 31–34.

14. See A. R. Johnson, *The Cultic Prophet in Ancient Israel* (Oxford: Oxford University Press, 1944), 41.

15. See "Foretelling and Forthtelling" above in chapter 2, "The Prophetic Message—What Is It?"

16. In John, Jesus is the "prophet like Moses" (Deut 18:15); see T. F. Glasson, *Moses in the Fourth Gospel*, Studies in Biblical Theology 40 (London: SCM, 1963). For the positive use of signs in John, see C. H. Dodd, *The Interpretation of the Fourth Gospel* (Cambridge: Cambridge University Press, 1953); and Raymond E. Brown, *The Gospel According to John I–XII: Introduction, Translation, and Notes*, AB 29 (Garden City, N.Y.: Doubleday, 1966), 525–32.

17. Crenshaw, *Prophetic Conflict*, 53.

18. For a list of such prophecies by Isaiah, Jeremiah, Second Isaiah, and others, see J. Lindblom, *Prophecy in Ancient Israel* (Philadelphia: Fortress Press, 1965), 199; also Crenshaw, *Prophetic Conflict*, 51.

19. Overholt, *Threat of Falsehood*, 37.

20. Overholt (*Threat of Falsehood*, 37) does an exhaustive study of "lie" (*šeqer* שֶׁקֶר) in Jeremiah.

21. John Skinner, *Prophecy and Religion: Studies in the Life of Jeremiah* (1922; repr., Cambridge: Cambridge University Press, 1963), 195.

22. H. H. Rowley, "The Nature of Prophecy in the Light of Recent Study," *HTR* 38 (1945): 33–34, 37–38.

23. On the importance of inner certainty for the true prophet, see Rowley, "Nature of Prophecy," 33–34, 37–38; Skinner, *Prophecy and Religion*, 195–96; Heschel, *Prophets*, 426–29; and Sheldon H. Blank, *Of a Truth the Lord Hath Sent Me: An Inquiry into the Source of the Prophet's Authority*, Goldenson Lecture 1965 (Cincinnati: Hebrew Union College Press, 1955), 7–8.

24. Overholt, *Threat of Falsehood*, 36.

25. Skinner, *Prophecy and Religion*, 191.

26. Johnson, *Cultic Prophet in Ancient Israel*, 30; Overholt (*Threat of Falsehood*, 77) calls it "private opportunism."

27. So Johnson, *Cultic Prophet in Ancient Israel*, 42; and Rowley, "Nature of Prophecy," 18–19.

28. See Crenshaw, *Prophetic Conflict*, 57–59.

29. Skinner (*Prophecy and Religion*, 187) says of the true prophet that "his moral character was not in question" (cf. p. 195). See also Davidson, "False Prophet," 16, on the true prophet's high ethical and moral principles.

CHAPTER 4

1. Robert Lowth, *Lectures on the Sacred Poetry of the Hebrews*, trans. G. Gregory (1787; Boston: Joseph T. Buckingham, 1815).

2. See Roman Jakobson, "Grammatical Parallelism and Its Russian Facet," *Language* 42 (1966): 403–5.

3. Christian Schoettgen, *Horae hebraicae et talmudicae* (Leipzig and Dresden: Christoph. Hekelii & Sons, 1733). Dissertatio VI: *De Exergasia Sacra*, 1249–63. For an English translation, see Jack R. Lundbom, *Jeremiah: A Study in Ancient Hebrew Rhetoric*, SBLDS 18 (Missoula, Mont.: Society of Biblical Literature and Scholars Press, 1975), 121–27 (2nd ed. [Winona Lake, Ind.: Eisenbrauns, 1997], 155–63).

4. James L. Kugel, *The Idea of Hebrew Poetry: Parallelism and Its History* (New Haven and London: Yale University Press, 1981), 85.

5. H. L. Ginsberg, "Ugaritic Studies and the Bible," *BA* 8 (1945): 55; William F. Albright, *Yahweh and the Gods of Canaan: A Historical Analysis of Two Contrasting Faiths*, Jordan Lectures in Comparative Religion 7 (Garden City, N.Y.: Doubleday, 1968), 8.

6. Jack R. Lundbom, *Jeremiah 1–20: A New Translation with Introduction and Commentary*, AB 21A (New York: Doubleday, 1999), 458–59.

7. Ibid., 454, 459.

CHAPTER 5

1. Samuel Noah Kramer, "Sumerian Similes: A Panoramic View of Some of Man's Oldest Literary Images," *JAOS* 89 (1969): 1–10; idem, *The Sacred Marriage Rite: Aspects of Faith, Myth, and Ritual in Ancient Sumer* (Bloomington: Indiana University Press, 1969), 23–48.

2. Sigmund Mowinckel, "Psalms and Wisdom," in *Wisdom in Israel and in the Ancient Near East: Presented to Professor Harold Henry Rowley by the Society for Old Testament Study in Association with the Editorial Board of Vetus Testamentum, in Celebration of His Sixty-fifth Birthday, 24 March 1955*, ed. Martin Noth and D. Winton Thomas; VTSup 3; Leiden: Brill, 1955), 206.

3. James M. Muilenburg, "A Study of Hebrew Rhetoric: Repetition and Style," in *Congress Volume: Copenhagen 1953*, VTSup 1 (Leiden: Brill, 1953), 97–111.

4. Nils W. Lund, *Chiasmus in the New Testament: A Study in Formgeschichte* (Chapel Hill: University of North Carolina Press, 1942; repr., Peabody, Mass.: Hendrickson, 1992), 40.

5. Muilenburg, "Study of Hebrew Rhetoric," 99.

6. Henry A. Fischel, "The Use of Sorites (Climax, Gradatio) in the Tannaitic Period," *HUCA* 44 (1973): 119–51.

7. William J. Brandt, *The Rhetoric of Argumentation* (New York: Bobbs-Merrill, 1970), 135–37.

8. See above in chapter 2 under "Covenant Disobedience."

9. Heschel, *Prophets*, 13.

10. A colon appears here to be missing; see my article "The Double Curse in Jeremiah 20:14-18," *JBL* 104 (1985): 589–600.

CHAPTER 6

1. H. Wheeler Robinson, "Prophetic Symbolism," in *Old Testament Essays*, ed. D. C. Simpson (London: Charles Griffin, 1927), 1–17.
2. Richard G. Moulton, *The Literary Study of the Bible* (New York: D. C. Heath, 1895), 372–79.
3. Jack R. Lundbom, "Elijah's Chariot Ride," *JJS* 24 (1973): 39–50.
4. Nils W. Lund, *Chiasmus in the New Testament: A Study in Formgeschichte* (Chapel Hill: University of North Carolina Press, 1942; repr., Peabody, Mass.: Hendrickson, 1992), 87–88.
5. See A. Bentzen, "The Ritual Background of Amos I 2–II 16," *OS* 8 (1950): 85–99.
6. George Buchanan Gray, *A Critical and Exegetical Commonetary on the Book of Isaiah I–XXXIX* (ICC; Edinburgh: T&T Clark, 1912), 345–46.
7. Hermann Gunkel, "The Israelite Prophecy from the Time of Amos," in *Twentieth Century Theology in the Making*, ed. Jaroslav Pelikan, trans. R. A. Wilson, 3 vols. (London: Collins; New York: Harper & Row, 1969), 1:52.
8. J. G. Herder, *The Spirit of Hebrew Poetry*, trans. James Marsh, 2 vols. (German original, 1782–83; Burlington, Vt.: Edward Smith, 1833), 48.
9. T. K. Cheyne, *Jeremiah*, vol. 1 (London: Kegan Paul, Trench, 1883), xv.
10. Walther Zimmerli, "The Fruit of the Tribulation of the Prophet," in *A Prophet to the Nations: Essays in Jeremiah Studies*, ed. Leo G. Perdue and Brian W. Kovacs (Winona Lake, Ind.: Eisenbrauns, 1984), 358–61.
11. Lundbom, "Elijah's Chariot Ride," 47–48.

BIBLIOGRAPHY

Albright, William F. *From the Stone Age to Christianity: Monotheism and the Historical Process.* 2nd ed. New York: Doubleday, 1957.

———. *Samuel and the Beginnings of the Prophetic Movement.* Goldenson Lecture 1961. Cincinnati: Hebrew Union College Press, 1961. Also in *Interpreting the Prophetic Tradition,* edited by Harry M. Orlinsky, 149–76. Cincinnati: Hebrew Union College Press, 1969.

———. *Yahweh and the Gods of Canaan: A Historical Analysis of Two Contrasting Faiths.* Jordan Lectures in Comparative Religion 7. Garden City, N.Y.: Doubleday, 1968.

Balentine, Samuel E. "The Prophet as Intercessor: A Reassessment." *JBL* 103 (1984): 161–73.

Barton, John. "History and Rhetoric in the Prophets." In *The Bible as Rhetoric: Studies in Biblical Persuasion and Credibility,* edited by Martin Warner, 51–64. Warwick Studies in Philosophy and Literature. London and New York: Routledge, 1990.

Bentzen, A. "The Ritual Background of Amos i 2–ii 16." *OS* 8 (1950): 85–99.

Berger, Peter. "Between Tyranny and Chaos." *Christian Century* 85 (October 30, 1968): 1365–70.

Blank, Sheldon H. *Of a Truth the Lord Hath Sent Me: An Inquiry into the Source of the Prophet's Authority.* Goldenson Lecture 1955. Cincinnati: Hebrew Union College Press, 1955. Also in *Interpreting the Prophetic Tradition,* edited by Harry M. Orlinsky, 1–19. Cincinnati: Hebrew Union College Press, 1969.

Blenkinsopp, Joseph. *A History of Prophecy in Israel.* Philadelphia: Westminster, 1983.

Bowman, Thorleif. *Hebrew Thought Compared with Greek.* Translated by Jules L. Moreau. Philadelphia: Westminster, 1960.

Brandt, William J. *The Rhetoric of Argumentation.* New York: Bobbs-Merrill, 1970.

Bright, John. *A History of Israel.* 3rd ed. Philadelphia: Westminster, 1981.

Brown, Raymond E. *The Gospel According to John I–XII: Introduction, Translation, and Notes.* AB 29. Garden City, N.Y.: Doubleday, 1966.

Campbell, Edward F., Jr., and David Noel Freedman, eds. *The Biblical Archaeologist Reader III.* Garden City, N.Y.: Doubleday, 1970.

Campbell, Ernest T. "An Open Letter to Billy Graham." *A.D.* 2/3 (March 1973): 6–8.

Cheyne, T. K. *Jeremiah.* Vol. 1. London: Kegan Paul, Trench, 1883.

Conley, Thomas M. "The Enthymeme in Perspective." *Quarterly Journal of Speech* 70 (1984): 168–87.

Crenshaw, James L. *Prophetic Conflict: Its Effect upon Israelite Religion.* BZAW 124. Berlin and New York: Walter de Gruyter, 1971.

Davidson, A. B. "The False Prophets." *The Expositor,* 5th ser., 2 (1895): 1–17.

Dodd, C. H. *The Interpretation of the Fourth Gospel.* Cambridge: Cambridge University Press, 1953.

Fischel, Henry A. "The Use of Sorties (Climax, Gradatio) in the Tannaitic Period." *HUCA* 44 (1973): 119–51.

Gilula, M. "An Egyptian Parallel to Jeremia I 4-5." *VT* 17 (1967): 114.

Ginsberg, H. L. "Ugaritic Studies and the Bible." *BA* 8 (1945): 41–58.

Glasson, T. F. *Moses in the Fourth Gospel.* Studies in Biblical Theology 40. London: SCM, 1963.

Graham, Billy. "Billy Graham Answers His Critics." *A.D.* 2/3 (March 1973): 10–11.

Gray, George Buchanan. *A Critical and Exegetical Commentary on the Book of Isaiah I–XXXIX.* ICC. Edinburgh: T&T Clark, 1912.

Gunkel, Hermann. "The Israelite Prophecy from the Time of Amos." In *Twentieth Century Theology in the Making*, edited by Jaroslav Pelikan, translated by R. A. Wilson, 48–75. London: Collins; New York: Harper & Row, 1969. German original, 1930.

———. "The Secret Experiences of the Prophets." *The Expositor*, 9th ser., 1 (1924): 356–66, 427–35; 2 (1924): 23–32.

Haldar, Alfred. *Associations of Cult Prophets among the Ancient Semites.* Uppsala: Almqvist & Wiksells, 1945.

Hallevy, Raphael. "Man of God." *JNES* 17 (1958): 237–44.

Hanson, Paul D. *Dynamic Transcendence: The Correlation of Confessional Heritage and Contemporary Experience in a Biblical Model of Divine Activity.* Philadelphia: Fortress Press, 1978.

Herder, J. G. *The Spirit of Hebrew Poetry.* Translated by James Marsh. 2 vols. Burlington, Vt.: Edward Smith, 1833. German original, 1782–83.

Heschel, Abraham Joshua. *The Prophets.* New York and Evanston, Ill.: Harper & Row, 1962.

Huffmon, Herbert. "The Origins of Prophecy." In *Magnalia Dei, the Mighty Acts of God: Essays on the Bible and Archaeology in Memory of G. Ernest Wright*, edited by Frank Moore Cross et al., 171–86. Garden City, N.Y.: Doubleday, 1976.

———. "Prophecy in the Mari Letters." *BA* 31 (1968): 101–24. Also in *The Biblical Archaeologist Reader III*, edited by Edward F. Campbell Jr. and David Noel Freedman, 199–224. Garden City, N.Y.: Doubleday, 1970.

Jacob, Edmond. "The Biblical Prophets: Revolutionaries or Conservatives?" Translated by James H. Farley. *Interpretation* 19 (1965): 47–55.

Jakobson, Roman. "Grammatical Parallelism and Its Russian Facet." *Language* 42 (1966): 399–429.

Johnson, A. R. *The Cultic Prophet in Ancient Israel.* Oxford: Oxford University Press, 1944.

Kramer, Samuel Noah. *The Sacred Marriage Rite: Aspects of Faith, Myth, and Ritual in Ancient Sumer.* Bloomington: Indiana University Press, 1969.

———. "Sumerian Similes: A Panoramic View of Some of Man's Oldest Literary Images." *JAOS* 89 (1969): 1–10.

Kugel, James L. *The Idea of Biblical Poetry: Parallelism and Its History.* New Haven and London: Yale University Press, 1981.

Lemke, Werner. "Revelation through History in Recent Biblical Theology." *Interpretation* 36 (1982): 34–46.

Liddle, Henry George, and Robert Scott. *A Greek-English Lexicon.* Revised by Henry Stuart Jones. 2 vols. Oxford: Clarendon, 1951.

Lindblom, J. *Prophecy in Ancient Israel.* Philadelphia: Fortress Press, 1965.

Lowth, Robert. *Lectures on the Sacred Poetry of the Hebrews.* 1787. Translated by G. Gregory. Boston: Joseph T. Buckingham, 1815.

Lund, Nils W. *Chiasmus in the New Testament: A Study in Formgeschichte.* Chapel Hill: University of North Carolina Press, 1942. Reprint, Peabody, Mass.: Hendrickson, 1992.

Lundbom, Jack R. "The Double Curse in Jeremiah 20:14-18." *JBL* 104 (1985): 589–600.

———. "Elijah's Chariot Ride." *JJS* 24 (1973): 39–50.

———. "Hebrew Rhetoric." In *Encyclopedia of Rhetoric,* edited by Thomas O. Sloane, 325–28. Oxford: Oxford University Press, 2001.

———. *Jeremiah: A Study in Ancient Hebrew Rhetoric.* SBLDS 18. Missoula, Mont.: Society of Biblical Literature and Scholars Press, 1975. 2nd ed., Winona Lake, Ind.: Eisenbrauns, 1997.

———. *Jeremiah 1–20: A New Translation with Introduction and Commentary.* AB 21A. New York: Doubleday, 1999.

———. "Jeremiah 15, 15-21 and the Call of Jeremiah." *SJOT* 9 (1995): 143–55.

———. *Jeremiah 21–36: A New Translation with Introduction and Commentary.* AB 21B. New York: Doubleday, 2004.

———. *Jeremiah 37–52: A New Translation with Introduction and Commentary.* AB 21C. New York: Doubleday, 2004.

———. "The Lawbook of the Josianic Reform." *CBQ* 38 (1976): 293–302.

Meek, Theophile J. *Hebrew Origins.* New York: Harper & Bros., 1950.

Moulton, Richard G. *The Literary Study of the Bible.* New York: D. C. Heath, 1895.

Mowinckel, Sigmund. "Psalms and Wisdom." In *Wisdom in Israel and in the Ancient Near East: Presented to Professor Harold Henry Rowley by the Society for Old Testament Study in Association with the Editorial Board of Vetus Testamentum, in Celebration of His Sixty-fifth Birthday, 24 March 1955,* edited by Martin Noth and D. Winton Thomas, 205–24. VTSup 3. Leiden: Brill, 1955.

Muilenburg, James M. "The 'Office' of the Prophet in Ancient Israel." In *The Bible in Modern Scholarship: Papers Read at the 100th Meeting of the Society of Biblical Literature, December 28–30, 1964*, edited by J. Philip Hyatt, 74–97. Nashville: Abingdon, 1965.

———. "Old Testament Prophecy." In *Peake's Commentary on the Bible*, edited by Matthew Black and H. H. Rowley, 475–83. London and New York: Thomas Nelson, 1977.

———. "A Study of Hebrew Rhetoric: Repetition and Style." In *Congress Volume: Copenhagen 1953*, 97–111. VTSup 1. Leiden: Brill, 1953.

Niebuhr, Reinhold. "The Test of True Prophecy." In Niebuhr, *Beyond Tragedy*, 89–110. New York: Charles Scribner's Sons, 1937.

Noth, Martin. "History and the Word of God in the Old Testament." *BJRL* 32 (1950): 194–206.

Orlinsky, Harry M., ed. *Interpreting the Prophetic Tradition*. Cincinnati: Hebrew Union College Press, 1969.

———. "The Seer in Ancient Israel." *Oriens Antiquus* 4 (1965): 153–74.

Overholt, Thomas W. *The Threat of Falsehood: A Study in the Theology of the Book of Jeremiah*. Studies in Biblical Theology, n.s., 16. Naperville, Ill.: Alec R. Allenson, 1970.

Petersen, David L., ed. *Prophecy in Israel: Search for an Identity*. Issues in Religion and Theology 10. Philadelphia: Fortress Press, 1987.

Pfeiffer, Robert H. *Introduction to the Old Testament*. New York: Harper & Bros., 1948.

Quintilian. *The Institutio Oratoria of Quintilian I–IV*. Translated by H. E. Butler. LCL. Cambridge, Mass.: Harvard University Press, 1969.

Rad, Gerhard von. *Old Testament Theology*. Vol. 2, *The Theology of Israel's Prophetic Traditions*. Translated by D. M. G. Stalker. Edinburgh and London: Oliver & Boyd, 1965.

Rhetorica ad Herennium. Translated by Harry Caplan. LCL. Cambridge, Mass.: Harvard University Press, 1964.

Robinson, H. Wheeler. "Prophetic Symbolism." In *Old Testament Essays*, edited by D. C. Simpson, 1–17. London: Charles Griffin, 1927.

Ross, James F. "The Prophet as Yahweh's Messenger." In *Israel's Prophetic Heritage: Essays in Honor of James Muilenburg*, edited by Bernhard W. Anderson and Walter Harrelson, 98–107. New York: Harper & Bros., 1962. Also in *Prophecy in Israel: Search for an Identity*, edited by David L. Petersen, 112–21. Issues in Religion and Theology 10. Philadelphia: Fortress Press, 1987.

Rowley, H. H. "The Nature of Prophecy in the Light of Recent Study." *HTR* 38 (1945): 1–38. Also in Rowley, *The Servant of the Lord and Other Essays on the Old Testament*, 91–128. London: Lutterworth, 1952.

Sanders, James A. "Hermeneutics in True and False Prophecy." In *Canon and Authority: Essays in Old Testament Religion and Theology*, edited by George W. Coats and Burke O. Long, 21–41. Philadelphia: Fortress Press, 1977.

Schoettgen, Christian. *Horae hebraicae et talmudicae*. Leipzig and Dresden: Christoph. Hekelii & Sons, 1733. Dissertatio VI: *De Exergasia Sacra*, 1249–63.

Shank, David A. *Prophet Harris, The 'Black Elijah' of West Africa*. Abridged by Jocelyn Murray. Supplements to the Journal of Religion in Africa 10. Leiden: Brill, 1994.

Skinner, John. *Prophecy and Religion*. 1922. Reprint, Cambridge: Cambridge University Press, 1963.

Smith, John M. Powis. "The Conservatism of Early Prophecy." *AJT* 23 (1919): 290–99.

Sundkler, Bengt G. *Bantu Prophets in South Africa*. London: Lutterworth, 1948.

Tillich, Paul. *Systematic Theology*. Vol. 1, *Reason and Revelation; Being and God*. Chicago: University of Chicago Press, 1951.

Towner, W. Sibley. "On Calling People 'Prophets' in 1970." *Interpretation* 24 (1970): 492–509.

Weber, Max. *The Sociology of Religion*. 4th ed. Translated by Ephraim Fischoff. Boston: Beacon, 1963. German original, 1922. Chapter 4: "The Prophet," 46–59.

Wilson, Robert R. *Prophecy and Society in Ancient Israel*. Philadelphia: Fortress Press, 1980.

Wolff, Hans Walter. *Joel and Amos: A Commentary on the Books of the Prophets Joel and Amos*. Translated by Waldemar Janzen et al. Hermenia. Philadelphia: Fortress Press, 1977.

Wright, G. Ernest. *God Who Acts: Biblical Theology as Recital*. Studies in Biblical Theology 8. London: SCM, 1952.

———. "The Nations in Hebrew Prophecy." *Encounter* 26 (1965): 225–37.

Zimmerli, Walther. "The Fruit of the Tribulation of the Prophet." In *A Prophet to the Nations: Essays in Jeremiah Studies*, edited by Leo G. Perdue and Brian W. Kovacs, 358–61. Winona Lake, Ind.: Eisenbrauns, 1984.

INDEX OF PASSAGES

Index of Passages

CPSIA information can be obtained
at www.ICGtesting.com
Printed in the USA
FFOW02n0637040917
39520FF